STATESMEN AND NATIONS

B

PAUL JOHNSON

Statesmen and Nations

SIDGWICK & JACKSON
LONDON

The author wishes to thank the Chairman and Board of Directors of the Statesman and Nation Publishing Company for permission to republish these articles, all of which, with the exception of the introduction, first appeared in the *New Statesman*.

SBN 283.48454.3

Printed in the Republic of Ireland by
Cahill & Co. Limited, Dublin
for Sidgwick and Jackson Limited
1 *Tavistock Chambers, Bloomsbury Way*
*London, W.C.*1

CONTENTS

Introduction PAGE

The Art of Political Journalism 8

Part One—Morals and Society

Bunny, Flockie and Co. 20
Sex, Snobbery and Sadism 23
America's Suez ? 27
Are Virgins Obsolete? 31
Rome Goes Left 35
Hunting and Humbug 41
The Menace of Beatlism 45
Make Mine Topless! 50
Strictly Vindictive 54
The Man Born to be Pope 60
Mugg Waits for Godot 68

Part Two—The Party Game

Rule Like Pigs 74
Lucky Mac and his Hons' Cupboard 78
No Sex for Johnnie 83
Was the Palace to Blame? 88
Sir Alec's Gravy Train 93
The Prime Minister 97

Part Three—Intellectuals

War Games 104
Lucky Jim's Political Testament 108
The New Spectre Haunting Europe 113
How Danny Saved the Dollar 120
Young John Bull, 1969 124

Part Four—Crowns and Coronets PAGE

Coronation Street 130
Square Deal for Bertie 135
A Lady in Mid-career 140
Uncle Taffy 145

Part Five—Men and History

The Historian as Radical 156
The Dark Youth of Disraeli 161
The Dumb Colossus 166
The Case for Curzon 170
The Art of Opposition 175
The Creed of the Pallisers 180
1086 and All That 185
Hamlet in Downing Street 190
The Key to Palmerston 195
A Very Bad Man? 200
Aubrey's Brief Life 204
The Sound and the Fury 209

Part Six—Bad News from Abroad

Murder in Caracas 218
The Trouble with Persia 222
In the Heel of Europe 227

Part Seven—Off Duty

No Path to Rome 242
The Pleasures of Fear 247
The Man Who Built a Cathedral 251
The Naked and the Red 257
Dining with Liz 261

Introduction

THE ART OF POLITICAL JOURNALISM

The Art of Political Journalism

SO FAR AS I KNOW, very little has been written on this delicate and important subject. In journalism, above all professions, he who can does; he who cannot teaches. Good political journalists rarely have the time, or the inclination, or – in the last resort – the skill, to tell others how to do it. An experienced editor, faced with an article which contains an effective substance, but a good deal of padding, and awkwardly presented, will know exactly how to set about cutting and re-writing it, and will perform the task with great dispatch. But he will seldom be prepared to explain to the writer exactly what he is doing, still less why he is doing it. The writer must simply take the trouble to compare the finished, printed product with his original typescript and see for himself where he went wrong. A journalist, like an actor, learns chiefly by watching others perform, and from his own mistakes.

I know of only one good journalist who had the patience and the ability to teach others. This was the late Aylmer Vallance, who was an assistant editor on the *New Statesman* when I joined its staff in 1955. I had by then learned most of the ordinary editorial skills (including the very difficult business of writing picture-captions – almost a lost art today, to judge by the Colour Supplements), and was quite capable of turning out a signed article on almost any subject. But I had never written a leader; and Aylmer taught me how to do so. The editor, Kingsley Martin, would in theory tell me what to say; but often he did not quite know himself, and would terminate an inconclusive discussion by saying: 'You seem to have it all in your head – go and write it.' I would do so, and then hand the typescript to Aylmer. It was always very long. There seemed so much to be said on the subject (the state of the Maltese economy, say, or the structure of commercial television, or the latest round of talks on Berlin). Moreover, much essential rhetoric had to be included, and formidable and lengthy conclusions to be drawn.

Aylmer would read it through carefully, then say: 'I admire your treatise. Now let us turn it into a leading article.' He would look at the important first paragraph, in which the premises of the problem were, I felt, clearly outlined, and say: 'You seem to be clearing your throat here. Shall we see if we can do without it altogether?' And out it would come. Then he would look at the last paragraph, in which the disastrous and earth-shaking consequences of failure to follow the *New Statesman*'s advice were solemnly put down. 'We mustn't frighten the readers too much,' he would say crisply, and out that would come too. Then he would look for a paragraph in the middle: 'You seem to be pausing for your second wind here. But we don't want the reader to know that, do we?' Out it went. Then he really got down to business, hacking about the windy rhetoric, excising what he called 'the seven-and-sixpenny words', stabbing relentlessly at the liturgical clichés which, I then thought, were part of the high-minded apparatus of a leader. 'Too much *tone*,' he said (out would come 'both national honour and natural justice demand . . .'). 'We don't want to sound like C. P. Scott' (out would come 'it is greatly to be hoped/feared . . .'). 'Or Old Garvin' ('Such a reckless course would inflict grievous injury upon . . .'). 'Or Geoffrey Dawson' ('Her Majesty's Government would be well advised to . . .'). 'Or Michael Foot' ('criminal folly'). Aylmer would then add a few characteristic flourishes of his own; he was particularly fond of using quotation marks to imply incompetence or sinister design. 'The new government's "housing policy" ', he would write, implying that the Tories were not only going to build no houses, but might actually start tearing some down. Or: 'Last week's "note" delivered by the Persian "Government" . . .' – the Persians, it seems, did not *have* a Government in any acceptable sense, and, whatever it was, it was unfamiliar with normal diplomatic practices. By the time Aylmer had finished with the leader, it was much reduced in length. 'Too short,' I would say. 'No,' replied Aylmer, 'we must leave room for the Editor to put in his *qualifying phrases*.' And so it was. Indeed, Kingsley Martin's qualifications were often so numerous, and so complex, that the whole thing had to be severely cut in proof, and many cherished points were cast into oblivion.

Kingsley could not teach one to write leaders; but he had a definite theory about them. 'There are times,' he told me, 'when the issue is so clear that you must go wholly onto the attack. Don't give the enemy a single inch. Don't concede him the scintilla of a case.

But this doesn't happen often. There are nearly always two points of view, and remember that a good many readers will take the view opposite to ours. The object of a leader is to reinforce the convictions of your friends and, if possible, undermine the convictions of your enemies. Admit to your friends that there is a case to answer; then demolish it. Permit your enemies the luxury of an argument; then show it's unsound. I always think it is best to concede as much to the opposite case as you possibly can – short of actual surrender. That will persuade people who don't initially agree with you, or are wavering, that you are fair-minded. They are then likely to attach much more weight to your final paragraphs, in which you ram your own case home. A good leader should, as it were, reflect an intelligent argument between two civilized people, *provided always that the right man wins in the last sentence*.'

This seems to me sound advice, which I have always tried to follow. It is futile to ignore objections to your case, or to brush them aside by purely verbal dexterity. Any political or economic problem can be solved in words in the final paragraph: but this will convince only the superficial reader, and him only for a time. The art of the leader is to produce workable conclusions in persuasive language. If you win over even one thoughtful person to your view, you have achieved something. The temptation is to achieve verbal victories. Any experienced leader-writer will know the tricks of the trade: the careful selectivity of expression which turns your opponents' virtues into faults, and your own handicaps into assets. There are certain words and phrases which can be alternated to load the argument one way or the other. Thus, a Labour 'militant' as opposed to a Tory 'fanatic'; your supporter is 'staunch', your opponent is 'bigoted' or even 'rabid'; where you are 'disinterested', the other man is 'indifferent'. Mr Wilson delivered a 'penetrating' speech, made more 'pointed' by the use of 'homely expressions', and ending with a 'vehement' peroration. Mr Heath's was 'prolix and overloaded with detail', 'marred' by 'coarseness of phrase', and ending in 'sheer abuse'. Where Mr Wilson was 'right to remind us', Mr Heath 'insisted on dragging up' (usually a 'red herring' or an 'ageing Trojan horse', or similar unclean beast). You have 'principles', the other man 'prejudices' or 'dogmas'; your arguments are 'weighty' or 'ingenious', his 'contrived' or even 'tortuous'. One could give plenty more examples. But perhaps the best way to illustrate what I mean is to give three extracts from imaginary leaders published immediately after the murder of Archbishop Thomas à Becket in Canterbury Cathedral. The first is an outraged condemnation by a clericalist and papalist newspaper, the second a somewhat forlorn attempt to put the best gloss on the King's action, the third a cool-headed summing-up in the best *New Statesman* manner (this leader-writing technique was developed by George Bernard Shaw in the early years of the paper; for a brilliant specimen, see his unsigned leader on the Marconi case in the very first issue, reprinted in the *New Statesman Anthology*). Here, then, are our three leaders.

I

The scandalous event which took place last Sunday evening in Canterbury Cathedral will be unreservedly condemned by the entire civilized world. Indeed it is likely to shock opinion even in those areas which have not yet accepted the beliefs and standards of Christianity – for sacrilege is repugnant to men of all faiths. That the Primate of All England should be murdered, dressed in full canonicals, on the steps of the High Altar in his own cathedral, is appalling enough in itself; but that those responsible should be knights attached to the court, acting on the express orders of a Christian sovereign, almost defies belief. We say 'almost': it must be admitted that the present occupant of the throne has behaved with such persistent disregard for the rights of the Church, and with such violent animosity towards those whose duty it is to uphold them, that the atrocious crime committed on Sunday is not wholly unexpected. The late Archbishop (it would be improper to anticipate Rome by calling him 'St Thomas') had been a faithful servant of the Monarch for many years. He had accepted the onerous duties of the Primacy with reluctance, and after warning his former master that he might be forced to differ from him on major principles. His reward was to be hauled before the royal courts on spurious charges of peculation, and later to be driven into an exile which was as unjust as it was illegal. He returned at the Monarch's insistence, and on a solemn guarantee of safe-conduct. On reaching Canterbury, he naturally felt bound to take measures to restore the temporalities of the see, to impose appropriate penalties on the 'bishops' who had usurped the Primate's function at the coronation of the Heir, and to rebuke a local crown official for a deliberate insult too barbarous to particularize. The sermon in which he dealt with the last point was typical of his robust style. We now know how the Monarch chose to respond, and we confidently await the retribution which, in the next world if not in this, will most certainly overtake him. The Archbishop died as he lived: full of righteousness and truth, fearing none but his Maker. It will come as no surprise to those privileged to know him well that his faithful monks, on preparing his violated body for burial, should have discovered, next to his skin, the hairshirt he invariably wore . . .

II

What precisely occurred last Sunday evening in Canterbury Cathedral is still far from clear, and the public would be well advised to suspend judgement until the authorities have had an opportunity to establish the facts. This may not be easy. A highly-coloured, indeed hysterical, version is already being circulated. The source of such a rumour seems to be monks from the chapter, not usually noted for their unprejudiced view of ecclesiastical controversy; and it is relevant to point out that, if the 'facts' were indeed as these monks claim, additional revenue could be expected to accrue to the chapter from pilgrims visiting the scene of such an event. What does seem beyond dispute is that the Archbishop had excommunicated, or rather attempted to excommunicate, those diocesans who took part in the enthronement of the royal heir last month; that he did so *ultra vires*, and in explicit breach of an agreement made with the Crown before his return from self-imposed exile; and that he followed this by an intemperate discourse, delivered in the cathedral on (of all occasions) Christmas Day. We do not yet have the full text of the sermon; but all accounts agree that during it he excommunicated a royal official (and, what is more, feudatory) without warning, without opportunity to answer the charges, without the customary formulary, and on a pretext which most sensible people would dismiss as frivolous. The tone of His Grace's recent utterances has become increasingly strident; their content openly disloyal, if not actually treasonable. Some response from staunch supporters of the Crown was to be expected, if only in the form of verbal remonstrations. In making such protests, they were understandably upset by the provocative (and quite possibly violent) behaviour of the chapter monks; indeed, as we have constantly pointed out, the essence of the controversy between the Archbishop and the Crown has been the inability of the ecclesiastical authorities to enforce respect for law and order among the criminal elements who claim benefit of clergy. In the atmosphere generated by His Grace's recent *pronunciamento*, a bout of fisticuffs was, perhaps, inevitable. What is difficult to understand is why the Archbishop found it necessary to intervene personally in such a scrimmage. If he so far forgot himself – some would say reverted to an earlier period of his career, about which the less said the better – the Crown cannot be held responsible for any injuries he may have received. That, we imagine, is likely to be the view all fair-minded people will take of this lamentable episode . . .

III

The conflict between the Archbishop and the King has come to an unpleasant but predictable conclusion. Granted the characters of both men, there was never much chance of a compromise. But before the hagiographers get to work, let us have a few plain truths. The King should never have made Becket his archbishop in the first place. Becket had warned him he could not double up the job with the chancellorship, and would feel bound to oppose the Crown over criminous clerks and advowsons. Why the King persisted with the nomination is a mystery, unless we attribute it to arrogance. On the other hand, once in office, Becket was clearly misguided in forcing the issue. Few of his fellow-bishops supported him; even the Pope was unenthusiastic. Where there is a conflict of laws, there must be give and take on both sides. In any case, Becket took no steps to improve the behaviour of the lower clergy, which would have made the issue far less acute. Right to the end he ignored the sensible advice of John of Salisbury. The King was perfectly entitled to promulgate the Constitutions of Clarendon (as even Becket admitted at first). Where he went wrong was to hound his former Chancellor over alleged financial abuses; the evidence looked flimsy, and the whole affair smacked of persecution. True, Becket's melodramatic 'flight' into exile was unnecessary. But the King was foolish to invite him back without securing his written agreement to terms. In fact the King's handling of the whole affair has been curiously slapdash, in striking contrast to his usual hard-headed methods. Becket was out of order in excommunicating the bishops; the King should have told them to ignore it. Instead, without consulting his coun-

> cil, he dispatched four knights, of low standing and with no legal or diplomatic experience, to force a retraction from Becket under threats. They had no written instructions, so we shall never know whether or not they exceeded them. Becket should have flatly refused to deal with such an unorthodox delegation. Instead he became involved in an angry debate which was bound to lead to blows. In effect he asked for martyrdom; and got it. Now wiser heads will have to clear up the mess. We note that a good deal of wine seems to have been drunk by all concerned at the crucial moments. One minor lesson of this deplorable affair is that delicate business should not be transacted after dinner.

The last leader would no doubt have irritated the King and angered the papal extremists; but the bulk of the episcopal bench, most of the tenants-in-chief, and the literate Anglo-Norman public would have conceded that it was a fair statement of the case. And John of Salisbury would certainly have nodded his head in approval (he probably wrote it; or at least briefed its writer). A good leader, in fact, always aims to conquer the middle ground of opinion.

I urge any aspiring leader-writer to develop the habit of writing such historical exercises, at any rate in his head. It is good practice; very instructive; and fun, too. He should try to develop a sense of history, and constantly widen his knowledge of the past, particularly of the 19th and early 20th centuries. He should acquire a library of historical works: not the instant books published today, which tell us a great deal about the sex-lives of people like Dilke and Parnell, and are serialized in the 'quality' Sunday newspapers, but the solid, multi-volume biographies, which give copious extracts from letters, speeches, debates, and articles: Moneypenny and Buckle on Disraeli, Morley on Gladstone, Gwendolyn Cecil on Salisbury, Churchill on his father, Lord Randolph; there are scores of others. The long chapter in the life of Salisbury which shows how Disraeli persuaded the Tory Party to pass the 1867 Reform Bill gives one an extraordinary insight into the way political processes actually work, and how they can be manipulated by a master. So do the two volumes of Cabinet diaries written by Tom Jones – perhaps the most precious glimpse into the mysteries of British government we are ever likely to get. The recent past is a rich repository of truth for the modern political writer. He cannot gain an exact knowledge of what is happening today; Cabinet secrets are extraordinarily well-kept in this country, and it will be many years, for instance, before we know the true story of the Wilson Government. But by studying the past, through letters, documents, and memoirs, the writer can create in his own mind an authentic picture of how government is carried on, how pressures are exerted and decisions reached. Into this picture he can fit the known factors operating today, and it is surprising how often this will enable him to conjure up the atmosphere and the mental processes of present-day Downing Street and Whitehall.

How far should a political writer – not just a leader writer – associate with politicians? He must know them personally. He must have a broad grasp of their characters. He should never confine himself to one particular faction, no matter how useful the information he thereby acquires. He must establish himself on easy terms with men and women of all parties. He must meet them often on social occasions. But he must never allow friendship to develop to the point at which his views are warped by prejudice or inhibited by the fear of causing offence. Nor should he ever purchase information at the cost of silence. I distrust politicians, especially Ministers, who talk too freely and are willing to divulge information 'off the record'. In the first place such information is often untrue, or hopelessly subjective, or deliberately slanted. In the second place, if it is true, it can usually be discovered by other means which do not prevent publication. The trouble is that journalists are often flattered out of their senses by contact with the great. They should develop a proper pride in the profession they represent, and deal with politicians on a basis of friendly and civilized equality. They must seek information, but never cringe for it; if they know their job, the politicians will always be prepared to meet them on fair terms. They should not have favourites or develop personal animosities; in either case the informed public will quickly spot the bias and discount their judgements accordingly.

Above all, they must not fall into the trap of regarding politics as a cynical game, played by people with unworthy motives. British politics is an honourable, even noble, profession, concerned with great issues of fundamental importance to the people of this country, and to many abroad too. Those who participate in it are, in the overwhelming majority of cases, people of genuine convictions, who really believe they are acting in the public service. British parliamentary politicians, it is true, are often vain, often boring, sometimes intolerable in the pursuit of their particular causes or obsessions. But their motives, in my observation, are rarely base. No man or woman in living memory ever made a fortune in British public life; most of them emerged the poorer. Democratic politics is, in some ways, a cruel business. A man can lose his seat, his job, his salary, his prospects, without warning, or notice, or pension, at the stroke of an elector's pen, indeed on the anonymous movement of an electoral swing. It is vital that this profession should continue to attract the best recruits. It will not do so if aspirants know they will be subjected to the cynical vilification which has been such a marked feature of political journalism, in the Press and television, during recent years. Journalism of this sort can inflict lasting damage on our public life. Political journalists must be fair-minded; if they find it impossible to control their pens, editors must have the courage to enforce a reasonable respect for individuals and institutions, even at the cost of losing gifted contributors. A country gets the politicians it deserves; if the Press teaches it to treat them with contempt, it will in time get contemptible politicians. This applies particularly to Ministers. However misguided they may seem, they are almost certainly acting from good motives, striving to do what they really believe is right for their country. A Minister's spirit can be broken – and his value to the public destroyed – by unfair, personal, and vindictive attacks. I have seen it happen. If the Press is to be treated as a fourth estate, it must accept the responsibilities that position implies. A political journalist, above all others, must be animated by a desire to serve the public.

All this may sound a little solemn. It is certainly unfashionable. But it is true and needs to be said. Political journalism is a splendid career: to describe great events, even to influence them; to inform the millions of the mass-electorate of what is being done in their name, and why; to seek to guide those who have charge of our affairs – what more can a young writer who cares about his fellow-humans ask? But to make such a career worthwhile requires dedication and unselfishness as well as ambition. It requires also a certain broadmindedness and variety of knowledge. Political writers should beware of tying themselves too closely to Westminster and Whitehall. They should go frequently to the provinces, and get to know their own country thoroughly. They should travel abroad at every opportunity, and write about what they see. Many problems which face British Governments are paralleled, often with fascinating variations, all over the world. They should be observed. The workings of foreign institutions should be studied. The political journalist should make a habit of reading the foreign press, and books published abroad, of forming contacts with leading foreign politicians. This may seem obvious advice; I give it because it is so rarely followed.

In fact, I suspect that the political writer's value to his paper and his country increases in direct proportion to his opportunities and ability to write, from time to time, about other countries. I am sorry that in this collection of articles I have been unable to include more than two or three examples of work done overseas, which in fact took up a great deal of my time during the last fifteen years. Alas, most of what I published has now lost whatever interest it once possessed. During this time I visited seventy or more countries, some on several or even many occasions, and wrote about nearly all of them. What I learned I found invaluable in writing about politics here, and essential in editing a political paper which dealt with the whole world. So I emphasize that a political journalist must insist that his editor allow him to travel. Indeed, if possible, he should spend two or three years as resident correspondent in a major country.

He should also – and this is my final piece of advice – write about subjects other than politics. He must never become enclosed in the parish and the assumptions of Westminster. Politics is ultimately about the everyday lives of ordinary people, which are infinite in their variety. A good political journalist should concern himself with industry and economics, with sport and the arts, with travel, fashion, society, and entertainment. And to do this effectively he must write about such subjects, even if they are frivolous and ephemeral. That way, he will acquire not just knowledge, but far greater flexibility in his style, and new insights into his craft. So I make no apology for including, in this book, some rather curious articles. They formed part of the process by which I learned to become a journalist. Remember, this is a journalist's book, no more. All these pieces were written for immediate publication in the *New Statesman*, most of them at speed, and some under great pressure. I have made no alterations, other than correcting a few silly mistakes of fact and cutting one or two passages now irrelevant or obscure. This book thus represents a small selection from some millions of words written over one and a half decades. How much interest it retains today is not for me to judge; all I will say is that nearly all these articles were enjoyable to write.

PAUL JOHNSON

1 July 1970

Part 1

MORALS AND SOCIETY

Bunny, Flockie and Co.

EXACTLY SIX WEEKS after Mr Macmillan's famous 'Savings Budget', four months after the imposition of the tightest credit squeeze since the war, and in the midst of a plethora of pious injunctions exhorting us all to save more and spend less, Miss 'Bunny' Esterhazy and Miss 'Flockie' Harcourt-Smith were, last week, solemnly and publicly 'brought out' at Claridges. This complicated and imperative operation cost, according to whether you believe the *Mail* or the *Express*, either £5,000 or £10,000. Its splendours were duly communicated to British workers, in goggling detail, by the daily press. A few days previously, they had been treated to an *hors d'œuvre*, in a more personal manner, when a hundred or so socially marginal junketers descended on the East End, armed, it is said, with everything from champagne to marijuana, and entertained the neighbours to an all-night jazz-session in a hired house.

We are, in other words, in the midst of the 1956 'Season'. For the first time since before the war, the British upper class has got the bit between its teeth. Not since the thirties has it consumed so much bad champagne and dubious caviare, trampled so much broken glass underfoot, and driven so many village dressmakers to profitable distraction. The *Evening Standard* night-reporting corps is worn off its feet. The worst dance bands in London are turning down engagements. Even the burglars are overworked. After years of war-time equality, Crippsian austerity, servantless mansions, travel allowances, dividend restraint and triumphant bureaucracy, the Butler Boom is beginning to take effect: Society is scrambling shakily to its feet again and cocking a tentative snoot at the masses.

Things, admittedly, are not what they used to be. The bandwagon is less exclusive than ever. Even minor heiresses from Milwaukee, even junior financiers from Frankfurt, even – Colonel Nasser notwithstanding – fourth secretaries from seedy Middle

Eastern embassies have got their feet in the door. If you have the money, there is a maze of short cuts to the Palace. Nor are the pillars of Society entirely easy about the future. Five years of handsome capital gains have primed the pump; but the deep financial wells no longer exist, and super-tax and death-duties continue to take their fearful toll. The rich are no longer really rich; but, thanks to Mr Butler – and in spite of Mr Macmillan – they at last have a little pocket-money to spend. Deep down, they all know it can't last. All the more reason, then, to spend it with a splash. Edwardian economics breed Edwardian vulgarity. The fake economic prosperity of Tory rule has bred a fake revival of the leisured class.

Ultimately, then, the upper-class spending-spree – of which the 1956 Season is the apotheosis – is a form of collective hallucination, a desperate attempt, on the part of Britain's financial and social elite, to persuade itself that nothing has changed. Every all-night party, every case of champagne, every hamper of *pâté de foie gras* is one more proof that the Welfare State no longer exists – has, indeed, never existed – that the Labour government was just a transitory nightmare, that equality is not merely not just around the corner, but receding into the remote distance.

In theory at least, this social hullabaloo, apart from its tedious bad taste, might be relatively harmless. The fact remains, however, that Britain is still in the midst of a financial crisis; that the government and trade unions are still desperately trying to hold down wages; and that the workers are still being implored, from all sides, to work harder. If, as we are so constantly told, Britain can never regain her industrial supremacy until the workers identify themselves more explicitly with the nation as a whole, do Bunny, Flockie and Co. really help matters? Nobody would go so far as to suggest that the battle of the export trade is being lost on the dance-floor of Claridges, but is it too much to ask, just once, that the people at the top should set something other than the worst possible example?

Also—and this is far more important—do we really want the sort of society of which the Season is the image? Must we continue to believe that a pyramid, whose only criteria are wealth and money, is the real form of social organisation? Are its values the ones to which we really subscribe? And if not, what do we propose to do about it?

It goes without saying that a Tory government cannot be expected to knock away the props which, in the long run, are its own foundation. It exhorts the workers, on the one hand, to exercise restraint, and, on the other, supplies the upper classes with the means to abandon it. But this is to be expected. The fundamental Tory image is not a prosperous Britain, but a prosperous leisured class. If a Tory chancellor set out to curb the Dockers and their kind, he would, in the long run, be destroying his own *raison d'être*. Nor, in combating the atavistic values of our society, can we expect much help from the intellectuals, who are, in the last resort, principally concerned with their own place on the pyramid. There is, however, something we can do. Our social pyramid is crowned by a series of paid functionaries whose social influence is decisive: one move from the Palace and the whole complex, hierarchic structure of the Season would collapse. We cannot set the pattern for the Bunnys and the Flockies; but the Royal Family can. They are obliged – if we take the trouble to assert our rights – to do exactly as we tell them.

Is this statement so very alarming? After all, members of the Royal Family have graciously consented to forgo the expense of equipping the Royal Flight with Britannias; they have even agreed to put up with their present waiting-room at London Airport; is it quite out of the question to ask them to adapt the pattern of their social life a little more closely to the needs of mid-20th century Britain? Are Presentation Parties at the Palace, Royal Ascot and incessant scurryings between country houses really necessary to the maintenance of royal dignity? On the contrary, they symbolize an outmoded social pattern and are at variance with the way of life which most of the Queen's subjects now find admirable.

Already, in other respects, royalty has been obliging: it gratifies the moralists by being unimpeachably respectable; it pacifies the politicians by pruning down its speeches to the barest bones of platitude; to encourage industry, it daily courts sartorial disaster by patronizing English dressmakers. Why not go a stage further? The British people are, by now, reconciled to a monarchy whose mental horizon is bounded by Newmarket and Drury Lane; they no longer expect any positive contribution to the welfare of the community; but have they not the right to demand, in return for their annual £750,000, the purely negative virtue of social responsibility? Mr Gaitskell reminded an American audience last week that the Labour Party officially supports the monarchy. True enough; but if such support is to continue to justify itself to the rank-and-file, there will have to be some big changes at Buckingham Palace when Labour returns to power.

—26 May 1956

Sex, Snobbery and Sadism

I HAVE JUST FINISHED what is, without doubt, the nastiest book I have ever read. It is a new novel entitled *Dr No* and the author is Mr Ian Fleming. Echoes of Mr Fleming's fame had reached me before, and I had been repeatedly urged to read his books by literary friends whose judgement I normally respect. When his new novel appeared, therefore, I obtained a copy and started to read. By the time I was a third of the way through, I had to suppress a strong impulse to throw the thing away, and only continued reading because I realized that here was a social phenomenon of some importance.

There are three basic ingredients in *Dr No*, all unhealthy, all thoroughly English: the sadism of a schoolboy bully, the mechanical, two-dimensional sex-longings of a frustrated adolescent, and the crude, snob-cravings of a suburban adult. Mr Fleming has no literary skill, the construction of the book is chaotic, and entire incidents and situations are inserted, and then forgotten, in a haphazard manner. But the three ingredients are manufactured and blended with deliberate, professional precision; Mr Fleming dishes up his recipe with all the calculated accountancy of a Lyons Corner House.

The plot can be briefly described. James Bond, an upper-class Secret Service Agent, is sent by his sadistic superior, M., to Jamaica, to investigate strange incidents on a nearby island. By page 53, Bond's bodyguard, a faithful and brutal Negro called Quarrel, is already at work, twisting the arms of a Chinese girl to breaking point. She gouges his face with a broken flash-bulb, and in return, he smilingly squeezes the fleshy part of her thumb (described by Fleming as 'the Mount of Venus', because if it is well-developed then the girl is 'good in bed') until she screams. ('She's Love Moun' be sore long after ma face done get healed,' chortles Quarrel.) Next, Bond's mysterious enemies attempt to poison him with cyanide-loaded fruit, and then insert a six-inch long venomous centipede in his bed ('Bond could feel it nuzzling at his skin. It was drinking! Drinking the beads of salt sweat!').

Bond visits the island, falls asleep, and on waking sees a beautiful girl, wearing only a leather belt round her waist ('The belt made her nakedness extraordinarily erotic'). Her behind, Bond notices, 'was almost as firm and rounded as a boy's'. The girl tells Bond she was raped at the age of fifteen by a savage overseer, who then broke her nose. She revenged herself by dropping a Black Widow spider on his naked stomach while he slept ('He took a week to die'). Bond rejects her urgent invitation to share her sleeping bag. Then the enemy arrives – huge, inhuman Negro-Chinese half-castes, known as Chigroes, under the diabolical direction of Dr No. Quarrel is scorched to death by a flame-thrower, and Bond and the girl are captured.

There follows a vague series of incidents in a sort of luxury hotel, built into the mountain, where Dr No entertains his captives before torturing them. This gives Fleming an opportunity to insert his snob ingredient. A lubricious bathroom scene, in which the girl again attempts to seduce Bond, involves Floris Lime bath-essence, Guerlain bathcubes and 'Guerlain's Sapoceti, *Fleur des Alpes*'. Bond, offered a drink, demands 'a medium vodka dry Martini' ('I would prefer Russian or Polish vodka'). A third attempt by the girl is frustrated only by Bond's succumbing to drugs inserted in his breakfast. At last Dr No appears, 6ft 6in. tall, and looking like a 'giant venomous worm wrapped in grey tin-foil'. Some years before, his hands had been cut off, but he is equipped with 'articulated steel pincers', which he has a habit of tapping against his contact-lenses, making a metallic noise. He has a polished skull, no eyelashes, and his heart is on the wrong side of his body; he is, needless to say, Chinese (with a German mother). His chief amusement is to subject his captives to prolonged, scientific tortures. ('I am interested in pain. I am also interested in finding out how much the human body can endure.')

Bond contemplates stabbing No's jugular vein with the jagged stem of a broken wine-glass, but reluctantly abandons the idea. The girl is taken off, to be strapped, naked, to the ground and nibbled to death by giant crabs. Bond is put through an ingenious, and fantastically complicated, obstacle course of tortures, devised by No. First come electric shocks. Then an agonizing climb up a steel chimney. Then a crawl along a red-hot zinc tube, to face twenty giant Tarantula spiders 'three to four inches long'. Finally Bond is hurled into the sea, where he is met by a 50-foot giant squid (everything is giant in *Dr No* – insects, breasts and gin-and-tonics). Having survived all these, Bond buries No alive under a mountain of bird-dung, rescues the girl and at last has a shot at a jugular vein, this time with a table-knife. He also shoots three Chigroes, one in the head, one in the stomach and one in the neck. The girl's feet get cut up, but they tramp to safety, 'leaving bloody footsteps on the ground'. The story ends with Bond biting the girl in an erotic embrace, which takes place in a special giant sleeping bag.

I have summarized the plot, perhaps at wearisome length, because a bare recital of its details describes, better than I can, how Fleming deliberately and systematically excites, and then satisfies, the very worst instincts of his readers. This seems to me far more dangerous than straight pornography. In 1944, George Orwell took issue with a book which in some ways resembles Fleming's novels – *No Orchids for Miss Blandish*. He saw the success of *No Orchids*, published in 1940, as part of a discernible psychological climate, whose other products were Fascism, the Gestapo, mass-bombing and war. But in condemning *No Orchids*, Orwell made two reservations. First, he conceded that it was brilliantly written, and that the acts of cruelty it described sprang from a subtle and integrated, though perverse, view of human nature. Secondly, in contrasting *No Orchids* with *Raffles* – which he judged a healthy and harmless book – he pointed out that *No Orchids* was evil precisely because it lacked the restraint of conventional upper-class values; and this led him to the astonishing but intelligible conclusion that perhaps, after all, snobbery, like hypocrisy, was occasionally useful to society.

What, I wonder, would he have said of *Dr No*? For this novel is badly written to the point of incoherence and none of the 500,000 people who, I am told, are expected to buy it, could conceivably be giving Cape 13*s*. 6*d*. to savour its literary merits. Moreover, both its hero and its author are unquestionably members of the Establishment. Bond is an ex-Royal Navy Commander and belongs to Blades, a sort-of super-White's. Mr Fleming was educated at Eton and Sandhurst, and is married to a prominent society hostess, the ex-wife of Lord Rothermere. He is the foreign manager of that austere and respectable newspaper, the *Sunday Times*, owned by an elderly nobleman called Lord Kemsley, who once tried to sell a popular tabloid with the slogan (or rather his wife's slogan) of 'clean and clever'. Fleming belongs to the Turf and Boodle's and lists among his hobbies the collection of first editions. He is also the owner of Goldeneye, a house made famous by Sir Anthony Eden's Retreat from Suez. Eden's uneasy slumbers, it will be remembered, were disturbed by (characteristically) giant rats which, after they had been disposed of by his detectives, turned out to be specially tamed ones kept by Mr Fleming.

Orwell, in fact, was wrong. Snobbery is no protection: on the contrary, the social appeal of the dual Bond-Fleming personality has added an additional flavour to his brew of sex and sadism. Fleming's novels are not only successful, like *No Orchids*; they are also smart. The *Daily Express*, pursuing its task of bringing glamour and sophistication to the masses, has serialized the last three. Our curious post-war society, with its obsessive interest in debutantes, its cult of U and non-U, its working-class graduates educated into snobbery by the welfare state, is a soft market for Mr Fleming's poison. Bond's warmest admirers are among the Top People. Of his last adventure, *From Russia, With Love*, his publishers claim, with reason, that it 'won approval from the sternest critics in the world of letters'. *The Times Literary Supplement* found it 'most brilliant', the *Sunday Times* 'highly polished', the *Observer* 'stupendous', the *Spectator* 'rather pleasant'. And this journal, most susceptible of all, described it as 'irresistible'. It has become easier than it was in Orwell's day to make cruelty attractive. We have gone just that much farther down the slope. Recently I read Henri Alleg's horrifying account of his tortures in an Algiers prison; and I have on my desk a documented study of how we treat our prisoners in Cyprus. I am no longer astonished that these things can happen. Indeed, after reflecting on the Fleming phenomenon, they seem to me almost inevitable.

—5 April 1958

America's Suez?

HAS THERE EVER BEEN a war which constitutes such a devastating compound of horror, futility and political poison as the Vietnam conflict? In the confusion which followed the end of World War II, a group of empire-minded French officers and administrators persuaded a divided and uncertain government in Paris to attempt to reimpose French rule in Indo-China. They were blind and foolish men, no doubt, but might not even they have hesitated if they could have foreseen the terrible chain of events they set in motion? More than 20 years of butchery, with no end yet in sight; the loss of France's honour; 2 million dead; the debauching of an intelligent and industrious people; the creation of a new market for fiendish weapons and a human laboratory in which to test them; a progressive erosion of the standards by which civilised nations wage war; the first wholesale experiments in chemical warfare and the systematic destruction of the earth-cover. Could they have guessed that this small country would become the chief impediment to understanding between the super-powers and, indeed, a possible detonator of nuclear conflict? That it would drag down in its agony the mightiest nation on earth, cover its armed forces with humiliation and dirt, imperil its currency, divide its people as never in this century, and cause decent men and women everywhere to revile its name?

Vietnam is a tragedy without mitigation, without a solitary redeeming feature. It has engulfed a whole nation in physical loss and spread subtle poisons many thousands of miles away. It was in Vietnam that professional French officers first learnt the systematic use of torture and first formed the attitudes which led them to kill the Fourth Republic. Their American brothers are now acquiring the same tolerance of evil, and the men who serve under them the the same indifference to life or human dignity of any kind. The blood daily spilt in Vietnam glitters, in full colour, from the TV sets in millions of American homes; it is reflected in a heightened domestic violence, which all condemn and none knows how to cure; it is a growing factor in the racial war which threatens to tear apart America's cities. It leads young men to renounce their country and turn to exile; to engage, in cities across the world, in brutal and senseless battles with the police. It turns universities into schools of hatred, writers and artists into vessels of propaganda for one side or the other, weak-minded social democrats – like our present government – into hypocrites. Vietnam is the corrupter of the world.

On the Vietnam stage the West enacts a kind of travesty of itself, spoken in Newspeak, performed by fake heroes and real buffoons. America protects the freedom of the Vietnamese by helicopters armed with batteries of machine-guns, which spray entire villages with bullets and 'flush out' – the clean, antiseptic military phrase – their inhabitants; by cumbersome, big-bellied aircraft which, every week, pour hundreds of tons of herbicides on growing crops. They drop steel-blades ('Hound Dog') by the thousand and clusters of steel balls, the size of hand-grenades, which break on impact and scatter lethal pellets through the thin partitions of the peasants' huts. In Vietnam the treasures of the American way of death are spread out as in a shop-window.

In normal times – if one can use such a phrase about a country at war for a generation – the shop window is brightly illuminated for the benefit of those Americans who sponsor the show from the security of Washington. An expensive and highly professional public relations machine maintains the willing suspension of disbelief. According to an illuminating article in the *Wall Street Journal* (25 January), over 2,000 American VIPs visited Saigon last year, and the season reaches its height over Christmas and the New Year.

But there are some physical facts which even the best-regulated PR machine cannot overcome, and for the Americans in Saigon the moment of truth must have come last week. No one can carry out his part in the fantasy when the Vietcong enter the American embassy, supposedly impregnable, and snipe at Pentagon East, General Westmoreland's own headquarters. And for the world outside, it is hard to maintain confidence in the fiction of America preserving democratic freedoms in Vietnam when a thousand newspapers carry photographs of the chief of the Vietnamese police shooting, in cold blood and without a pretence of a trial, an unarmed man whose hands are tied behind his back. The fact that this crime was carried out in front of photographers suggests that America's 'allies' no longer believe the fiction is worth the trouble.

Of course those who are determined to delude themselves will cling to it tenaciously. Mr Bernard Levin tells readers of the *Daily Mail* that the Americans are dying in Vietnam so that he can enjoy Wagner. Mr Peregrine Worsthorne in the *Sunday Telegraph* thinks the events of last week will 'boost America's conscience', 'go a long way towards removing America's debilitating sense of guilt' and unleash 'a truly terrible spirit of righteous revenge'. Those who find such concepts credible are beyond the reach of argument, or indeed of ocular evidence. But there can't be many of them left.

How many, for that matter, are left in the American high command and in the White House?

The propaganda trumpets still sound but they give forth an uncertain note. 'It is felt that we now have the initiative,' said a Pentagon East spokesman, 'and that we are no longer reacting to enemy-initiated actions but are seeking out the enemy'; even as he spoke the bullets were whistling round Westmoreland's ears. The general himself felt that the 'enemy is running out of breath'; but another of his spokesmen, the next day, disagreed: the offensive had just begun. Saigon issues figures of enormous Vietcong casualties; but who believes them? Does Lyndon Johnson? The atmosphere in which the President negotiates with his generals may be measured by the fact that he now demands written assurances from them on the feasibility of military operations. And what remains of the central fiction – the very foundation of America's presence in Vietnam – that it is winning the hearts and minds of the people? What became of 'pacification', if the Americans cannot even hold the major cities? Even the French contrived as much. If this fiction, too, must be abandoned, then the war will be seen for what it is, a naked power-struggle, in which the Vietnamese themselves are expendable pawns. Or, as the late Harold Holt put it: 'It is bad luck on the Vietnamese people that the cold war should be fought out on their territory'.

How long can the American people be persuaded to continue a war, which is costing them so much, and dividing them so bitterly, if the last shred of moral respectability which clothed it is snatched away? They are indeed capable of great self-deception, and great cruelty and ruthlessness in pursuing what they see to be an honourable cause. But they must have an ideal; if this is no longer seen to be credible, the will to continue the struggle will collapse. France abandoned the attempt to subdue Indo-China because she suffered military defeat, and her people did not possess the belief in her mission to recover from the defeat. The Americans are unlikely to suffer a Dien Bien Phu, and the analogy is in any case misleading. What faces them, rather, is the choice which baffled the Tory leadership at Suez: whether to continue a war whose moral justification was dubious but which might wreck the currency and plunge the nation into real economic hardship. Mr Harold Macmillan spoke at one time of 'selling the National Gallery' to ensure that the Canal remained British; but when the point came, he, like the rest, meekly put economic self-interest first. In the long run the Americans are likely to make the same choice. The war will end, I suspect, not with a bang but with a chink of devalued dollars.

—9 February 1968

Are Virgins Obsolete?

ONE OF THE MOST STRIKING phenomena revealed by the scientific study of history is the astonishing stability of sexual morals. In this respect, at least, we do not get better or worse: we have sinned evenly across the centuries. On the public surface of life, of course, attitudes change sharply. Waves of puritanism are followed by gusts of excess. A Savonarola begets an Alexander VI, a Cromwell provokes a Charles II. In every age, self-appointed arbiters of public morals have denounced the degeneration of their times and prophesied social doom. In the Edwardian era, for instance, a celebrated Jesuit preached eloquently on the Sins of Society to fashionable London congregations, predicting catastrophe. The Great War obligingly occurred, but brought no improvement in sexual morals – indeed, it was soon blamed for the further decline which allegedly followed.

But beneath these torrents of words and threats, the great mass of the ordinary people follow patterns which seem to be immutable. Fashions in public attitudes, though they arouse great heat among the *bien-pensants,* have remarkably little connection with what the majority actually do – or do not do – in bed. The one reliable index of morality – the statistics of illegitimate births – suggests that the volume of sin varies only with the size of the population.

This fact is equally annoying to popes and social psychologists, suggesting as it does severe limitations in their respective fields of professional activity. Perhaps this explains why both are obsessively interested in the subject and draw alarming – though often diametrically opposed – conclusions from what they claim to have discovered about it. Just after the war, a learned *abbé* asserted to me that it was the existence of military brothels which led to the collapse of the French army in 1940. Shortly afterwards all brothels in France were shut, but the French did not fight any better in Indo-China. Social experts, it seems to me, are equally pessimistic in attributing frustration, mental breakdowns and even crime to sexual restraint. Professor Carstairs, in a recent B.B.C. lecture, appeared to suggest that greater sexual licence among the young induced more charitable behaviour towards each other. Why should it? Early love affairs – especially when one partner has no 'honourable intentions' – are apt to lead to bickering and often to cruelty. Here, as in the pronouncements of clerical authorities, the experts often appear to be dealing with a world utterly remote from one's own experience. And both categories of men approach the subject from what one might term a crisis viewpoint.

Is there a sexual crisis among the young? Glancing back at history, one tends to doubt it. Sexual habits are notoriously impervious to change. For nearly a millennium the Catholic church has tried to enforce sacerdotal celibacy, using ever more formidable sanctions; but the present-day customs of the clergy in, say, Ireland and Spain, suggest that the campaign has met with indifferent success. The apostles of free love, active now for over a century, have done no better. The great majority seem firmly attached to the marriage system, but equally firmly determined to break its rules when they judge it desirable. The evidence for a sudden and dramatic change in sexual morals, among teenagers or anyone else, seems flimsy.

Yet there is a crisis of sorts – induced largely by the public arbiters of morals, both clerical and lay. Young people are given no firm guidance from above, since their elders are bitterly divided on the issue. But one thing which is impressed upon them from the earliest age is that sex is of transcendental importance. It is the dominant theme in virtually every book, play or film which achieves notoriety. It is imparted to them in a thousand subtle ways through advertisements and T.V. It is a moot point whether the publication of *Lady Chatterley* will damage the morals of young people; what cannot be disputed is that the trial reinforced the impression that sex is the dominant issue of the age. The secular experts deplore the ravages of teenage sex – attributing them, oddly enough, to the indifference or timidity of parents – and then promptly supply sub-editors with the controversial headlines which increase the sense of claustrophobic obsession. Clergymen inform us that young people place too much importance on sex, and then settle down to the far more serious business of haggling about contraceptives.

The bitter conflict among supposedly responsible adults is bound to induce acute schizophrenia among the young. The reformers have undermined the moral barriers against extra-marital sex, but have utterly failed to shake the paramountcy of marriage. Their fierce struggle with the orthodox has been resolved by a series of ludicrous compromises which the young must find bewildering and cynical. A film may portray adultery in the most lascivious detail, provided the adulterers are suitably punished. Contraceptives are freely on sale; but a teenage girl who approaches a guidance clinic for advice on how to use them – and who has not taken the precaution of buying a wedding-ring from Woolworth's – will be quickly shown the door. Pop-singers howl invitations to promiscuity from the juke-boxes, and then appear on T.V. to agree with their elders that there is no substitute for putting up the banns. Perhaps the most bizarre example of this moral confusion (with strong commercial overtones) is a London twist-club catering mainly for teenagers which provides rows of beds for its clients; they are, however, permitted to sit only on the edges.

The practical result of this confused compromise between the advocates of sexual reform and the defenders of the established moral system has been to reverse the movement towards sexual equality. It is the girls who suffer, all the time. They are encouraged to break the rules – but only up to the point when they get themselves pregnant. From then on, they are strictly on their own, and let them find what comfort in Professor Carstairs' words they can. Progress has got *Lady Chatterley* into the bookshops and puffed a wind of change into the Reith Lectures, but it has done nothing to change the law of abortion or improve the predicament of the unwed mother. Deserted by the progressive, the young pregnant girl finds that her only friend – today as throughout history – is still the illegal abortionist.

Statistics are unobtainable, but from what I can gather there has been a huge and continuing increase in illegal operations, most of them carried out under appalling conditions. If the truth were told, many respectable parents would be shocked to discover what their daughters have secretly suffered. This is one of the areas of life in which class distinctions mean nothing. Debutantes used to announce their engagements during or shortly after Goodwood; now they slip off to some discreet 'clinic' – abroad if they are lucky. Young factory girls go to an obliging old hag round the corner. Comparatively few of them suffer permanent physical effects, but the mental and psychological consequences of their experience are often disastrous. This is something which both those who encourage them to fornicate and those who deny them instruction in contraceptives and the right to a legal abortion choose to ignore.

In this period of sexual confusion, one sometimes has the impression that the girls themselves are trying, instinctively, to formulate a new code of sexual ethics, based on the facts of their predicament. A girl can no longer afford to refuse a young man liberties; but she employs carefully-graded restrictions which she knows to be accepted among her friends. This journal recently published, in the *This England* column, an extract from a Sunday paper. A young girl is giving evidence:

> 'He asked if I would like to go to bed with him and I said: "Only married people do that." When he asked if I wanted intercourse I told him only engaged couples did it.'

At first reading this seemed puzzling. But the girl was in fact drawing a firm distinction between sexual intercourse in bed – a luxury permitted only to those actually married – and intercourse performed in less comfortable surroundings, which even so, in her view, could only be allowed if the couple were going steady.

Such folk-rules are unacceptable to the clerics and irritating to the reformers, whose belief is that there shouldn't be any rules at all. But the fact is that the great majority of people need an established system of conventions. If the Top People fail to agree as to what these should be, lesser people will devise their own and, within the limits of human frailty, observe them. Ideally, of course, the law and the teaching of the churches should be adapted to what the mass of the people think workable. But for the moment there is an immense gap. So long as that gap exists, her virginity will remain a girl's best friend.

—4 January 1963

Rome Goes Left

WHAT HAPPENS when a dictatorship is abruptly transformed into an oligarchy? When Stalin died in 1953 there were no precedents to guide his colleagues on the Central Committee, and in the ensuing rough and tumble at least one of them was killed. But the Roman Catholic Church has been doing precisely this sort of thing for a thousand years, and the events of the past fortnight in the Vatican, though scarcely very edifying, have at least been predictable and even relatively peaceful.

Some hard blows, however, were struck and received. Nineteen years is a long reign for a pope; and Pius XII was a man of strong views and idiosyncrasies. An autocrat who loathed delegating authority – he never appointed a Secretary of State – he was nevertheless very susceptible to advice from personal attendants and hangers-on, and during the last ten years of his life a distinctly Byzantine atmosphere permeated the papal apartments. Among the people around Pius who counted, there was only one – Tardini, the pro-Secretary of State – who commanded any respect in the Church. The rest were courtiers pure or simple. There was Sister Pasqualina, the German housekeeper, whose help in fixing a private audience was often essential and who encouraged Pius in his drift to Mariolatry. There was Galleazzi-Lisi, the Pope's doctor; his brother, Count Galleazzi, the papal architect; and other strange medical figures, such as Niehans, the Swiss expert on rejuvenation, who injected the Pope with animal-glands. There were two German Jesuits – the Pope's confessor and chaplain – and the powerful Jesuits of Vatican Radio. Finally, there were the three papal nephews, Princes Carlo, Giulio and Marcantonio Pacelli, all active in the legal and financial labyrinth of the Vatican.

Naturally, this set-up was resented by the Cardinals – and in particular by Cardinal Tisserant, the Dean, and the five big magnates of the Curia, led by Cardinal Canali, who runs the financial Congregation (they are known, collectively, as the 'Pentagon'). Though they still controlled the congregational committee-system, they were virtually excluded from decisions affecting diplomacy or dogma (all six French cardinals, for instance, bitterly opposed the dogma of the Assumption). Pius was often too busy to see his cardinals, particularly the foreign ones on their rare visits to Rome; and he sometimes flatly refused to receive senior bishops and archbishops, even though they might have journeyed thousands of miles. On the other hand, as they pointed out bitterly, he always seemed to have time to deliver long speeches to visiting delegations of gynæcologists or plumbers and never declined a private audience with Catholic film stars (his very last one was with Alec Guiness). Finally, Pius appeared to indicate his dislike for the Sacred College by refusing to fill its vacancies – there were fifteen at the time of his death.

Hence, when Galleazzi-Lisi finally brought himself to sign the death certificate, Tisserant, his beard flowing fiercely, descended on Castel Gandolfo with flaming sword. The Pasqualina was given exactly seven hours to pack her Gladstone bags. The princely nephews were told to make themselves scarce and not to talk to the Press. Lisi might have proved a more difficult proposition, for he held innumerable official appointments, but he played straight into Tisserant's hands. First, he sold his medical diary to the Press. This is not necessarily a serious offence in the Vatican, for many officials have to supplement their meagre stipends by selling information, but it provided a technical excuse for dismissing him. Secondly – and fatally – he botched the papal embalmment. Instead of using the traditional Egyptian method, in which the intestines are removed, he attempted to embalm the body entire, and the consequences were both disastrous and very discernible. This turned the Romans against him, and within forty-eight hours the police – as well as Tisserant – were advising him not to show his face in the city. What happened to the German Jesuits is not known; they seem just to have disappeared. (A rumour, started by the Communist *Unita,* that the Pope's secret diary had been smuggled out of the Vatican and sold to the German embassy, may have made their position difficult.)

Having cleared out the courtiers, the cardinals then got down to serious haggling among themselves. Tisserant received an initial setback, for he failed to secure his election as Chamberlain: the post went to the more popular Masella. During the week before the conclave opened the cardinals met every morning and, as their colleagues streamed in from all parts of the world, two distinct schools of thought began to emerge. The Curia cardinals, having suffered under Pius for two decades, were anxious to choose a healthy reactionary like themselves, who would allow them to play their traditional policy-making role, but at the same time would keep a firm grip on the overseas provinces and slap down experiments. The *autonomisti,* on the other hand – led, naturally, by the French – wanted more devolution. Both groups could muster a blocking vote of 17, but neither the 35 votes necessary for an election. Three further factors contributed to the impasse. Pius in his Bull, *Vacantis Apostolicae Sedis,* had laid it down that the balloting for his successor must be secret, and this made the bargaining process much trickier. He himself, so the cardinals complain, had failed to keep any of his private election promises, so this time they were naturally more suspicious of each other. Finally, and most important, by failing to fill up the College, Pius had narrowed the choice of *papabili.* In 1939, there were about thirty cardinals who, by reason of their age, training and background, were suitable compromise candidates, and only three ballots were required. This week, there were scarcely half-a-dozen *papabili* and the only suitable 'neutral', Roncalli, was seventy-six. The *autonomisti* would undoubtedly have preferred a youngish active man with progressive ideas, such as Montini or Agagianian. But the first was not a member of the College and the second was a 'foreigner'. I suspect, therefore, that they switched at an early stage to Roncalli who, though elderly, is still vigorous, is a firm friend of the French, a supporter of the worker-priest movement, and carried his own personal vote of four or five Italians. From then on, at each successive ballot, more and more cardinals must have climbed on his bandwagon. He was, moreover, elected on two reasonable assumptions: first, that his reign would be short; second, that he would appoint a progressive Secretary of State – with Montini as the favourite – who would eventually succeed him. Inevitably, then, his papacy will inaugurate an era of change.

Indeed, the desire for change was undoubtedly increased by the actual circumstances of his election, which even the hardened Roman clergy were finding distasteful. In the Piazza, the vast, excited crowds ate ice-cream, drank beer, chewed olives and beans. For some reason, a mobile blood-donation unit had arrived and played *The Ride of the Valkyries* over a loudspeaker. Communist agitators, placed at strategic points in the crowd, started spicy rumours. A ludicrous note was introduced by the failure of the smoke-signalling apparatus. The cardinals had no choice but to use this absurd system, for it is laid down in the Bull; but since a new stove was being used (the old one had been stolen and sold as a potential relic) the failure to try it out seems inexcusable.

Within the conclave the atmosphere must have been unbearable. Nearly all the cardinals are over seventy (one is ninety-six), and they were living in conditions of acute discomfort: the grandeur of

the Vatican Palace is mainly visual – it does not extend to such simple amenities as modern bathrooms, lavatories and soft mattresses. Twenty brought their private doctors to Rome, but were not allowed to bring them into the conclave. Four are in very fragile health, four are deaf, one almost blind, two unable to write, one is in plaster; some are extremely rude. An hour before they were due to meet, one of their number collapsed and died. The rest, as they trudged slowly into the Sistine Chapel, can hardly have been easy in their minds, for there is a Roman tradition that 'three cardinals must die to elect a pope'. Even Vatican democracy finds it hard to function in such conditions, and as I left Rome many forward-minded *monsignori* were saying openly that such an election must never be allowed to happen again; that the entire system should be changed and the choice left to a small committee who would not themselves be eligible.

John XXIII can be expected to make other, far more important, changes. There is general agreement that, in future, the Vatican finances should be publicly audited, if only to eradicate scandal and ensure that some sort of order is kept. In many of the 'backward areas' of Catholicism, the Church is dying for lack of money, although the Vatican has funds of around £14 thousand million in New York, London, and Swiss banks. Cardinal Spellman, whose church has virtually financed South American Catholicism since the war, is determined to impose a centralized 'Marshall Plan' on the Curia. Plans are also being discussed for the enlargement of the College and the introduction of a compulsory retiring age; for regular cardinals' conferences and a Civil Service Commission for Vatican appointments.

But transcending these administrative details is the problem of the role the Church should play in the mid-20th century. Slowly but surely, Pius had been steering Catholicism towards a policy of peaceful co-existence in the Cold War, and of positive neutrality in the colonial struggle. His encouragement of the Wyszynsky-Gomulka agreement and his public disapproval of both the Suez expeditions and the Jordan-Lebanon landings testify to this; whilst, in Algeria, the Church has remained the most consistent European opponent of *colon* extremism. From my conversations in Rome, I believe that such tendencies will become more marked under John XXIII, and for one very simple reason. Although the Church, with its 450 million adherents, is by far the largest in the world, 90 per cent. of them are concentrated in Europe and the Americas; less than 10 per cent. live in the two 'continents of the future' – Asia and Africa – where the demographic revolution is just beginning. By 1980, therefore, the Church's percentage of the global population will have fallen from a fifth to less than one-eighth. Yet it is precisely in the coloured areas – notably West, Central and East Africa, India and Indo-China that its chances are brightest. The Afro-Asian provinces still, however, retain their missionary flavour and carry little weight in the Vatican (there are only two coloured cardinals). All this will now be changed, and one of the first acts of the new Pope will, it is expected, be the appointment of more cardinals and archbishops in the ex-colonial regions. But the shift of emphasis will be much more than bureaucratic. It will affect points of dogma: the prelates from the east will compel the Vatican to abandon its opposition to artificial birth-control, just as the Indian bishops swung round the Lambeth Conference. It will also affect political policy. By striving to retain and justify its claim to universality, in an age in which the world balance of power is changing, the Church will increasingly be obliged to act as a mediator between the two great secular blocks, and the Vatican – that citadel of anti-Communism – may yet find itself the spokesman of a Third Force.

—1 November 1958

Hunting and Humbug

FEW HUMAN ACTIVITIES have aroused such contentious passions, over so long a period, as the hunting of animals. Fifty years before the birth of Christ, Cicero was snorting contemptuously that he found it impossible to understand how an educated man could take pleasure in so disgusting a pursuit. A thousand years later, the Normans imposed over a third of England a complete legal, social and economic system exclusively designed to protect the sport. Nothing in our early legal history aroused greater savagery and class-bitterness than the forest laws. Cottars, ceorls and free men alike were branded, maimed, flogged and slaughtered in their hundreds for defying them; in turn they frequently murdered wardens and sheriff's men. The decline of forest law merely shifted the battlefield. From the Tudor age onwards, the poaching class – that is, virtually everyone in England below the gentleman farmer – waged continuous and violent warfare against the game laws, which were brutally upheld by magistrates on behalf of their fellow-gentry.

With the invention of modern fox-hunting by Hugo Meynell, and the perfection of the shotgun, the controversy was raised to a more exalted, one might say intellectual, plane – and there it has stuck. The country-folk closed ranks, but had to face an acrimonious verbal assault from high-minded townsmen (and women) who objected to bloodsports on moral grounds. The arguments on both sides are by now notorious, indeed threadbare from prolonged use. Almost exactly 100 years ago they were fully set out in *The Fortnightly* by Trollope, on behalf of the hunting interest, and the historian Freeman, speaking for the humanitarians. Little has changed since, except in one vital respect. Trollope wrote with the easy assurance that behind him were the overwhelming majority of the House of Commons, still largely composed of country gentlemen. Today the anti-hunting lobby has not only numbers but time on its side. It is poised for victory. If Labour is returned at the coming election, it is on the cards that most forms of bloodsports will be made illegal.

Before this happens, I would like to make one last attempt to strip the subject of the extraordinary layers of illogicality, emotion and sheer humbug with which it is burdened. None of us is objective about it and very few of us consistent: I exempt from this general charge the small band of idealists who refuse willingly to take any form of life, and who are vegetarian both in food and apparel. I also exempt the hunting man who honestly admits that he pursues and kills animals purely for pleasure. But between these two categories lies every variety of specious justification, self-deception and gross dishonesty. Foxes 'like' being hunted. No: they would much prefer to be shot (or poisoned?). Game must be 'kept down' (then why raise it?). Hunting preserves the balance of nature. No: it destroys it. If animals were not hunted they would die out. No: they would flourish. Hunting is a class sport. No: it is the chief pleasure and delight of the entire rural community. Hunting coarsens and corrupts. No: it keeps the younger bumpkins from the bingo-halls and other dens of vice. It is unfair. No: the fox has an even chance (and: 'Your wily cock-pheasant knows how to fly over the bad guns').

The truth is that for those, like myself, who view hunting with a mild but governable distaste, it is awfully difficult to be consistent. Thoreau, in his book on Walden Pond, argues reasonably that for a young man to learn the disciplines and privations of hunting (in the widest sense) is, on the whole, desirable; but that the pursuit should be abandoned with full manhood. He goes on to say that it is natural and right to hunt in order to survive but that hunting purely for sport is unconscionable. This position seems acceptable, but it completely ignores the sufferings of the animals, which are likely to be far less under sporting rules than under a natural free-for-all. A clear instance is East Africa, where the detested figure of the White Hunter at least kills swiftly and with discrimination. The tribesmen themselves, morally justified by their intense hunger for flesh, inflict frightful cruelties on the animals and would certainly wipe out whole species, were not game laws enforced by rich sporting interests.

Even if we ignore the welfare of the animals, and argue on the score that killing debases the hunter, we are still in difficulties. The red-faced Master of Foxhounds may be debauched, but what of the patient and solitary fisherman – often a kindly clergyman or doctor, occasionally even an intellectual? The fisherman himself is inconsistent, for he will throw the small fish back into the water and abuse Frenchmen, for instance, as immoral for not doing likewise. Yet there can be no doubt that salmon-fishing, to give one example, is both cruel and brutal; and there is nothing, I believe, quite so unnerving as the cries of a harpooned baby whale. For that matter, how are we to judge the lepidopterist, usually represented as timid, myopic, absentminded, a symbol of humane, civilized, even Quixotic, values? We teach our children that it is wrong to tear the wings off flies, but we cheerfully subject thousands of millions of creatures to the agonies of modern insecticides – and with a clear conscience too, for our values equate hygiene with morality.

Why do we respect some creatures and hate others (even vegetarians, in panic, have been known to kill harmless grass-snakes)? Our eclecticism is governed purely by instincts, however we seek to rationalize them. Snakes have no more and no less moral rights than foxes. Indeed one of the curators at the Butanta Institute in Brazil where all kinds of poisonous creatures are bred and studied, told me that it was perfectly possible to have an affectionate relationship with a boa-constrictor, and that he had warm feelings towards even some of his tarantulas.

But supposing we all agree that hunting debases, does that automatically give us a right to stop it? Here we touch at the heart of the conflict between libertarianism and social morality in English life. At what point should the state intervene to prevent an activity which harms those who indulge in it and is, in a general sense, noxious to society? There are all kinds of things – smoking, drinking, driving private motor-cars – which bring death and misery on the widest scale, but are allowable. All of us would like to legislate against activities we deplore; all of us would like unlimited freedom to indulge in those we enjoy.

In this respect, there is blind inconsistency on both sides of the hunting fence. The hunting fraternity are notoriously lascivious and, in the season, the night air of Melton Mowbray is loud with the sighs of adulterers. But the same people are overwhelmingly in favour of draconian legislation against, say, homosexuals and nudists, and they deplored the publication of *Lady Chatterley's Lover*, more particularly since it portrays the amorous triumph of a gamekeeper over a member of the landed classes. Inconsistent? Of course. But what of those well-meaning humanitarians who would bring legal relief to the deviant but seek to prevent the hunting of foxes by consenting adults? The trouble is that English people form their opinions in huge, inbred chunks – there is a reactionary set of views and a progressive set, with very little cross-voting. Who ever heard of a prominent homosexual or nudist riding to hounds? What MFH has ever turned Conscientious Objector?

I fully admit that my own position is as muddled as most other people's. I used to watch a lot of bullfighting and believe that, at its best, it is one of the noblest spectacles created by man (at its customary worst it is horrible). But I find it intolerable that a great and beautiful animal like the stag should be hounded to death in a river-bed, or that red deer should be shot with powerful modern rifles. I hated seeing brown bears killed in Scandinavia (they were awoken at dawn by beating tins outside their lairs and shot as they emerged, dazed with sleep). But I see nothing against hunting the grizzly in the natural conditions of the Rockies.

Nevertheless, in this confusion, I hold strongly to two principles. First, in determining the relative rights of man and animal, we must concede the paramountcy to man. His interests – and they include his reasonable diversions – should come first. Animals are entitled to our concern in so far as they serve, delight and comfort mankind. Those which serve man most, such as the horse, and dog, and have the closest relation with him, thereby earn a degree of consideration and protection inferior only to that we extend to human life itself.

If we accept this, then a second principle emerges. Man is a creature of infinite variety, particularly in the pursuit of pleasure. Some of these activities are harmful; but they may also contribute to the riches of our civilization. We must beware of uniformity, even under the most exalted moral aegis. Before we suppress any manifestation of the human spirit, we must weigh its contributions as well as its evils – and the onus of proof must lie heavily with the suppressors. Hunting has always played a distinctive and colourful role in our history. It has given us some of our best songs and ballads, wonderful pictures by Morland and Stubbs, Pollard, Herring and Rowlandson, some of the finest chapters in Trollope and countless other valuable and pleasing things. It may well in time be swept away, and no doubt England will be a better place for it. But a happier place, a richer place? I wonder.

—12 July 1963

The Menace of Beatlism

MR WILLIAM DEEDES is an Old Harrovian, a member of the cabinet and the minister in charge of the government's information services. Mr Deedes, it will be remembered, was one of those five ministers who interviewed Mr Profumo on that fateful night and were convinced by him that he had not slept with Miss Keeler. Now any public relations man, even a grand one who sits in the cabinet, can use a touch of credulity; but even so I remember thinking at the time: 'If Deedes can believe that, he'll believe anything.' And indeed he does! Listen to him on the subject of the Beatles:

> 'They herald a cultural movement among the young which may become part of the history of our time . . . For those with eyes to see it, something important and heartening is happening here. The young are rejecting some of the sloppy standards of their elders, by which far too much of our output has been governed in recent years . . . they have discerned dimly that in a world of automation, declining craftsmanship and increased leisure, something of this kind is essential to restore the human instinct to excel at something and the human faculty of discrimination.'

Incredible as it may seem, this was not an elaborate attempt at whimsy, but a serious address, delivered to a meeting of the City of London Young Conservatives, and heard in respectful silence. Not a voice was raised to point out that the Emperor wasn't wearing a stitch. The Beatles phenomenon, in fact, illustrates one of my favourite maxims: that if something becomes big enough and popular enough – and especially commercially profitable enough – solemn men will not be lacking to invest it with virtues. So long as the Beatles were just another successful showbiz team, the pillars of society could afford to ignore them, beyond bestowing the indulgent accolade of a slot in the Royal Variety Performance. But then came the shock announcement that they were earning £6,250,000 a year – and, almost simultaneously, they got the stamp of approval from America.

This was quite a different matter: at once they became not only part of the export trade but an electorally valuable property. Sir Alec Home promptly claimed credit for them, and was as promptly accused by Mr Wilson of political clothes-stealing. Conservative candidates have been officially advised to mention them whenever possible in their speeches. The Queen expressed concern about the length of Ringo's hair. Young diplomats at our Washington embassy fought for their autographs. A reporter described them as 'superb ambassadors for Britain'. It is true that the Bishop of Woolwich has not yet asked them to participate in one of his services, but the invitation cannot be long delayed. And, while waiting for the definitive analysis of their cultural significance by Messrs Raymond Williams and Richard Hoggart we have Mr Deedes' contribution on behalf of the cabinet.

Of course, our society has long been brainwashed in preparation for this apotheosis of inanity. For more than two decades now, more and more intellectuals have turned their backs on their trade and begun to worship at the shrine of 'pop culture'. Nowadays, if you confess that you don't know the difference between Dizzy Gillespie and Fats Waller (and, what is more, don't care) you are liable to be accused of being a fascist.

To buttress their intellectual self-esteem, these treasonable clerks have evolved an elaborate cultural mythology about jazz, which purports to distinguish between various periods, tendencies and schools. The subject has been smeared with a respectable veneer of academic scholarship, so that now you can overhear grown men, who have been expensively educated, engage in heated argument on the respective techniques of Charlie Parker and Duke Ellington. You can see writers of distinction, whose grey hairs testify to years spent in the cultural vineyard, squatting on the bare boards of malodorous caverns, while through the haze of smoke, sweat and cheap cosmetics comes the monotonous braying of savage instruments.

One might, I suppose, attribute such intellectual treachery to the fact that, in jazz circles, morals are easy, sex is cheap and there is a permissive attitude to the horrors of narcotics. Men are, alas, sometimes willing to debauch their intellects for such rewards. But I doubt if this is the real reason. The growing public approval of anti-culture is itself, I think, a reflection of the new cult of youth. Bewildered by a rapidly changing society, excessively fearful of becoming out of date, our leaders are increasingly turning to young people as guides and mentors – or, to vary the metaphor, as geiger-counters to guard them against the perils of mental obsolescence. If youth likes jazz, then it must be good, and clever men must rationalize this preference in intellectually respectable language. Indeed, whatever youth likes must be good: the supreme crime, in politics and culture alike, is not to be 'with it'. Even the most unlikely mascots of the Establishment are now drifting with the current: Mr Henry Brooke, for instance, finds himself appointing to the latest Home Office committee the indispensable teenager, who has, what is more, the additional merit of being a delinquent.

Before I am denounced as a reactionary fuddy-duddy, let us pause an instant and see exactly what we mean by this 'youth'. Both TV channels now run weekly programmes in which popular records are played to teenagers and judged. While the music is performed, the cameras linger savagely over the faces of the audience. What a bottomless chasm of vacuity they reveal! The huge faces, bloated with cheap confectionery and smeared with chain-store makeup, the open, sagging mouths and glazed eyes, the hands mindlessly drumming in time to the music, the broken stiletto heels, the shoddy, stereotyped, 'with-it' clothes: here apparently is a collective portrait of a generation enslaved by a commercial machine. Leaving a TV studio recently, I stumbled into the exodus from one of these sessions. How pathetic and listless they seemed: young girls, hardly any more than sixteen, dressed as adults and already lined up as fodder for exploitation. Their eyes came to life only when one of their grotesque idols – scarcely older than they – made a brief appearance, before a man in a camel-hair coat hustled him into a car. Behind this image of 'youth', there are, evidently, some shrewd older folk at work.

And what of the 'culture' which is served up to these pitiable victims? According to Mr Deedes, 'the aim of the Beatles and their rivals is first class of its kind. Failure to attain it is spotted and criticized ruthlessly by their many highly-discriminating critics.' I wonder if Mr Deedes has ever taken the trouble to listen to any of this music? On the Saturday TV shows, the merits of the new records are discussed by panels of 'experts', many of whom seem barely more literate or articulate than the moronic ranks facing them. They are asked to judge each record a 'hit' or a 'miss', but seem incapable of explaining why they have reached their verdict. Occasionally one of the 'experts' betrays some slight acquaintance with the elementals of music and makes what is awesomely described as a 'technical' point: but when such merit is identified in a record, this is usually found to be a reason for its certain commercial failure.

In any case, merit has nothing to do with it. The teenager comes not to hear but to participate in a ritual, a collective grovelling to gods who are themselves blind and empty. 'Throughout the performance,' wrote one observer, 'it was impossible to hear anything above the squealing except the beat of Ringo's drums.' Here, indeed, is 'a new cultural movement': music which not only cannot be heard but does not *need* to be heard. As such I have no doubt that it is, in truth, 'first class of its kind'.

If the Beatles and their like were in fact what the youth of Britain wanted, one might well despair. I refuse to believe it – and so I think will any other intelligent person who casts his or her mind back far enough. What were we doing at sixteen? I remember the drudgery of Greek prose and the calculus, but I can also remember reading the whole of Shakespeare and Marlowe, writing poems and plays and stories. It is a marvellous age, an age of intense mental energy and discovery. Almost every week one found a fresh idol – Milton, Wagner, Debussy, Matisse, El Greco, Proust – some, indeed, to be subsequently toppled from the pantheon, but all springing from the mainstream of European culture. At sixteen, I and my friends heard our first performance of Beethoven's Ninth Symphony; I can remember the excitement even today. We would not have wasted 30 seconds of our precious time on the Beatles and their ilk.

Are teenagers different today? Of course not. Those who flock round the Beatles, who scream themselves into hysteria, whose vacant faces flicker over the TV screen, are the least fortunate of their generation, the dull, the idle, the failures: their existence, in such large numbers, far from being a cause for ministerial congratulation, is a fearful indictment of our education system, which in ten years of schooling can scarcely raise them to literacy. What Mr Deedes fails to perceive is that the core of the teenage group – the boys and girls who will be the real leaders and creators of society tomorrow – never go near a pop concert. They are, to put it simply, too busy. They are educating themselves. They are in the process of inheriting the culture which, despite Beatlism or any other mass-produced mental opiate, will continue to shape our civilization. To use Mr Deedes' own phrase, though not in the sense he meant it, they are indeed 'rejecting some of the sloppy standards of their elders'. Of course, if many of these elders in responsible positions surrender to the Gadarene Complex and seek to elevate the worst things in our society into the best, their task will be made more difficult. But I believe that, despite the antics of cabinet ministers with election nerves, they will succeed.

—25 February 1964

Make Mine Topless!

SOME VERY FUNDAMENTAL ISSUES of human freedom are involved in the business of topless dresses. It is true that the origins of the affair are trivial and in some respects mercenary. Thanks to Sir Alec Home's decision to postpone the election until the Autumn, the silly season started nearly eight weeks early this year and newspapers are desperate for lively copy. Topless dresses give editors a wonderful running story which fascinates lubricious and censorious readers equally. The dresses themselves were, in origin at least, a mere gimmick. For some time, certain dress designers have been disturbed by the apparent unwillingness of women to accept dresses with very low necklines. They launched the idea of the topless dress in order to push the frontiers of respectability a stage further and make very low-cut dresses seem, by comparison, conventional. The trick certainly succeeded: few women with the figures for it will now hesitate to bare nine-tenths of their bosom. What the designers did not foresee, however, was that women would be prepared to wear the topless dress itself. In fact very few were made; the story was a promotion stunt which existed largely on paper. Yet where such dresses are available, they have sold exceptionally well. Evidently, a surprising number of women want to wear these dresses, at least in private.

This has shocked and dismayed many designers. It is a threat to their livelihood. The art of female fashion depends basically on only two variables: hemlines and necklines. By juggling artfully with them from season to season, the designer can persuade women to buy many more clothes than they need or want because these two lines date the dress infallibly. It is the original and classic illustration of the theory of planned obsolescence. But if the neckline disappears altogether, the designer's basic resources are automatically halved. From his point of view, the awful thing about the topless dress is that it does not date. Possibly in time he may find ways of getting round this problem – but for the moment it is not surprising to hear that Dior is planning high necklines for his autumn collection. It is an instinctively defensive act.

Meanwhile, the topless dress is being worn, and this is where the social and moral problems arise. Let us look at the line-up on both sides of the controversy. In favour of the topless dress are, of course, a few models and starlets who need a little free publicity. But, to judge from the press-clippings not only in this country but elsewhere, the great majority of women who have actually worn them in public are perfectly ordinary housewives and working girls who happen to possess elegant breasts and who like to display them for the benefit of us all.

On the other side, by contrast, we have a curious alliance. Naturally, all the *dramatis personae* of puritan authoritarianism – policemen, magistrates, clergymen, communists, Tory councillors and others whose professional business it is to limit the public's opportunities to enjoy itself – have united in an outraged chorus of abuse. I have always regarded the Public Baths Superintendent as a particularly unattractive and totalitarian figure, and on this occasion one of them has obliged with a characteristically revealing comment. Topless bathing suits, he said, would be banned in his baths on the grounds that 'they might embarrass the children'. A more conventional expression of the anti-sex viewpoint was provided by the Prosecuting Counsel in a case in California. According to him, a very pretty young woman who had exposed her breasts on a beach was guilty of 'throwing filth in the faces of the police and the public'. This extraordinary remark was apparently made in tones of genuine passion.

However, the authoritarians have also been joined by those whose professional business it is to operate on the forbidden side of the sex-barrier. Fanatical nudists are furious at the topless cult, which they denounce as obscene. Call-girls hate it. Striptease dancers fear (needlessly, I should have thought) that it will put them out of business, and when one of their number in Australia actually wore one, she was beaten up by her colleagues and fired. Whores and pimps – anyone in fact who makes money out of the frustrations imposed by conventional morality – have a vested interest in keeping the sex-barriers high. At all costs the public must not get its sexual enjoyment free. Throughout history the puritan and the professional dispenser of sex have joined in unholy and unacknowledged wedlock. If another Gibbon comes to write the history of Christian civilization, he may note in an ironic aside that the night Oscar Wilde was convicted and gaoled, the West End tarts danced in the streets for joy. Ex-prostitutes, I'm told, make the best nuns, and one might say that inside every whore there is a Joynson-Hicks or a Henry Brooke struggling to get out.

Women who wear topless dresses in public risk prosecution, and plans are seemingly afoot to stage a test-case. It is not yet known precisely what charge will be made against a woman behaving in this fashion, but clearly the essence of the crime committed depends on the view that a woman's breasts are obscene: however the charge is framed it does not make sense except on the basis of this proposition. But can any lawyer explain, in rational terms, why a woman's breasts are obscene? My dictionary defines the word as 'repulsive, filthy, loathsome, indecent, lewd'. What possible bearing do any of these expressions have on the breasts of a normal and healthy young woman? If breasts are repulsive, filthy or loathsome, why are we invited to admire the Venus de Milo? Surely the answer is precisely the opposite: a woman's breasts, far from being repulsive, filthy and loathsome, are, or can be, attractive, beautiful and desirable. The obscenity, if any exists, must and can only lie in the eyes and mind of the beholder. What the law is in fact saying is that women must not expose their breasts because men are obscene.

And here we come to the heart of the matter. The law is made by men and for men; the woman is, as it were, incidental to it. She is regarded more in the nature of an instrument, an impersonal property, without legal consciousness of her own, whose significance consists solely in the way men react to her. We have laws about drugs, firearms and dogs; and we have laws about women. One of them prescribes the portions of her anatomy she is forbidden to display: but the intention behind it is not to protect her person or her virtue, but to inhibit the supposedly unrestrained lusts of the men who may look at her. The interests of the woman are rejected as irrelevant. The law, being entirely masculine in orientation, cannot conceive that a woman may wish to show her breasts without any other motive than that she is proud of them.

Here, it seems to me, we have a very simple and straightforward issue of personal liberty, which goes straight to the heart of the continued subjection and subordination of women in our society. The law permits a woman to display her breasts in a dingy basement club for the obvious, express and sole purpose of exciting the sexual appetites of men. What she must not do, however, is to display them in public for her own satisfaction. Perhaps I am naïve, but I regard this as flagrant and selective injustice. We rightly condemn the customs of South Arabia, and other backward parts of the Arab world, which forbid a woman to reveal any portion of her body except to her husband. We recognize that this is the direct consequence of social and religious teaching which denies woman a soul and relegates her to the level of a mere plaything and property of men. The most important contribution of Christianity to civilization was its establishment of the spiritual equality of the sexes. Yet where is the difference in principle between the ethics of the harem and the refusal to allow a young Englishwoman, in the mid-20th century, to display one of the most attractive parts of her body in the streets? Women have got the vote and much else of the formal impedimenta of equality; they have yet to break through the social mould which still treats them as objects rather than persons. A silly season stunt or a revolt of the still-inferior sex? It depends which way you look at it. But my guess is that a girl who wears a topless dress in the streets of Coventry or Nottingham could be doing as much for her sex as any Mrs Pankhurst.

—24 July 1964

Strictly Vindictive

THE WEEK BEFORE Cecil King was dismissed as chairman of the world's largest publishing company, I arrived, rather late, at a party given at 11 Downing Street. By the doorway was Hugh Cudlipp. In all innocence, I said: 'Hugh, I think it is time you got rid of King. He is turning the *Mirror* into a proprietor's newspaper.' Cudlipp looked startled, as well he might; by then the *putsch* must have been in its final stages of preparation, and any leakage could – indeed must – have been fatal. But the secret was kept; King fell; and those who trouble to read this curious volume of memoirs (*Strictly Personal* by Cecil King, Weidenfeld & Nicolson 45*s*.) will realize why his fall was inevitable.

Not that Mr King discusses the episode or reproaches his assassins. But he produces sufficiently startling insights into his character to convince me that while he had the courage and ability to build an empire, he lacked the magnanimity and balance to rule one. He also shows that his temperament was such that his removal could only be accomplished by a palace revolution. This is one of the most candid and self-damning autobiographies of our time.

King's vanity is breathtaking. 'By the time I was thirteen I had read more books than most people in a lifetime.' 'At school . . . I knew what remarks to make or questions to ask to silence anyone . . . a devastating weapon . . .' 'I have always had a wider general knowledge than anyone I have ever met . . . I have a greater gift of foresight than anyone I have met, and my life has been such that it has been helpful to keep this faculty in constant use.' Some people, he adds, 'have thought me the best talker in London.' He is also 'to [his] astonishment' regarded by his 'colleagues as a master of timing' – one suspects before the *putsch* – 'and I have been told that my sense of time is "geological" '. Best of all, 'my judgement is very good and over a very wide range' – especially of people: 'The fact that I am a good judge of people has helped me enormously in my career, and partly explains why I am such a good administrator.' What is more, King has the gift of passing on these talents, notably to Cudlipp:

> 'Over the years [Cudlipp] has acquired an excellent education, and picked up from me a habit of looking ahead which, once acquired, cannot be forgotten.'

There is even a supernatural element in King's range of accomplishments. He has told us his wife has the capacity to stop trains and aircraft. He himself can become invisible, as he makes clear in a passage reminiscent of Boswell:

> 'Never express your real thoughts. Throw out amusing or controversial ideas but leave no hint of your own convictions. As you are shy or frightened, you have to try to be invisible and, anyway, to learn courage . . . To become invisible sounds impossible and, of course, in any complete sense it is, but it is surprising to what an extent one can become invisible it one sets one's mind to it.'

There may be some truth in this last claim. Shortly after King's memoirs were serialized, Lady Gaitskell and I were discussing his iniquities at a diplomatic reception. We were hemmed in on one side by a door, on another by a sturdy sofa, in front by the mob; behind us a blank wall. Suddenly I became conscious of a presence behind us and, half turning round, I saw King, gazing not at us, but through us. Shortly, by the same agency, he vanished. It is, I think, equally *ad rem* that the door porter at the Midland Hotel, Manchester, once mistook King for Malcolm Muggeridge's personal detective.

Mr King's vanity extends itself to the *Daily Mirror*, of which he was, according to his own account, if not the onlie begetter, at least the chief one:

> 'As a result [of my efforts] over the years we have acquired better sources of information over the whole field, political, diplomatic, financial, scientific, etc., than any other paper.'

The *Mirror*, he says, has been a major and at times decisive force in politics:

> 'In fact we were what opposition the government had in the war years. Attlee was merely supine, and the opposition consisted of Nye Bevan in the House of Commons and ourselves outside it.'

In fact, to use Mr King's expression, Mr Attlee was the Deputy Prime Minister. However, the *Mirror* went on to win the 1945 election, just saved Labour in 1950, just failed to save it in 1951 and just squeezed it past the post in 1964. Labour was bent on supporting Eden over Suez in 1956, but happily, 'Hugh Cudlipp went down to Brighton to the T.U.C. conference and persuaded them to pass a resolution hostile to any military intervention . . .'

Vanity is perhaps pardonable in an autobiography; persistent malice less so. *Strictly Personal* should have been entitled *Strictly Vindictive,* though the abuse becomes less frequent as the book proceeds and the laws of libel begin to apply. Since proof copies of the book were sent out, some prudent excisions have been made. But a good deal of mud still spatters the pages, and phrases such as 'A short, dark, common little woman' and 'Bertha Bartholomew was a vulgar old thing' are accurate indices of the manner in which it is thrown. His headmaster at Winchester was a 'humbug', the second master 'a pleasant nonentity with a stone-deaf wife'. One don 'owed his position to his attractive wife. He made no pretence of doing anything for his pupils.' Dawson, of *The Times*, got his job because 'his mistress was a friend of Molly's'; Caird, of the *Mail,* was 'a mean, penny-pinching Scotsman'; Marlowe 'a dignified nonentity'; Cowley 'a man without ability . . . His value to Rothermere was that he would do whatever Rothermere told him to do, however foolish or dishonest.' Bartholomew, the real creator of the *Mirror,* comes in for the coarsest treatment. He was 'nearly illiterate . . . usually incoherent by 9.30 a.m. . . . He enjoyed spying on people, and so our telephones were tapped and our letters read . . . Setting different members of the staff – or the board – at each other's throats was a real pleasure for him.' Churchill was a 'gifted adventurer' who surrounded himself with 'men of no calibre'; Lord Buckland was said to be so much disliked by his staff that 'when he died out riding, a party was held to drink the health of the horse that killed him'. There are miscellaneous sideswipes at men as diverse as J. F. Kennedy ('a compulsive womanizer'), Harriman ('a rich man, full stop'), Rusk and Henry Fowler. Various acquaintances, apart from the hapless Bart, seem to have died of drink, their failings remorselessly noted by this mordant chronicler.

But it is when King comes to his own family that he really lets fly. Grandfather Alfred, Northcliffe's favourite mistress, Uncle Rothermere, Uncle Leicester, and Uncle Cecil all succumbed to the bottle, as did Northcliffe's illegitimate son, who died in an asylum to boot. Even Grandma Harmsworth, in her middle nineties, was 'sustained by the brandy bottle'. King's father was 'irascible' with 'no imagination and no enterprise that I ever noticed'; but then King's mother had 'devitalized him and squashed him flat'. Northcliffe's wife 'had various amorous affairs'; Rothermere indulged in 'very crude womanizing . . . most of his affairs were one-night stands'; Emily Harmsworth was a 'sinister figure. Her first two children died, it was said, of neglect . . .' She had a 'ghoulish' habit of 'hovering around deathbeds' and was to be seen 'struggling on the sofa with young officers, or wandering about the upper floors in her undies'. Hildebrand 'married a lady he was said to have picked up on Brighton front'. Aunt Violet, King's godmother, 'pursued me from my adolescence with all the malice at her command'. Uncle Charles was a 'high-grade mental defective'. The only attractive member of the family seems to have been Uncle Vyvyan. When Northcliffe upbraided him for doing no work, he answered: 'What is the use of having a brother like you if I have to work?'

The central figure in King's demonology was, as the reader will by now have guessed, his mother. She had married 'for social reasons' and 'was no mother to her children and no wife to her husband . . .' 'She was very beautiful' (the photograph King prints does not bear this out) 'and very intelligent, but lazy, selfish and quite hopeless at handling people . . . she showed no interest in me, my character, my abilities or anything of the kind.' She was 'violently racist' and 'fell violently for other women', though King doubts that she was a lesbian. He adds two horrific sentences:

> 'Looking back on my life, I feel as though I were an orphan brought up by step-parents, a stepfather who was completely null and a stepmother who was loveless, capricious and occasionally cruel.'
>
> 'I have no wish to do anything with my hands and it seems to me that this was because in early childhood I had wanted to strangle [her] with them.'

How much of all this ought we to believe? I ask this because a great deal else Mr King writes is silly or just inaccurate. It is silly, for instance, to say that 'For anyone to want the Presidency as much as John Kennedy is a sign of immaturity.' It is silly to say that Nixon 'leaves our ministers looking like fumbling schoolboys' or that 'In English politics one could see [Humphrey] going straight to the top.' Equally, no one who has read *My Early Life* should find it surprising, as King does, that Churchill had an inferiority complex about his education. Some of King's statements seem highly dubious but are difficult to check. Did Northcliffe really give King's father a knighthood to please his mother? Did Uncle Leicester really commit bigamy in his constituency? Or make a fortune out of oil in Egypt, though oil was not discovered there until a generation after his death? King states that Rothermere took no interest in politics until he acquired the *Mail*; but this happened in 1922, and Rothermere was already Secretary for Air in 1917. It may be true, though I greatly doubt it, that Lady Rothermere 'financed both Gide and T. S. Eliot when they were both quite unknown'; but she cannot have persuaded her husband 'to finance the ballet when it first came to London in the Twenties with Diaghilev'. Nor do I believe the story that Rothermere installed one of the ballerinas 'in a large suite, but to her indignation nothing happened!' – for which party could have any interest in advertising the fact?

Plain errors abound. Consider, for instance:

> 'It was [Northcliffe's] revelation of the shell shortage which brought Asquith down. Beaverbrook tried to take the credit, but his books detail only the backstairs intrigues that actually removed Asquith.'

King is here confusing and telescoping the May 1915 crisis, which led to the formation of the First Coalition, with the December 1916 crisis, which led to Asquith's resignation. In seeking to rebuke Beaverbrook, always scrupulous about his facts, he makes an ass of himself. Even contemporary certitudes elude him. Beuve-Méry is not the editor of *Le Monde*, but its *directeur*; the Christian name of M. Lazareff of *France-Soir* is Pierre, not Paul; M. Pompidou does not come from the Auverone, wherever that may be, but from the Auvergne; it is not true that 'the only newspaper [in Italy] worth talking about is the *Corriere della Sera*'. And so on. The man 'who has always had a wider general knowledge than anyone I have ever met' must have a very limited acquaintance.

All the same, one finishes this book feeling neither angry with nor contemptuous of Mr King: just compassionate. From early manhood he has suffered from a fearful skin disease called psoriasis, which periodically is acutely painful or violently irritating. 'For most of my life,' he says, 'it has been like wearing a painfully uncomfortable hair shirt.' With an unhappy home, followed by the usual crucifixion at school, it is not altogether surprising that he grew up to be what he terms 'a formidable and unattractive acquaintance', repelling would-be friends and acquaintances. At least until recently, he says, 'I have hated myself and have always wanted to commit suicide'. There is a curious analogy here with De Gaulle, whose halitosis led him to fend off people before they got the chance to fend off him. King seems to have chosen power as a substitute for people, and its pursuit as an alternative to loving. I think this is why he is so callous in his judgements of men and women, for power is an abstraction which can feel no pain. *'Alors, Soustelle, changez vos amis!'* But power is no substitute for friendship; and in the end solitary power even becomes dangerous. The pawns moved obediently across the board for many years, but in the end they ganged up to checkmate the King.

—30 May 1969

The Man Born to be Pope

THE PONTIFICATE OF PAUL VI has proved a catastrophe for his Church and a personal tragedy for himself. That a pope should be repudiated, even reviled, by great masses of his followers; that his teachings on birth control, a major point of doctrine, should go unheard by a majority of the educated laity; that thousands of priests, and even princes of the Church, should accept it, if at all, with reluctance and with qualifications that make it meaningless; and that the Church itself, which has preserved its unity and discipline through two millenia, should now be a bickering shambles – all this would have been inconceivable five years ago, and all is largely the work of one man.

The irony is that no pope has been so assiduously prepared and trained, by himself and by his superiors, for the supreme office. If ever a man was born to be pope, it was Giovanni Battista Montini. The village of his birth, Concesio, in the foothills of the Italian Alps, is a nest of clericalism that has given four bishops to the Church. The nearest town, Brescia, is one of the most Catholic in all Italy, and Montini's father was its chief Catholic layman. A well-to-do minor aristocrat, married to a woman from the same background, Giorgio Montini had the means and the leisure to devote his life to the propagation of liberal Catholic principles. For thirty years he was publisher-editor of the Catholic daily *Il Cittadino*. He helped to form the Catholic Popular Party in 1919 and was deputy from Brescia until 1926. His pious wife, Giuditta Alghisi, was noted for her leadership of the area's catholic women's organizations.

Such Italian families train their sons in a way similar to that of the British aristocracy in its heyday. The eldest administers the property and enters parliament, the second joins the Church, the third, a profession. Giovanni Montini's elder brother became a senator, his younger, a doctor; he himself was marked out for the Church not only because of his position in the family but because of his evident taste for religious matters. He was his mother's favourite, and his links with her were unusually intimate. His health was considered poor (an assumption soon belied by his energy and prodigious capacity for work), and his childhood and youth were marked by special privileges. Even when his decision to become a priest was made, the local bishop, an old family friend, took the extraordinary step, in defiance of the Council of Trent, of allowing him to remain at home while studying for the priesthood. Young Montini thus missed both the rigours and the comradeship of seminary life.

The privileged career moved smoothly onward. The bishop, unwilling to subject him to the drudgery of parish work, sent him to the Lombard College in Rome, where he took courses at both the Jesuit Gregorian University and the faculty of letters at the University of Rome (he is, incidentally, an exceptionally well-read man). But before completing his courses, he was brought to the attention of the Vatican undersecretary of state, who placed him in the Pontifical Academy of Noble Ecclesiastics, the training centre for the Vatican's diplomatic service, then exclusively Italian. Again, before he had completed even this course, strings were pulled; he was summoned to the undersecretary of state and appointed *addetto*, or second secretary, to the nunciature of Warsaw. After a few months he was brought back to the Vatican and in 1925 promoted to *minutante*, or summarizer of incoming dispatches, in the Secretariat of State. There he worked for thirty years, steadily climbing the official ladder. At one stage he was assigned to organize the Catholic student militants but, when they came into frontal conflict with the fascist youth, Montini was quickly snatched back to the Vatican; he was too valuable to be allowed to fall foul of Mussolini.

Montini had progressed under the highly conservative Pius XI, but it was not until after 1939, when the Roman diplomat Eugenio Pacelli ascended the throne as Pius XII, that he became a real power-figure. His relationship with Pius XII was extremely close – or, rather, as close as this austere, demanding, imperious, short-tempered pope was capable of making it. But it had a love-hate element. Pius may well have regarded Montini as his natural successor, but if so, he treated the younger man in an odd way. Not only was he his own secretary of state, but he also 'double-banked'

Montini with a second prosecretary, the self-effacing Domenico Tardini. Moreover, he gave neither of them a red hat. It is true that on one occasion he announced that he had offered to make them cardinals and they had refused in a spirit of humility. But it is inconceivable that the refusal would have been accepted had Pius really wanted them in the sacred college; and difficult to believe, in Montini's case at least, that it was ever really made, for he has never been diffident about accepting responsibility and position.

Finally, in 1954, Pius awarded Montini the greatest benefice in his gift, the archbishopric of Milan, the historic see of Saint Ambrose and the largest and richest in Italy. But again, oddly, he 'forgot' to accompany it with a cardinal's hat; this not only offended the Milanese, and was no doubt resented by Montini himself, but it also had dramatic consequences. When Pius died, Montini could not take part in the conclave to elect his successor and was not, therefore, in practice eligible for election. Had he succeeded Pius, he would not have held a council, and the whole history of the modern church would have been different. As it was, a much older man, Angelo Roncalli, the patriarch of Venice, was elected as John XXIII, to act as a stopgap and keep the seat warm for Montini.

If Montini felt that Pius had treated him badly, he did not show it; on the contrary, he has always hotly defended his old master, particularly in the matter of the extermination of the Jews. In a letter to the London *Tablet* about Rolf Hochhuth's highly condemnatory play, he said that for Pius to attack Hitler publicly would have been an act of 'political exhibitionism' that would have unleashed 'still greater calamities'. By this he meant a Nazi occupation of the Vatican and the arrest of the pope—small coin, one might think, balanced against the lives of six million. It is clear that Montini himself was heavily involved in the policy of compromise with Hitler.

At Milan, Montini set about establishing himself as the unquestioned successor to Pope John. He organized a massive campaign against the Communist unions in the big factories, the success of which won him approving nods from the more conservative Italian prelates. He befriended Enrico Mattei, Italy's leading industrialist, and strengthened his position among the secular establishment. He built seventy-two churches in eight years and vastly expanded the recruitment of priests, thus establishing a reputation as an ecclesiastical administrator as well as a diplomat. All his acts were carefully balanced: on the one hand he suppressed the Catholic paper *Adesso* because of its connections with the liberal French journals *L'Esprit* and *Témoignage Chrétien;* on the other, he sent a telegram to Generalissimo Franco begging clemency for political prisoners. In public at least, he gave unreserved approval to Pope John's decision to call an ecumenical council, but he played a muted part in its deliberations. John had doubts about Montini's suitability as his successor – he thought him indecisive – but on the whole he was inclined to agree that he should get the job. He promptly gave Montini a red hat and privately cautioned him against speaking too often at the council or committing himself on important issues, for fear (it seems ironic now) of alienating the moderates and conservatives.

When John died, Montini played his cards coolly and well. Once inside the conclave, a cardinal is forbidden to make electoral promises to win votes (though this has been done); but there is nothing to stop him from issuing a cautious manifesto before it begins. The Friday after John died, Montini, preaching in his own cathedral, said: 'John has shown us some paths which it will be wise to follow. Can we turn away from these paths so masterfully traced? It seems to me we cannot.' These words were widely interpreted as a pledge that Montini, if elected, would continue John's policies.

There was never much doubt about Montini's election. Even as he was progressing into the sealed conclave area, he was greeted by murmurs of 'the Pope, the Pope!' from the Romans.

The authorities had prepared the conclave with scrupulous care. The sealed area was guarded like a fortress and stocked like a city under siege. Apart from the eighty cardinals and their personal staffs, crowded into the rambling palace were seventy-five attendants and servants, twelve nun-cooks, a doctor, a surgeon, a confessor, two barbers, and – oddly – two architects. Prodigious quantities of food and drink were stored, including 1,600 pounds of pasta, 4,000 pounds of potatoes, 1,500 litres of wine, and 3,000 bottles of beer. They were ready for a long conclave, though few really expected one. Nevertheless, things did not go altogether smoothly for Montini. After an abortive attempt by Cardinal Cushing of Boston to have Montini elected by acclamation, none of the four ballots cast on the first day gave him the majority he needed. But overnight there was some frantic clambering onto the bandwagon, and on the first vote the next morning he got an overwhelming seventy-nine votes. His acceptance of the tiara was prompt; his announcement of his title unhesitating and firm: 'Paul.'

Does power corrupt and absolute power corrupt absolutely? Certainly, in theory, there is no power so absolute as that of 'Christ's Vicar on Earth'. But in practice it is a different matter. A modern pope has to contend, on the one hand, with an immensely conservative and entrenched Vatican bureaucracy, backed by the bulk of the Italian episcopate, and on the other, with a vast liberal tide, from cardinals to laymen, washing against the breakwaters of orthodoxy all over the world. Pius XII had held the two in balance by a policy of masterly inactivity and one-man rule. But even he could not have done the trick much longer. Pope John set the lines of battle by summoning his council, thus superimposing on an absolute monarchy a kind of temporary parliament. Paul inherited this constitutional anomaly, and it soon became evident that he would have to resolve it one way or the other. Either he must accept permanent limitations on his powers, and progress slowly through a collegiate to a democratic system, or he must risk an explosion – even civil war – by trying to restore the monarchy in all its plenitude. In the end he took the second course. He never had much chance of carrying it through successfully, and his evident hesitation before attempting to do so made failure certain. This strategic error was compounded by the gross tactical blunder of making the issue of contraception a decisive one.

Yet, given the nature of the man, it is almost inconceivable that he could have taken any other course. He is plainly a man of the highest ambition. Imbued since early childhood with the principles and mystique of an authoritarian religion, accustomed to operate within the machine with all its severity and certitudes, the protégé and disciple of a masterful pope, how could he, when he finally inherited power over the machine, take the terrifying risk of dismantling it? As he weighed the arguments in the solitude of the Vatican, how could he be made to see that the risks of a restoration were even greater?

There were soon portents of which way he would turn. Under cover of a great deal of diplomatic activity – missions to India, Jerusalem, the United Nations, Portugal, and Latin America – which gave a misleading progressive flavour to his actions, the pope moved steadily into the conservative camp, his natural home. Two items, clerical celibacy and contraception, were removed from the deliberations of the council. And the council itself eventually came to an anticlimactic end, with no provision made for its succession by a permanent body endowed with real authority. Paul's speeches showed an increasing preoccupation, gradually becoming an obsession, with the prestige of his office.

Privileged at school, denied the community spirit of the seminary, never a parish priest, thirty years a bureaucrat, and finally given pastoral work only in the politico-ecclesiastical macrocosm of Milan, Paul has had curiously little contact with the problems of ordinary human beings. This may explain his notable lack of sensitivity. In November 1964 for instance, he placed his tiara on an altar in St Peter's as a symbolic gift to the poor; later, however, it was handed over to New York's Cardinal Spellman, of all people, presumably as a reward for the immense sums he had raised for the Vatican. Again, he recently lectured the Latin-American rich for not paying their taxes – while the Vatican was fighting a ferocious, though losing, battle to escape paying its own. Most important of all, only a profound ignorance of people could have led Paul to nail his pontifical colours to the mast on the issue of contraception. What followed needs no re-telling. Here was one battle he could not hope to win; indeed, it is already clear that he has lost it, setting the stage for a progressive, and cumulatively dramatic, erosion of papal authority.

This authority has been further challenged by the raising of the still more sensitive issue of clerical celibacy. The Catholic laity may defy the pope by using artificial contraceptives, but their defiance is necessarily secret, and the pope can claim, even if he is not widely believed, that his diktat has been generally respected. Clerical celibacy is a different matter. When a priest leaves the church and marries, his act is public; it is news; it is widely, often sensationally, reported. The pope has repeatedly and unequivocally emphasized that celibacy is an absolute condition of the priesthood and that in no circumstances can this rule be relaxed.

In the past, there has been no recorded case of a priest who has married since ordination being allowed to say Mass and perform other priestly duties. Now the situation is entirely different, and changing almost from day to day. In Holland, for instance, a pacesetter in reformist ideas, the number of priests leaving the church to marry exceeds the total of new ordinations, and with the natural wastage of death, the ranks of the clergy are steadily diminishing. This has led some Dutch bishops to take the view that priests should be allowed to marry and still carry on with their normal duties. There is a similar crisis in the United States and, indeed, throughout the Catholic world. In Latin America, where the shortage of priests outside the big cities has always been acute, the hierarchy is in despair. It has repeatedly, and with growing emphasis, petitioned the pope to relax the celibacy rule as the only way to save large areas from a reversion to paganism. So far he has not yielded.

And so his troubles multiply; but his response to them shows a remarkable combination of tactlessness and obstinacy. His decision to summon a special synod of bishops this past autumn, without defining its powers or allowing its composition to be determined locally, was a major strategic error.

Meanwhile, the pope spends a lot of time busying himself with trivial matters that stir up wholly unnecessary controversy. Last May he authorized the issue of a new liturgical calendar that downgraded certain popular saints and declared others to be, in all probability, spurious. Saint George, patron of England, Saint Patrick, patron of Ireland, Saint Christopher, patron of travellers, Saint Barbara, and many more – all the subject of cults for countless millions of simple Catholics – had official doubt cast on their very existence. A good practical case could probably be made for this belated act of liturgical reform. But its inevitable, and plainly foreseeable, result was to anger and confuse many of the pope's most faithful and uncritical admirers. At a time when the power and numbers of the progressives grow daily, it is difficult to conceive of a more calculated insult to the pope's own supporters. What is more, if certain traditions that rest on a dubious factual basis are to be questioned, where is the process to stop? The beliefs and practices of the Catholic Church are an inextricable mingling of myth and reality, of truth and superstition; the very *magisterium* itself, the basis of papal absolutism, is no more than a tradition, a euphemism for the irresponsible (in the constitutional sense) exercise of personal authority, and cannot stand up to strict historical analysis. Indeed, the pope gratuitously placed in the hands of his adversaries a devastating, perhaps fatal, weapon.

His wisest course now would be to abdicate and make way for a less divisive successor, who could try to pick up the pieces. But this his temperament seems to forbid. He will continue to fight a rearguard action, and if his pontificate is prolonged, the best his Church can hope for is an armed truce between the factions. The new man, when the time comes, will probably be a non-Italian. He will almost certainly be elected only on the understanding that he introduce a permanent and formalized system for the devolution of power. The man born to be pope may prove to be the last of his line.

—July, 1969

Mugg Waits for Godot

MALCOLM MUGGERIDGE'S RETURN to Christian belief is one of the more exotic show-biz events of our age. Not since Dr Joad renounced the flesh and the devil has an old entertainer made such a turnabout; a Rector of Stiffkey in reverse. The show is already playing to packed houses and seems set for a long run. But it is all too easy to forget how recently it went on the road. What a short time ago it was that I saw Malcolm take the chair, in a London theatre, at a veritable *talkfest* of permissiveness! Of course in those days there were no naked happenings (how long ago that seems, you may say), not even a single four-letter word. But the speaker was Norman Mailer and what he had to say, incoherent though it seemed, was clearly not on the side of the angels. From the back row, the late Robert Pitman, and an Indian gentleman of indeterminate politics, raised the occasional objection. In the front row sat Ken Tynan, and I recall (I hope accurately) a singular exchange across the footlights:

MAILER: 'A penis is really a pistol-symbol.'
TYNAN: 'N-no, N-Norman, a p-pistol is really a p-penis-symbol.'

Over these festivities Malcolm presided with beaming benevolence.

Since then a good deal has happened. Malcolm has been to Lourdes, where he experienced, so he tells us, a tiny miracle of his own, has chatted up Cardinal Heenan, has traced the footsteps of Jesus, has applauded the Pope on the Pill, and has preached sermons and written articles, now garnered into a slim paperback (*Jesus Rediscovered* by Malcolm Muggeridge, Fontana 6*s*). Rereading these articles, two points strike me: one concerns faith, the other charity. On the first, I do not think Malcolm is a Christian in any meaningful sense. He says he accepts the historical fact of Jesus as the God-man, and the crucifixion as the act and symbol of redemption for mankind. For most Christians who think at all about the matter, this is the hardest thing to swallow, and archaeological research, combined with biblical exegesis, makes it daily more difficult. Malcolm swallows it whole, but then proceeds to brush aside the majestic edifice of conclusions piled logically on this fundamental premise. If Christ lived, if the gospels, which Malcolm accepts, contain even a kernel of truth, then it follows that His work was to be carried on by the church He founded. It is irrelevant that the church became fissiparous; that some fragments may or may not be closer to His intentions. What does matter is that Christ (if He existed) intended the church, or churches, to be the primary instrument of His religion. They were the flesh and blood of His spirit. Salvation is to be found outside the church; but not Christianity. Yet Malcolm rejects all churches, and indeed takes wry delight in what he believes to be their imminent dissolution.

Equally he rejects theology. He dismisses Aquinas as comprehensively as did the scholars of the Renaissance. Yet theology is as essential to Christianity as the organized churches. Granted, again, the premise of gospel truth, theology is the needful architecture to be imposed upon it. The New and Old Testaments, imperfectly recorded, riddled with *lacunae,* often contradictory and obscure, require the continuous process of theological interpretation and debate. One might as well say: 'I accept physics, but the second law of thermodynamics is irrelevant.' Or: 'Of course I believe in economics, but whether Keynes or the Chicago School is right is not worth worrying about.' The truth is that, once one gets involved with a church, or begins to take theology seriously, one becomes a professional Christian; and Malcolm is determined to remain an amateur. Alas, there is no such thing as an amateur Christian – merely a religious dilettante.

And that is precisely what Malcolm is. He reminds me of those pious Anglican clergymen who 'poped' in the middle decades of the 19th century. They were beguiled by the certitudes of Rome, no doubt, but still more so by the whiff of incense, the laced surplices, the heavy chasubles embroidered with gold and crimson and silk, the red lamp forever burning over the sanctuary, the relics lying on their velvet cushions in the sacristy, the swinging censers, the myriad wax candles, the smells and sights and chaunts of a religion unashamed of its flamboyancy and superstition. Not for a moment do I accuse Malcolm of succumbing to the temptations of such baubles. No: for him the serpent is the Word. He is in love with it. No man of his generation, except the late Evelyn

Waugh, has cherished words so deeply, or used them with such fastidious exactitude. He has made his living by the word, written and spoken; but he longs for a world in which the word, grand, true, eloquent, dramatic, elegant, is wholly divorced from commercial rewards. And there is no flowering of civilization so rich in the financially-uncontaminated word as Christianity. When Christ spoke the Sermon on the Mount, no TV company fed him. St Paul, writing his epistles, had no thought for the Roman serial rights. There was no film option on Pascal's *Pensées*. The four evangelists were not in desperate competition to get their Instant Biographies out first. It is notable, in these essays, that Malcolm is extremely selective in the Christian authors he quotes. Not a word from St Peter, who knew Christ better than any man, but was a dull dog; on the other hand, St Paul, who made up his religion as he went along, but was a writer of distinction, gets a good showing. *Le style, c'est la réligion*. Plenty of Simone Weil but, as I say, no Aquinas. That would be hard pounding, and Malcolm is not a hard pounder. He is essentially a literary convert, just as the 19th-century parsons were liturgical converts. If the lost *Testament of Beelzebub,* written in the cadences of Milton, were suddenly to emerge from a heap of Dead Sea scrolls, I am not entirely sure where Malcolm would stand.

So much for faith. As for charity, Malcolm, as all who know him will testify, is the most charitable man in private. But seated before the typewriter, or standing before the cameras, it is a different matter. His rediscovery of Jesus has been accompanied, and clearly influenced by, his growing detestation of the 'permissive society' and his contempt for the efforts of organized religion to 'meet the challenges' of 'the contemporary world'. Not content with this, he also selects as prime targets the legion of 'do-gooders' and, like the odious Pius X, sees liberalism as the archetypal sin of the world today. Progressive prelates who hold pop services, women who campaign for abortion law reforms, doctors who would rather distribute birth pills than minister to hysterical pregnant teenagers, priests forced by an evil doctrine to choose between service to God and human love – all these are first caricatured, then brutally scourged by his tongue.

It is at this point that he becomes hopelessly confused: inside his Savonarola, a St Francis is struggling to get out, and sometimes succeeds. Malcolm can recognize the necessity, say, for an abortion in the case of a friend's daughter whom he knows; he cannot accept the generality of abortion for social reasons. A priest with whose good work he is familiar, and who needs a wife for moral and physical sustenance has his sympathy; priests who demand the same privilege *as a class* are 'rebellious or randy clerics come to the microphone to tell us of the doubts which have assailed them and of the hazards of priestly celibacy'. A naked Indian dying of hunger in Calcutta has his pity and his annas, the nun who takes the creature in has his blessing; but scientists in white coats seeking to devise better pills, economists seeking to raise the GNP – a key item in the Muggeridge anti-litany – have nothing but his scorn and, worse, his derision. Such consciences as his are tender within the charmed circle but untroubled by things unseen. Malcolm is the lord of the manor who dispenses alms but votes against the welfare state. For him, a 'do-gooder' is a person who may do good but whom he doesn't happen to know. He refuses to admit that to be truly charitable is to ensure that charity is superfluous.

'Graham Greene,' I once heard Malcolm say, 'is a saint trying to be a sinner. I am a sinner trying to be a saint.' I suppose we all are. One way to begin is not to impute unworthy motives to opponents whose attitudes grate on the nerves. It is all very well to meditate, as Malcolm does, on the prose of Pascal or Bunyan, basking in a sense of communion with higher things, without the irritating intrusion of theological *minutiae* or inconvenient pastoral injunctions. This literary religion can induce bliss, of a kind, but so can tobacco and alcohol, with which it has a great deal in common. To give up the latter two and embrace the former is to exchange one type of drug for another. Far more difficult is to arrest the hand as it reaches out for the typewriter to savage a progressive bishop or a humanist don. 'One notes,' writes Malcolm, 'the grimaces of sacerdotal faces as, holding their noses, they try to swallow *Humanae Vitae*'. But does one note this? I note the agony of men torn between their vows and their consciences, between comfortable but hypocritical obedience, and spiritual exile, often actual penury. Surely it requires little imagination to see this? Or to recognize that the 'antics' of clergymen trying to get someone, anyone, to come to their churches are prompted not so much by self-advertisement as by a sense of duty? St Francis himself met the same sneers from the conventional and established Benedictines. Malcolm is fond of quoting Jesus's saying that His kingdom is not of this world. But this does not mean Christians should not be social reformers. On the contrary, they are enjoined to do so: Thy will be done on earth as it is in heaven. The welfare state is the ante-room to the city of God. A socialist need not be a Christian; but a Christian must be a socialist, and if necessary a socialist revolutionary.

I suspect that Malcolm knows this perfectly well, and during another phase might admit it publicly. But his chosen métier is to be the articulator of the minority view and the castigator of the prevailing wisdom. And at present he sees a world bloated with affluence, obsessed with sex and devoted to the pursuit of material happiness, led by power-crazy politicians and urged on by apostate clergymen. So he goes for it, red in tooth and pen. This is not charity. But then charity makes unreadable articles and dull scripts. Enforce charity on Malcolm and Othello's occupation is gone indeed! But having discussed faith and charity let us end on a note of hope. The great redeeming feature about Malcolm is that he never occupies the same position for long. At any moment now, just as Pope Paul and his frightened monsignori scramble up the communications trench to join Malcolm gratefully in his dug-out, he may swing his Gatling through a 180-degree arc and riddle them with verbal dum-dums. Meanwhile, the Mugg waits for Godot.

—13 June 1969

Part 2

THE PARTY GAME

Rule Like Pigs

MORE THAN ANY OTHER town in England, what matters in Blackpool is people: the vast, vulgar, guzzling, uproarious hordes which swarm in annually from the great industrial towns of the north and midlands. Without people, Blackpool is just an obscene shell of desolate boarding houses and shuttered arcades, an abandoned, ransacked ghost-town waiting for the miracle of Spring. So I found it last week. The Big Dipper was still. Montmartre in Blackpool ('The Show They Tried to Close') was locked-up and silent; so was The Strangest Girl in the World ('It Was All Her Father's Fault'). Along the gigantic promenade a bitter wind whipped up discarded ice-cream papers and the relics of funny hats. At the end of the deserted North Pier, a handful of old men and boys fished pessimistically into an angry sea. 'It's no use', said one of the old men philosophically, 'they've all gone' – as if the fish, too, abandoned Blackpool with the October gales.

But weren't the Tories there? Of course: 10,000 of them, including camp followers; not enough to fill Blackpool, but enough to make it seem inhabited, one would have thought. And yet the ghosts remained unexorcized: in some curious way, the Tory militants, though undoubtedly human beings, are not people. This may seem a perverse remark. The Tories claim to be a national party, above sectional interests, and in a sense they are right. Many millions of Britons, from retired sergeant majors to frail widows living on £2 10s. a week, vote Tory because they think they are voting for England. Tory delegates, when they claim to speak for their country, are not trying to kid anyone, least of all themselves.

During the last ten years, too, the upper-class impedimenta – 'the second magnum and the third cigar, the chauffeur kept waiting at the door till dawn', as Evelyn Waugh put it – have been swept away, or at any rate tidied out of sight. I saw only one Rolls last week, and not a single Brigade tie. True, the platform is still unmistakably Old Etonian, with more than a hint of strawberry leaves (its solitary trade unionist looked as if he had contracted out not merely of the political levy, but of life itself). But in the great body of the hall, it is possible to explore all the myriad ramifications of the British middle class: near-gentry and near-proletarians, provincial barristers with strange accents, military gents with limps acquired in India and the East, bumptious young men from LSE and the anonymous regiment of the minor public schools, young girls training to be air hostesses and gym mistresses, matrons in hand-knitted cardigans, clutching huge, bursting handbags – even a Tory teddy-boy, with Brando cut, check drapes and an exquisite pale-blue tie. Not a party of wealth or privilege, by any means.

But a cross-section of England? Only in a strictly limited sense. The Tory militants offer an image of England, but it is a distorted one: an image of our prejudices and our atavisms, our unreasoning acceptance of unproved truths, because they are comfortable and established, our dislike of controversy, our unwillingness to ask questions when we know the answers may be unpleasant – all the factors which militate against independent intellectual inquiry. Conservatism, in fact, is an authoritarian church of platitudes, a party of proverbs. 'Spare the rod and spoil the child', 'A bird in the hand is worth two in the bush', 'More haste, less speed' – such maxims, which seem incontrovertible until one begins to think about them, evoked roars of approval last week. Indeed, a lady delegate even coined a new one: 'A flogging today may save a hanging tomorrow' – and this went down well, too. This is England, of course, but it is only part of England: the English id, magnified out of all proportion, dominating the whole. The Tories, in short, are atrophied Englishmen, lacking certain moral and intellectual reflexes. They are recognizable, homely – even, on occasions, endearing – but liable to turn very nasty at short notice.

Now the Tory leadership knows this perfectly well, and they are getting some pretty shrewd advice from the Berkeley Square publicity experts on how to handle the problem. Sailing serenely towards their third election victory, they must at all cost make people forget that they still carry a flick-knife. Last week, the Tory catchword was 'civilized'. 'The British,' Lord Hailsham intoned, 'are a highly civilized and very sophisticated people, and we are a very British party.' This being the slogan, the debates required a good deal of stage-managing to make it seem true. Knowing that the old beast had to roar sometime, the platform skilfully threw a few tasty, but safe, morsels into the cage. There was a good howl over Iceland, a screech for Mrs. Castle, an ovation for our boys in Cyprus. The flogging debate posed a problem, but the platform dealt with it in masterful fashion. It was pared down to an hour, fixed for a time when most of the nice, savage old ladies are thinking of tea and crumpets, introduced by a singularly dull and dim delegate, and concluded by Mr Butler with such skill that the hall gave him an ovation for his harmless suggestion that, if more corporal punishment were needed, then perhaps it had better be administered by parents.

And, to let off the remaining steam, on Saturday morning Hailsham treated the conference to the most accomplished piece of oratorical demagogy since Nasser's Suez Canal speech, which brought delegates roaring to their feet, but which was confined throughout to such harmless objectives as 'storming the robber castle of Socialism' – whatever that may mean. By lunchtime, with the special trains already lined up at Blackpool Central, and with only Harold's ovation to come, the party managers were breathing well-earned sighs of relief.

But, as they should have known, the flick-knives had to come out sometime; and it happened at the worst possible moment. As the clock ticked towards two, the Winter Garden filled to bursting, and Reg Dixon at the organ regaled the happy, relaxed delegates with tunes from an age when the Union Jack really mattered: *Daisy, Daisy, If You Were the Only Girl in the World,* and *Pack Up Your Troubles.* The Tories, indeed, had already packed up their bags and were waiting only for the ritual genuflection to the leader. The choice greenery and chintz which once separated platform from delegates had been removed, and there sat all the assistant masters beaming benignly, with Dame Florence Elliot, the matron, suitably playing the fool. Promptly, as the clock struck two, the head arrived, the whole school rose and caps were flung high.

Then it happened. As conquering Harold rose to speak, there came a first blast of the trumpet from the gallery, and the old, familiar battle cry of the League of Empire Loyalists. The sheer caddishness of letting off a stink bomb on speech day froze the audience with horror; ample bosoms and manly chests heaved with indignation as the scoundrel was dragged off. By the time the second interruption came, horror had turned to fury: a group of delegates held the intruder's arms while a military gent smashed his fist in his face. The third was flung over his seat, had his face kicked and was dragged out moaning. Another – a middle-aged woman – was punched in the chest and hauled along by the hair by delegates who, forty-eight hours before, had shouted their indignation at attacks on defenceless women. Yet another was dragged, screaming for the police, behind locked doors and detained for some minutes: his bloodstains spotted the stairs. The Old Adam, the secret little Tory hobgoblin, had come out with a vengeance.

In that disturbing little play, *Live Like Pigs,* the author subtly hints that what makes the respectable council estate tenants fear and hate the awful family which has moved in among them is their unconscious realization that the Sawney family exhibits, in a vastly magnified form, all the degrading instincts which they themselves possess. The Sawneys personify, and finally unleash, the forces of anarchy lying dormant around them. When the outraged housewives storm their house, Col Sawney, peering through the keyhole at the oncoming hordes, cries out in fear 'They're not people, they're bloody *animals*!' Last Saturday; the political Sawneys exposed Conservative civilization for the shabby and dangerous myth that it is. And afterwards, a battered Loyalist, still trembling with shock, told me: 'Communists, Socialists, Liberals – they're nothing by comparison. Them Tories, they're bloody *savages*!'

I left the Winter Gardens as soon as possible, and came upon a scene of strange transformation. While we had been listening to Hailsham and Macmillan, great convoys of coaches had been steadily streaming into Blackpool from all points of the compass, bringing with them joyful, earthy battalions from Stoke and Oldham, from Manchester, Liverpool and Sheffield, from St Helens and Bradford. The Golden Mile was lit up, the pin-tables whirred, Montmartre in Paris was packed, the piers blazed, the Strangest Girl was revealing her charms again. They were only half-day trippers up to see the illuminations, but they were people. As the Tory trains steamed magisterially away, Blackpool came alive again.

—18 October 1958

Lucky Mac and his Hons' Cupboard

AT THE RISK of seeming ponderous, I am getting a little tired of the picaresque image which Mr Harold Macmillan – and his faithful Admen – crams daily down our rising gorges. That Britain should have to go through the painful slimming process of the 20th century is inevitable: but Lucky Mac has managed to turn it all into an elderly debutante's joke. It is rather like watching the last act of a crumbling country-house play from the servant's quarters: Ivy Compton-Burnett jazzed up by P. G. Wodehouse. I can forgive Mr Macmillan most of his props: the misty crofter grandfather, the American mother, the ducal wife with her gardening gloves, the endearing tribes of grandchildren (though what the government will look like when *they* come onto the political labour market I shudder to think). But I draw the line at the patches on the hacking-jacket, the Edwardian cricket-boots, the carefully darned undergraduate waistcoats, the thumbed volumes of Trollope (has he ever read *The Way We Live Now,* I wonder?) and, most of all, those peculiar shooting-gaiters. For a highly-successful, super-rich, cast-iron unflappable political Houdini, this carefully-contrived atmosphere of down-at-heel gentility is just about the last cheese-straw.

Indeed, from what I hear, Mac's Edwardian charade no longer evokes the ripples of unaffected mirth even from those for whose delight and profit it was originally contrived: the hard-faced gents of the Tory party. It was all very well to be pulled from the brink of the Suez pit by a pyrotechnic display of aristocratic *sang-froid*; but Suez, as we all know, is a dead duck now, while the *sang-froid* is still with us – or, rather, with them. Julian Amery was fair enough; and Cousin What's-his-name and Uncle That; so, perhaps, was the Earl of Home – though nobody could ever remember actually meeting him – and even the Earl of Cromer. But the Duke of

Devonshire? Who exactly *was* he? One elderly Parliamentary Under-secretary, who has been unable, in umpteen years' service, either to rid himself of a Midlands accent or to form the useful habit of reading a page or two of Debrett before composing himself to sleep, seemed to think that the Duke was the man who dished Gladstone in 1886, adding: 'For all I know, the fellow's *still* a Whig'.

Indeed, it is gradually being realized by a widening circle of Tory hopefuls that they are positively not welcome in the Hons' Cupboard; that they are, in short, Horrible Counter-Hons, and had better get used to the fact. Short of scrounging an invitation to the right sort of shooting-parties – City syndicates are distinctly not good enough – the Tory self-made member must be content with an occasional airy pat on the back as the Prime Minister passes through the lobbies on his way to the Dukeries. And even this symbolic gesture, though well-intentioned, is occasionally taken amiss – as, for instance, by the Tory member who reckons he spends £5,000 a year on his constituency, who has never been invited to a ministerial dinner-party, and who was recently slightly miffed to be congratulated by Mr Macmillan on 'the splendid way you chaps are standing by Hugh Gaitskell'.

But if life is hard for the Tory under-dogs, it is often disconcerting for their superiors, too. In the increasingly vague feudal world he inhabits, the Prime Minister does not always draw the proper distinction between a Duke and his valet – a failure which Arthur Balfour might have relished. Mr Macmillan's favourite form of relaxation, nowadays is the dispensing of patronage: there is nothing he enjoys more than discussing the merits of rival contenders for a post he has at his disposal. Unfortunately, so the story goes, he is not over-particular in the partners he chooses for such deliberations. Tory wits tell the tale of the senior peer who, the evening before, had been gratified by the Premier's confidence in debating ——'s suitability for the bishopric of ——, and who was perturbed to overhear, early the next morning, the same conversation being conducted with a puzzled under-gardener. At the country houses the Premier honours, butlers and gamekeepers, beaters, still-room maids, second footmen and other feudal figures are often astonished to be asked their views on the attainments of, say, a potential Regius Professor of Ornithology. And, to judge by some recent appointments, advice of this type is not without weight.

But while all this is going on at the Big House, what of the estate? It is here, alas, that the joke ceases to be funny. Nowadays, this country gives the impression of a torpedoed liner settling slowly into the water. Upstairs, the band is still playing, the captain is on the bridge, the cocktail-shakers are still rattling in the First Class Lounge: only in the boiler-room is there any sign of panic. Whenever I return from abroad, I bring back with me a deepening sense of the gross incompetence of British industrial management. In Santiago, recently, I heard a group of British businessmen blaming their failures on the Labour government, as if Sir Stafford Cripps was still twisting their arm at the Board of Trade.

Any excuse will do; indeed, it must do, for senior directors are kept too busy arranging for the purchase of a tax-fiddle house in Bermuda, or for a company Rolls to take their wives shopping, to bother about such minor matters as competing with the Germans or the Japanese. Fat men with big cigars fight paper battles over vast blocks of property; while in the Midlands, it appears, we cannot even make enough of that elementary commodity, the brick. Presumably somebody forgot to order the straw. While the death of the *Chronicle* and *Star* is debated in terms of morality, or blamed on the printing unions, or the price of paper, nobody seems to notice that it was a colossal failure of 'enlightened' capitalist management.

The government's answer to failure is, of course, to launch a fresh advertising campaign, thus further fostering illusion at the expense of reality. Indeed, taking the cue from our Premier, we are becoming a society of illusions, of mechanically contrived happiness concealing an abyss of – what? Of inner loneliness, perhaps, the inevitable consequence of a surrender to egotistical materialism. The new rich, who haven't quite made the Dukeries, spend their money on building grotesque villas on the fringe of all-Aryan golf-courses, aping their American superiors in Nassau, or, stung by their supine cultural consciences, on buying bad Impressionists, as valueless as the hideous canvases Lord Duveen once foisted on the Morgans.

The middle classes, whose primary concern is morality, are diverted by such issues as hanging, birching and the prosecution of *Lady Chatterley,* while the government quietly allows the One-Armed Bandit, together with its two-armed masters, to take over the underworld. At the bottom of the rubbish-dump the workers are encouraged to grovel among the ever-growing litter of electric gadgets, cosmetics, detergents and nasty chocolate bars, while their rulers, deploring at intervals the decline of religion, pocket their tax-free capital gains.

Indeed, it is curious that, as a student of Trollope, Mr Macmillan does not recognize his hero's favourite image: the old estate which is living on capital. The guards at the Palace are still as smart as ever; but there is no second battalion in the barracks. Falling exports are 'balanced' by paying medieval rates of interest on hot foreign money – or by selling off an occasional slab of sterling assets. To pay for our independent nuclear deterrent – the current equivalent of keeping a coach-and-four – we run down our conventional forces, on the assumption that nobody will notice. Lacking a positive international strategy or a real voice in world affairs, we have Mr Macmillan's increasingly motiveless publicity trips, punctuated by a new brand of verbal *legerdemain* which Lloyd George, for one, might have envied, and which has led Mr Krushchev, for another, to carry a tape-recorder whenever the Premier accords him a private audience.

Carlyle described Disraeli as a conjuror, leading the British people 'by the nose, like helpless, mesmerized somnambulant cattle'. But Disraeli, at least, had a shrewd idea of where he wanted the herd to go: he possessed a consistent philosophy of class, a coherent view of the world and Britain's place in it. I see no evidence that Macmillan has any planned design – beyond the misty euphoria of a Ramsay MacDonald. Anxious, on the one hand, that Britain should take the lead in settling the Cold War, he cheerfully hands over absolute control to America of the British-based Polaris. A public opponent of the class war, he conducts his government on an ideological class basis, and has created the conditions for a steady widening of the gap between incomes. A sentimental conserver of the past, he has turned the speculators loose upon the English countryside. It is both ironic and significant that the Scottish crofters have never had it so bad as under Lucky Mac.

History, I think, will write Macmillan off as a plunger, a seeker after the fast buck of popularity, a gambler who concentrates on enjoying his winning streak. One day, soon perhaps, the luck will run out; and I think that he is smart enough to know it. On Monday he took the unusual step of giving a dinner party for his noble colleagues. It was an impressive and numerous gathering, for his government now includes one duke, one marquess, six earls, two viscounts and seven barons. What, I wonder, passed through the Premier's mind as the port circulated and the glow of cigars lit up the pink cheeks clustered admiringly around him? Did he reflect that Lucky Mac had had his turn, that the time had come to cash his winnings, pocket his earldom, and get out of the racket? Or did he decide to linger a moment longer in his private Ruritania – and wait for the broker's men to batter down the door?

—10 December 1960

No Sex for Johnnie

EVEN IN ENGLAND, no activity arouses a higher degree of passion and ambition than politics. Westminster brings out the best and worst in a man more faithfully than any other institution. Yet few novelists have gone there in search of material, and fewer still have succeeded in finding it. The English political novel is a lunar landscape, in which one or two giant protuberances survey desolate plains of failure. Only Disraeli and Wells have produced enduring novels of political ideas, only Trollope convincing novels of political fact. True, these three were outstandingly successful. Disraeli's *Sybil* and *Coningsby* came at a time when an aristocratic oligarchy was reluctantly surrendering power to an aggressive and self-righteous middle class. In them, he caught the pathos of the struggle, and perceived, with astonishing foresight, that the aristocrats could conjure up new allies from the depths. The novels not only mirrored the age, they influenced it; and, a generation later, the vision of Tory Democracy materialized. This is why Disraeli will always be read, at any rate by the young. The characters are dead – they never really lived – but the ideas tremble with life, marry, divorce, beget children. Disraeli wrote novels purely to make money and win notoriety. But in the process he became a political thinker.

In *The New Machiavelli* Wells also straddled a watershed. In 1906, the working class first won a measure of direct political power. The Liberal *élite*, still echoing the aristocratic Whig tradition of public service, reinforced now by the spirit of middle-class 'leadership' created by Arnold and Jowett, held the offices, but their authority was being steadily undermined by unsmiling men and women armed with blue-books and statistics, the unromantic impedimenta of gas-and-water Socialism. Once again, Wells mirrored this transformation and projected it into the future, adding a personal note of criticism by describing, with relish, the triumph of sex over duty. Wells was a born novelist and his story has a technical excellence which Disraeli never attained; yet, although he was at heart a more serious man, he lacked Disraeli's political instinct and failed to grasp the crucial importance of Westminster: thus his novel has no geographical centre of gravity.

At the other end of the spectrum – the novel of political fact – Trollope is quite alone. He was a traditionalist and a successful civil servant who believed that politics was the science of administration, and that men mattered more than measures. For him, the House of Commons really was the best club in the world; his unsuccessful attempts to enter it left him chagrined, but still respectful. (His description of the broken millionaire's drunken speech in *The Way We Live Now* is the best House of Commons scene in English fiction.) Trollope, like Wells – and Disraeli at the time of the novels – lived on the political fringes and was fascinated by the mystery at the core. As he lumbered heavily through the clubs and salons of Mayfair, his mind pondered on the rise and fall of reputations. Who was up, or down; and why? What went on in the Prime Minister's mind? How exactly was Lord —— squeezed out of the cabinet? Untrammelled by any concern over issues, Trollope was able to resolve these questions with passionless accuracy (it is not surprising he is the favourite reading of Mr Macmillan). In *The Prime Minister* he presented an utterly convincing portrait of a great Whig statesman, and of the central dilemma which lies at the heart of English politics: the conflict between duty and principle. The Whig magnate believed he had a duty to retain office, but at the same time was bound in honour to relinquish it if a principle, however minor, was jeopardized; the clash, moreover, was complicated by the corrupting effect which the exercise of power has even upon men of the highest character, for principles seem less vital as office endures. In the Duke of Omnium, Trollope traces the struggle phase by phase, as it was, in fact, fought out within the minds of the Marquess of Hartington, Lord Rosebery, Lord Derby and – in our own day – Lord Salisbury. Here is a rare, perhaps unique, example of a novelist's imagination creating political truth.

Yet the list, as we have seen, is a brief one and the question remains: why are English political novels so difficult to write? Young politicians, with a literary flair and no prospects of office, continue to write them. Recently we had Wilfred Fienburgh's

No Love for Johnnie and now comes a fresh attempt by Maurice Edelman – a galvanic colonial crisis in Africa, complicated by love and jealousy at cabinet level. (*The Minister, Hamish Hamilton* 16*s*.). Both, within their limits, are readable books; but, apart from a few technical details, both could have been written by somebody who had never set foot in the House of Commons. Partly, I suppose, this is a failure of talent; but mainly the immense, inherent difficulties of the task. There is the initial obstacle of names. How does one create authenticity? When I wrote a political novel set in France, I was criticized for employing the names of real ministers, off-stage. True, some readers find this dishonest, and it has the further disadvantage of limiting the action to back-benchers, for clearly real ministers cannot play a major role in the plot. But what is the alternative? One's hackles of disbelief rise instinctively when Mr Edelman introduces 'Mr Geoffrey Melville, Secretary of State for Commonwealth and Colonial Affairs', and when the guests at his cocktail party assemble, credibility vanishes:

> ... Bagnari the sculptor, the Lord Chamberlain, Gregory Broome, three young MPs, two of them with model girl wives, Sir Brian Upjohn, Marcus Prebble-Keir, Sir Gareth Meade, the Curator of the National Gallery, Lord Claddishe, Lord Ardrossan, Sir Julian Greenhill Waters ...

One expects to see Sir Alec Guinness acting them all, simultaneously.

The second, more serious difficulty springs from the almost total absence of drama from English political life. Our politics not only are, *but are known to be* both honourable and dull. The novelist must have a certain basic diet of wickedness and incident; forced to invent these, against the character of the world he describes, he raises the barrier of disbelief still further. The French and the Americans do not suffer from this deficiency. *All the King's Men* and *Advise and Consent* may be criticized on various grounds, but not on credibility; while, since 1945, France has had sixteen major political scandals, each stranger than fiction.

But in Britain even historic moments are played in a minor key. Lord Dalton recently dredged up the worst anecdotes of Labour's rule and misrule; but his narrative was singularly lacking in real drama, if not in malice. When Lord Randolph Churchill sent in his disastrous resignation, the only intimation the inhabitants of Hatfield received was when Lord Salisbury failed to appear at breakfast – scarcely a scene of high tension. The histrionics of English politics have an irritating way of failing to materialize. The plot is laid, the cast assembled; then all dissolves in a mist of good manners. At the height of the struggle to replace A. J. Balfour, the two contenders, Walter Long and Sir Austen Chamberlain, almost came to blows on the steps of the Carlton Club. Almost; in fact, they shook hands and agreed to compromise on Bonar Law. When Lord Curzon was cheated of his life's aim, the premiership, his instinct was to gnaw the carpet and, like Lear, invoke cataracts and hurricanes; in fact, he pulled himself together and made a charming speech welcoming the elevation of Mr Baldwin. Only rarely do the characters reach the level of the history they are making, and when this happens – as in the overthrow of Asquith in 1916, or the Suez crisis in 1956 – the novelist is otiose; the historian collects the spoils.

The third great obstacle an English political novelist faces is sex. The conventions of the modern novel demand that sex play a major role and that it be extra-marital, if not unnatural. Here again, the French and the Americans are at an advantage.

The career of the late Earl Long shows that an American public man can still openly consort with bubble-dancers while preserving popular esteem. English politicians enjoy no such liberty, nor, I should add, do they seriously seek it. How can they seduce a woman when, at the climateric hour of 10 o'clock, they must hurtle back to Westminster to answer the division bell (French parliamentarians can vote by proxy, while Americans rarely vote at all)? How can they, like French Deputies, enjoy the delights of an afternoon in bed when all important ministerial statements take place at 3.30?

The novelist, alas, must leap these barriers, and the result is invariably comic. Mr Fienburgh asks us to believe that his hero was dallying with his girl-friend when the Speaker called his vital Question. But I can think of no Member, however dissolute, who would hesitate an instant between his mistress (always supposing he had one) and the chance of snatching a headline in the *Evening Standard*. Still less do I believe Mr Edelman when he obliges his harried Colonial Secretary to spend hours in the bed of an actress while Africa is seething. It is exceptionally difficult for a British Minister (who is not protected, like his French colleagues, by a discreet *cabinet* of intimates) to conduct any sort of liaison, however innocent. I myself know of only one member of the present cabinet who has had an affair while in office (admittedly, it was with a peeress). No: in the light of these limitations, we can safely assume that English politics will never provide the novelist with his bread and butter.

—28 July 1961

Was the Palace to Blame?

A NUMBER of minor criticisms, of fact, emphasis and judgement, can be made of Mr Iain Macleod's account of the Tory leadership crisis. But one sentence, thrown out almost as an aside, calls for immediate contradiction. 'There is no criticism whatsoever,' he writes, 'that can be made of the part played by the crown.' This sentence is all the more remarkable in that it is, by implication, refuted by the rest of Mr Macleod's article. For his whole thesis is that the procedure used to select a new prime minister was unsatisfactory; that a mistake was made and the wrong man chosen. True, his accusing finger is pointed principally at Mr Macmillan and Mr Redmayne, and if the advice tendered by these gentlemen was ill-judged, tendentious or misleading, they must accept some share of the responsibility. But the right of the Monarch to select and appoint the prime minister is the one unqualified, executive privilege still enjoyed by the crown. If Lord Home was an unsuitable choice as Prime Minister – and Mr Macleod claims he was – then the Monarch was at fault. To adapt the anguished cry of Laertes, 'The Queen, the Queen's to blame!'*

Indeed, Mr Macleod's exoneration of the Palace reveals a serious, though common, misunderstanding of the way in which a prime minister is chosen. The only limitation on the Monarch's unrestricted choice is that the person selected should be able to command a majority of the House of Commons, and so carry on the business of government. As a rule, following a general election, the choice is automatic, though Queen Victoria did not take this view in 1880. Again, when there is already a clearly designated successor to replace a retiring prime minister, the Monarch is not

*A leading article in one morning newspaper seeks to place the full responsibility on Sir Michael Adeane. But this is to misunderstand the relation between the Monarch and the Private Secretary.

called upon to exercise a choice. Asquith, Balfour, Chamberlain and Eden were all appointed as a matter of course. Equally, where a party has a precise and constitutional procedure for electing its leader, the Monarch has no alternative but to accept the man so chosen, for there would be a presumption that anyone else would not receive the requisite support. But when the absence of such a procedure creates an element of doubt, the onus of choice falls squarely on the Monarch's shoulders.

What is more, though the Monarch is clearly prudent to take advice before designating a new prime minister, there is no obligation to do so, still less to seek it from any particular quarter. There is no foundation whatsoever for the often-repeated myth that the Monarch must consult the retiring prime minister. Queen Victoria declined to do so in 1894, and seems to have appointed Rosebery without taking formal advice of any kind; Edward VII did not consult Campbell Bannerman in 1908, and in 1916 George V sent for Lloyd George at the suggestion of Bonar Law, the Colonial Secretary. King George may have acted on advice from Bonar Law in 1923 (the matter is still in dispute), but if so it was at his own insistence, for Bonar Law, who had been correctly advised on the point by Lord Crewe, was not anxious to proffer it. When Chamberlain resigned in 1940, George VI indeed consulted him; but, as his diary records, he had made up his mind to send for Churchill before Chamberlain was given an opportunity to suggest his name.

In the case of Macmillan's own appointment, we do not know whether Eden was consulted (it is possible that, in view of his health, he declined to advise), but the Queen's choice seems to have been made as the result of advice tendered by Lord Salisbury and Sir Winston Churchill, and soundings carried out by the Lord Chancellor and the Tory whips. All these precedents make it clear that the role of a prime minister in choosing his successor is limited or non-existent, and that, in any event, his advice is never mandatory.

In the light of this, Mr Macmillan's behaviour appears truly extraordinary. He was an elderly man, who had recently undergone a serious, if successful, operation; he was in fact in the very early stages of recuperation and, as Mr Churchill tells us, had just emerged from heavy sedation. He had had a gruelling year, during which, many observers agreed, his physical powers and political judgement had deteriorated. A more diffident statesman might well have concluded that, in all the circumstances, he might honourably discharge himself from the duty of tendering advice in so complex and important a matter and, still more, of assembling and collating the evidence on which that advice would, supposedly, be based. This was the view that, in similar circumstances, Bonar Law very properly took in 1923. But Mr Macmillan suffered from no such doubts or inhibitions. From the very start of the crisis, he seems to have determined that his advice should not only be given, but given in all its plenitude. As Mr Churchill tells us, the document he eventually presented (and indeed read) to the Queen was 'magisterial'.

It is true that he sought to justify his temerity by presenting to the cabinet a paper describing in detail the lines on which party soundings should be conducted. Mr Churchill tells us that the cabinet approved the paper, but this is not precisely the impression of some of its members. In any case, if the procedure itself was to be invested with the weight of cabinet authority, had not the cabinet an equal right to be shown, and to check, its findings before they were presented to the Queen? The cabinet, as we now know, had no such opportunity. It does not appear that anyone, outside Mr Macmillan's personal secretariat, saw the memorandum in its final form.

Once the Queen had received Mr Macmillan's memorandum, argues Mr Macleod, she had no alternative but to send for Lord Home: 'Presented with such a document, it was unthinkable even to consider asking for a second opinion.' Mr Macleod, of course, is anxious to protect the Queen, and to lay the blame fairly on Mr Macmillan for presenting, as the collective view of a party, what was in fact the advice of one man. But, I repeat, the Queen was under no obligation to follow such advice, however presented – or indeed to ask for it in the first place. Throughout the crisis, which had now lasted nearly two weeks, the results of independent soundings taken by her Private Secretary had no doubt been given to her. She can read, and she must have seen in the newspapers, circumstantial information that the impression of unanimity conveyed by the document was open to doubt. Had Mr Macmillan been tendering formal and constitutional advice to her, she would of course have had no choice but to accept it. But his advice was, in the constitutional sense, informal, and her acceptance of it optional. If there was any question of its validity, to take a second opinion, far from being unthinkable, was her positive and compelling duty.

We now know, from Mr Macleod, that there was indeed question as to its validity. The case for Lord Home, from first to last, rested on his attractiveness as a compromise candidate: he emerged as the man most likely to break the deadlock. If the deadlock could be broken by other means, then the arguments in his favour would largely disappear, and the arguments against him – his lack of experience, his supposed unwillingness to renounce his peerage and, not least, the fact that such renunciation would contravene the intention, if not the letter, of the Peerage Act – would become unassailable. But Mr Macleod tells us – and no one has contradicted him – that the deadlock was in truth broken by other means. For, after all, the essence of the dispute was simple: there were three contenders, Butler, Hailsham and Maudling. If two of them could be persuaded to serve under a third, then the dispute ceased to exist and the Queen need have no hesitation in sending for him, for a candidate so powerfully supported would have no difficulty in rallying the party. It could then be argued that the Home candidacy had served its turn by forcing the three principals to agree among themselves.

This process, as Mr Macleod relates, culminated on Thursday 17 October, when Hailsham and Maudling declared they were opposed to Lord Home and pledged themselves to serve under Butler. The true crisis was over and Mr Redmayne, the Chief Whip, was asked to convey the information to the Prime Minister. Here we come to the heart of the affair. Did Redmayne fail to carry out this mission? It seems almost inconceivable. Did Mr Macmillan, despite this knowledge, fail to qualify his clear recommendations to the Queen – or even to alert her to the fact that they might be so qualified? If so, he was guilty of misleading her.

But was the Queen in fact misled? The newspapers on Friday morning were available to her. Their reports of the meeting the previous night were incomplete and in some ways incorrect, but they plainly indicated that there was substantial opposition to Lord Home among senior ministers. Was it not her duty to discover the truth of these reports from the men principally concerned? As it happens, such inquiries may have been unnecessary, for it is now known that one of those who was privy to the tripartite agreement telephoned the Palace at 7 a.m. on the Friday morning and gave the news to Sir Michael Adeane, the Queen's private secretary. It would seem, therefore, that both Mr Macmillan and the Queen were fully informed of the events of the previous twenty-four hours. This being so, one might have expected them to move on the

Friday with the greatest deliberation and caution. In fact, they acted with speed, one might say haste: the whole process had been completed and Lord Home was at the Palace by lunchtime. It could be argued that the gravity of the crisis made its early resolution imperative. But their movements are clearly open to a different interpretation: both of them wanted Lord Home and were determined to have him.

And is this very surprising? Mr Macmillan had raised Lord Home from obscurity and had given him the Foreign Office in the teeth of opposition. The experiment had been pronounced, by some at least, a success. As a statesman, Lord Home was thus very largely a creature of Macmillan's contriving. Why not continue the role of Pygmalion and make him prime minister? As for the Queen, Lord Home must have seemed, by his background, lineage and opinions, a most suitable candidate: if she could secure positive advice in his favour, why hesitate? Most of her friends are in, or connected with, the House of Lords; and, as Mr Macleod wrily observes, the Lords formed the one section of the party which, one could confidently accept, was overwhelmingly for Home. Why, then, be deterred by last-minute warnings from mere cabinet ministers? In short, if the salient facts are as Mr Macleod has stated them, and there was indeed a conspiracy to foist Lord Home on the nation, it is hard to escape the conclusion that the Palace was a party to it.

—24 January 1964

Sir Alec's Gravy Train

EIGHTY YEARS AGO, Mr Gladstone – at an age at which Mr Harold Macmillan is thought too old for office – descended on Scotland and invented modern electioneering. His Midlothian campaign was a gigantic and successful personal attempt to re-light the torch of reform and sweep the left back to power on a sea of moral righteousness. Re-reading his speeches, one is amazed at their high philosophical tone, the complete absence of materialistic appeal, the remorseless concentration on absolute standards of conduct.

What a contrast with Sir Alec Douglas-Home's campaign in Perthshire and Kinross! It is true that the Prime Minister, paying a dutiful call at church last Sunday, got a blistering earful of Scottish moral indignation from the pulpit. But that was the only occasion, so far, in which spiritual issues have made even a token appearance in the highly mundane campaign. It is Midlothian in reverse. With the Tory Party threatened with disaster, Sir Alec has chosen one of the most backward and conservative constituencies in Britain for a desperate attempt to reverse the radical tide. His methods are elementary, his appeal very basic indeed. More hydro-electric dams? Certainly. Higher subsidies for farmers? Of course. An extra £3,500 million for higher education? Yes, indeed. State subsidies, loans, grants, anything you care to mention – Sir Alec is for it. No modern prime minister, and certainly no socialist, has ever been so guilelessly free with the public purse.

I say guilelessly because it is by no means clear to me that Sir Alec is fully aware of what he is promising. One has the impression that, having succeeded to his inheritance, he is content to leave the account-books to the estate bailiff. This is a new rake's progress, though conducted with richly comic undertones. Sir Alec began his campaign in an appropriately bizarre setting, the sanded ring of the cattle auction room in Perth. Behind high steel bars, in place of the steers, were hunched rows of journalists; at the auctioneer's rostrum Sir Alec himself; there was a powerful smell of disinfectant. The last celebrity to appear in this room was a prize Aberdeen Angus bull, which was knocked down for £63,000 a few weeks ago. Sir Alec, not to be outdone, was dealing in hundreds of millions. But among the accomplishments he has yet to acquire is the ability to read accurately from a typewritten script: his sentences vanish disconcertingly in a mist of subordinate clauses, verbs oscillate from singular to plural without warning, and paragraphs are liable to end in syntactical chaos. This is no great handicap before an audience of farmers; but it is a little daunting to realize that Sir Alec's grasp of economic realities is even more slender than one had been led to suppose. 'Production' becomes 'productivity', and Sir Alec calmly informed us that a new hospital was being started and completed every 19 days – a fact which, if true, would indeed be remarkable.

Sir Alec's desire to please the electors is exceeded only by his positive anxiety to win over the Press. No trouble – be it press-conference, personal interview, smiles and postures – is too great for him. Last Monday, on a misty morning, he met the Press at the house of Major Drummond-Moray, where he is staying. Looking like an elongated rhesus monkey, he obediently skipped and trotted through the garden at the behest of the photographers, and one felt that, if they had asked him to stand on his head amid the Major's chrysanthemums, he would have obliged cheerfully.

Confronted with this travelling circus, even the Prime Minister's professional competitor, Mr William Rushton, is being pushed off-stage. True, I saw him, early this week, in the centre of an admiring crowd in the main square of Crieff: but most of those who composed it were schoolgirls asking for autographs; cross-faced electors scuttled by disapprovingly. Even more curious figures have emerged for this by-election. There is Mr Smith, a retired Wing-Commander, who believes that, by defeating Sir Alec, he can somehow help the Tories to win the general election. There is Mr Wort, a Wimbledon schoolmaster, who argues that the Prime Minister, by a misuse of the Peerage Bill, has brought the House of Lords into contempt. I listened carefully to his case, but it has much of the obscurity of Jarndyce v. Jarndyce, and I admit that I have not yet mastered his point.

Then there are the Scottish Nationalists, accompanied by miscellaneous impedimenta of sporrans, kilts, tartan waistcoats, bagpipes, and pamphlets with titles like 'Britain's Forgotten Satellite'. Scottish Nationalism is a new phenomenon to me but, having been ruthlessly brainwashed by two of its adherents last weekend, I am happy to announce that they have invented an entirely new kind of boredom, have achieved a sort of technological break-through into the higher reaches of tedium. After this, it was good to learn that the amiable Mr Grimond underwent a similar experience: in the course of a lightning visit on Saturday, the Nationalists trapped him in the corner of a hotel, from which he emerged, glassy-eyed, some considerable time later.

The serious issues, in fact, are being left largely to the Liberals and the Labour Party. Mr Duncan Millar, the Liberal, is the only candidate with a genuine local base. As a hydro-electric engineer and a sheepfarmer, he is well known and liked in the region, and is burrowing away industriously into the Tory farming vote; indeed, he appears to be the only one the Tories are taking seriously. Mr Forester, the young Labour man, struck me as, on the whole, the most articulate of the group, but he faces a discouraging task. Labour has put up five different candidates in six elections, and its vote has fallen from over 7,000 in 1945 to a mere 4,000 last time. With both a Liberal and a Nationalist in the field, he will do well to save his deposit.

The truth is, it is quite beyond the Prime Minister's capacity to lose this seat. The whole vast area, stretching from the outer suburbs of Perth to the high glens of the north-west, stinks of the genteel decay on which Toryism thrives. Everyone is vaguely in favour of 'bringing in the industry'; nobody really knows how, in practice, this can be done. The farmers grumble about a mysterious thing called 'winter keep'; but, with a Mercedes or a Jaguar in the garage, they are not the stuff from which mass revolts are made. Besides, there are leases to be renewed and, in this part of the world, the laird in his castle is still a fearsome thing. There are no jobs, but no unemployment either. The young people just push off to Perth or, more likely, to Glasgow and the south. The angry men are the small tradespeople and shopkeepers; but, whatever they may do in the secrecy of the ballot-station, they are not going to voice their wrath publicly and lose big Tory customers. There is no Poujade to give them collective courage. And then, Sir Alec is the devil they know and, secretly, revere: Scotsmen love a lord – even when he has renounced his title.

The Tories, in fact, have this region in their grip. The big lairds are buying out the smaller farmers and consolidating their estates. Every year, there are more animals and fewer men. The rivers leap with salmon, the fields are dark with pheasants pecking at the stubble, huge hares lope drunkenly across the narrow roads, where they are squashed flat by the racing tyres of journalists and TV-teams. This is a country where a gentleman can still exact his due. Whatever the Perthshire man may think in his heart, he can still be relied upon, for some time to come, to doff his bonnet and give three respectful cheers for Sir Alec.

—1 November 1963

The Prime Minister

THIS ELECTION has focused essentially on men rather than measures. The question that has been put to the voters boils down to this: is Harold Wilson the right man to be placed in charge of our affairs for the next five years? Constitutionalists may deplore this drift towards a presidential referendum, but I would suggest that there are three good reasons why it is logical. First, the issues facing electors – Rhodesia, the Common Market, defence, the incomes policy, the management of the economy, housing, education, trades union reform (to mention only eight of the most important) – are of such variety and complexity that it is almost impossible for most people to make a balanced judgement on the policies produced by the rival parties: inevitably they are forced to make a personal estimate of the man who will be called upon to deal with them.

Secondly, the power of the Prime Minister has increased, is increasing and will certainly increase still further in the next five years. He now stands on an altogether different constitutional level from the rest of the cabinet, who are becoming essentially prime ministerial assistants, rather than ministers in their own right. Thirdly, Harold Wilson exercises a personal dominance over his own party which is well-nigh complete and which is, I believe, altogether without precedent. To an ever-increasing extent he *is* the Labour Party – and the government. The electorate instinctively grasps this point, and in voting for or against Wilson they are responding to structural changes in our political system.

These developments are, in some ways, unwelcome to many members of the Labour Party. In the first place, the concentration of power in the person of a single man runs contrary not only to the party's constitution but to its moral spirit, which is essentially collectivist. Labour believes in internal democracy and debate; it distrusts the personal mandate; unlike the Tories, it rejects the mythology of leadership; and, in addition, it has a profound suspicion of the whole machinery of power. Labour is, by its very nature, an underdog's party; it is a novel and somewhat alarming experience to find itself led by a man who plays so convincingly the part of the overdog.

There are more particular reasons why many Labour supporters view a Wilson mandate with apprehension. Wilson is a man whose political expertise is universally recognized and admired. But his political principles are virtually unknown. It could be said of Attlee, for instance, that he had two absolutely central beliefs – that mass-unemployment was wicked, unnecessary and could be eliminated; and that India must be given her freedom. These two causes sprang direct from his own personal experience; they were inseparable from the man. What can we say of Wilson? What bedrock body of political doctrine can be associated with him? He is a politician who used the left of his party to overcome the right and then planted himself firmly in the centre. Nothing wrong in that; but one must ask – what are the beliefs of the centre? To hold the party together? To stay in office? These are admirable objectives, but they are not beliefs. Wilson is associated with the concept of efficiency, if with anything. This again is excellent in itself, but as a political proposition it is morally neutral. Efficiency for what? I think the hesitations of many on the left can be summed up quite simply: 'We know we are fortunate to have a leader of such capacity. But where is he going to take us over the next five years? And what will be left of the party, as a moral crusade, at the end of them?'

I confess I share these hesitations. But there is a case for the Wilson style of leadership, and I propose to put it. First, the man himself. I do not doubt for an instant that Wilson is one of the half-dozen ablest men in the country. For sheer brain-power, and (more important) the ability to direct it into practical channels, there is perhaps nobody to beat him. Granted all the accidents of politics, it is almost incredible that, at this moment of supreme peril in our economic fortunes, the nation should be led by the cleverest man in the kingdom. Just as Britain found Churchill in 1940 so, by some intervention of democratic providence, we have got Wilson now. Together with brain-power goes a capacity for administrative work which is formidable, and which allows him to achieve the correct balance between intense activity and reflection – a very important quality in a prime minister. I am tempted to recall Bagehot's words on Palmerston:

> 'His objects were common objects: what was uncommon was the will with which he pursued them. No man was better in action, but no man was more free from the pedantry of business . . . He knew that the real essence of work is concentrated energy, and that people who really have that in a superior degree by nature, are independent of the forms and habits and artifices by which less able and active people are kept up to their labours.'

The second most important thing about Wilson is his genius for compromise, which is linked to his ability to handle men. The role of the conciliator in politics is unexciting and sometimes ignoble. But it is essential to the well-being and success of a political movement. It was something which Gaitskell, for all his great gifts, never possessed: indeed, it was perhaps incompatible with his fiercely held convictions. He not only wished to beat his opponents within the party: it was his nature to force them to stand up and publicly admit their defeat. This produced righteous drama, which the Labour Party loves, but it made unity impossible. It is difficult now to recall the misery and bitterness which infected the party at all levels until Wilson took over. So much of its energy was spent in internal battles; so little in thinking about its policy and preparing for government. We often talk of the 'thirteen wasted years' of the Tories. But what of Labour's wasted years? How many of them were spent spilling fraternal blood on the altar of doctrinal purity, how few devoted to the practical blueprints of social change?

When Wilson assumed the leadership, the change of morale and spirit within the party could be felt within a matter of weeks; and, despite eighteen exceptionally difficult months in office, the sense of unity is now stronger than ever. We take it, indeed, for granted, and so dismiss the magnitude of the achievement. Was it brought about by a certain deviousness, an occasional willingness to be all things to all men? No doubt. But politics has little to do with perfection: it is the art of balancing comparative good – and evil. The experience of the last sixty years or so shows that unity is the most precious gift a political party can possess. It is, in fact, the key to electoral victory. But it cannot be purchased without certain sacrifices of doctrine and principle. We can be purists, yes – but only by living, like hermits, in the wilderness.

This brings us to the central fact about Wilson: his attitude to power. He likes power. He enjoys it. But his enjoyment of it is severely practical. Not for him the ability to sway the ideas of millions. I doubt if he will ever exercise one-tenth of the power over men's minds that, say, Aneurin Bevan possessed. For Wilson, power means office: the physical possession of the executive machine. This is unglamorous; it is also realistic. A politician should never flinch from office, or relinquish it lightly. Too many of our greatest political talents have spent most of their lives in sterile opposition. Fox had only three brief spells of executive power. Disraeli did, indeed, climb to the top of the greasy pole; but only when he was an elderly man, the fire extinguished, the fertility of ideas almost gone. Parnell never got office at all; Lord Randolph Churchill for only a year. His son, for great periods of his life, was powerless to direct events. Lloyd George, perhaps the ablest of them all, spent his prime in frustrated impotence, while lesser men brought the country to the brink of ruin. Bevan's political life was a failure, except for his years as Minister of Health, when he accomplished a great work. What a prodigal wastage of political energy and genius! What missed opportunities! Should we not be grateful to a man like Wilson, who scorns the emotional indulgence of opposition, and who is quite determined to exercise his political skill not just through Westminster, but through Whitehall too?

There is a wider lesson in this for the Labour Party. In the past it has feared office, held it without confidence and surrendered it almost gratefully. There is some truth in the Tory jibe that Labour 'runs away' from power. Perhaps Harold Wilson's greatest contribution to the Labour movement is that he is gradually exorcising this fear, is teaching the left that power is not necessarily an agent of corruption, but a neutral instrument: something which a working-class party must learn to use, and can only use effectively by prolonged experience. We have apathetically come to regard Tory rule as the 'normal' form of government. Wilson's aim is to shake this rooted defeatism, to convince, not just the electorate, but the movement itself that Labour is the governing party. If he achieves this – and the prospects are excellent – then this most unrevolutionary man will have brought about a fundamental change in our political system. And, over the years, this change will be reflected in every aspect of our national life.

There can be no question that all of us on the left – not just those of us who belong to the Labour Party – have a duty to ensure that the government receives a decisive mandate this Thursday. This journal has, over the past month, amply demonstrated that Labour's case for a further period of office is unanswerable. I shall vote Labour on Thursday and I would exhort all our readers to do the same. Having said all this, however, I admit that my doubts about Wilson remain. He is, in a sense, a statesman without a cause. It is up to the left to supply him with one. All the resources of the Labour Party's democratic constitution, every organ of opinion on the left, must be employed to ensure that the machinery of power Wilson has created is devoted to the cause of progress at home and abroad. Wilson uses power; and we must use Wilson. In short, we can risk the dangers inherent in the Wilsonian revolution – and reap its potential benefits – only by a conscious revival of democracy within the progressive movement. The battle does not end this Thursday. It is only just beginning.

—1 April 1966

Part 3

INTELLECTUALS

War Games

PLATOON HQ in a forward battalion. L/Cpl Toynbee, P., from his advanced observation post, has just reported a strong concentration of Blue Army troops in the vicinity. A mile or so to the right, Colonel Crossman has announced he is already engaging a column of the 'New Obscurantist' Brigade. On the left, Brigadier Sartre, O/C Allied Forces, signals that he is in difficulties. Sitting on an upturned orange-juice crate, Major Biggs-Smith, who served with distinction under General Webb in the Twenties, is discussing the situation with the Platoon Commander, Lieutenant Carruthers, a young veteran of the Laski Irregulars. They have just heard a very alarming report: Marshal Bevan is a prisoner-of-war and may be treating with the enemy. At this moment, Corporal Tom Maschler arrives with the latest batch of recruits; he hands their documents (Declaration. Edited by Tom Maschler. Macgibbon & Kee. 18s.) *over to Carruthers.*

BIGGS-SMITH: Got to be careful in selecting this lot, Carruthers. Some of the ones they've been sending us recently caught Beaver's Disease and went over to the enemy. Trouble is, they pay more. Well, who's the first?

CARRUTHERS: Doris Lessing, Sir. Roman Catholic education, ten years of Communism, transferred to us suffering from Hungarian shellshock. Bit over-age for this lot, but then years in the C.P. don't count. Five novels, goodish. The Divisional Psychiatrist, Dr. C. P. Snow, says he's prepared to 'bet heavily' on her. She has sound views on Chinese, Indians, Africans; says we'll be impoverished by cutting ourselves off from the Communist third of mankind. Admits things are difficult, just now, but thinks that if the writer makes the imaginative effort to comprehend change, then despair and self-pity can be conquered. Claims she has a still, small voice, but speaks for the inarticulate many.

BIGGS-SMITH: Excellent. Can she shoot?

CARRUTHERS: Oh, yes, Sir. Writes very well: in fact I was quite moved by her piece.

BIGGS-SMITH: Good, put her down as a rifleman, then. Next?

CARRUTHERS: Colin Wilson, Sir. His training sergeant reports: 'An unruly case, but no use giving him CB. Virtually immune to punishment, critical or physical. Joined the ranks with recommendation for a commission from Captain Connolly (Rtd) but failed to justify expectations. On his own admission, writes letters to the Press.'

BIGGS-SMITH: Barrack-room lawyer, eh? Can't have that. Next thing we know he'll be writing to his M.P.

CARRUTHERS: Yes, Sir. And he seems to have read Shaw, Spengler and Toynbee either too soon or too late. In consequence, says our civilization is in decline and is therefore challenged to produce 'a higher type of man'. I don't like the sound of that.

BIGGS-SMITH: Neither do I. Anything else?

CARRUTHERS: Yes, Sir. He writes: 'So we want a room in which we can lock ourselves tightly, and barricade the windows and bar the doors. Then experience pounds harmlessly outside, like volleys of wind, and we can sleep.'

BIGGS-SMITH: That puts a different complexion on things. There speaks the authentic voice of first-class Pioneer Corps material. Put him on fatigue, but don't give him a rifle yet. Next?

CARRUTHERS: John Osborne, Sir. Sound, pubsy working-class background, no inhibitions, hates religion, middle class, Tories, Suez and royalty. Excellent sense of timing, splendid parade-ground voice and superb command of invective.

BIGGS-SMITH: Perfect. Make him the platoon sergeant immediately. Next?

CARRUTHERS: John Wain, Sir. Welfare State upbringing, then pedagogy. Wrote a good first novel, but nothing much since. Says he believes art should be serious and that writers should work hard and hasten slowly.

BIGGS-SMITH: Seems to know what's wrong with himself, then. Well, if he really believes it, put him down as a probationary rifleman. By the way, where's this Amis I hear so much about?

CARRUTHERS: He's not in the group, Sir. It says in the Introduction that he refused to join because he suspects anyone 'who wants to buttonhole me about my role in society'.

BIGGS-SMITH: Fiddlesticks! We're not asking for volunteers. What do we have conscription for? Send him his papers. Next?

CARRUTHERS: Kenneth Tynan, Sir. Used to be Kenneth Peacock Tynan, but he's dropped the middle since undergraduate days. Seems a bit unnecessarily pro-American – in fact he's had himself photographed in this book against a background of Coca-Cola bottles. Brilliant marksman: his essay is far and away the best. The N.C.O.s down at the training depot thought he was a bit of a lightweight, but he's vastly improved since he went on that course at the *Observer* small-arms school. He now asks for a society 'Where people care more for what you have learned than for where you learned it; where people who think and people who work can share common assumptions and discuss them in the same idiom; where art connects instead of separating people . . .'. Question is, does he *believe* it?

BIGGS-SMITH: We'll soon find that out in action. Give him a rifle.

CARRUTHERS: Next is Bill Hopkins, Sir. Has a grave handicap to begin his career with: Private Wilson says he's the only other genius alive besides himself. The fact is, he's rather a dark horse. His first novel is due to appear in a few weeks' time, but I can't make head or tail of his piece in this book – except that it shows he's a very poor shot.

BIGGS-SMITH: Well, hold him down at depot until his book comes out.

CARRUTHERS: Next is Lindsay Anderson, Sir. A good lefty from a middle-class background. Makes films about foot-and-mouth disease and slums. Thinks that liberal day-dreams are no good, that we should all get out and push. A good party man: 'All points of view are *not* equally right, and to suppose that it is somehow narrow-minded to opt for one consistent line of action rather than for all policies simultaneously is the shortest way to render oneself politically ineffective.' Unfortunately – I hardly like to mention this, Sir – he has some hard things to say about the NEW STATESMAN.

BIGG -SMITH: What! Insulting the regimental mag.? Mutinous swine!

CARRUTHERS: But, Sir, isn't that just what it stands for?

BIGGS-SMITH: Quite right, Carruthers, I was forgetting myself. Make the fellow a corporal.

CARRUTHERS: Finally, Sir, there's Stuart Holroyd. Only twenty-four. He published his first book, *Emergence from Chaos*, this year. It didn't do so well as *The Outsider*, but everyone who actually read it says it was much better. Says he was an agnostic in his teens, 'when I had not yet liberated myself from my inherited humanist thought-habits'. Doesn't believe in representative government. He says: 'Waking up consists first of all in waking up to oneself (religious awakening), and only secondarily in waking up to the world (political awakening). This should always be the sequence: first organize yourself, and only then consider yourself sufficiently mature to attempt to organize the society.'

BIGGS-SMITH: Well, has *he* organized himself?

CARRUTHERS: I don't think so, Sir. He says that in his next two books he's going to 'broaden and deepen the definition of religion by returning to its dynamic centre in the human psyche'.

BIGGS-SMITH: We haven't got time to wait for that. Send him back to depot. Next?

CARRUTHERS: That's the lot, Sir, except for a word of thanks to Corporal Maschler for getting them all on parade.

BIGGS-SMITH: Good. Not a bad little bunch, all in all. Don't seem to like each other much, but then that's all to the good. Remember the regimental motto: 'Strength is disunity.' But most of them could do with a sharp course of arms drill. The balloon will be going up any minute.

CARRUTHERS: By the way, Sir; are these just manœuvres or the real thing?

BIGGS-SMITH: That, Carruthers, is what we never know until they start.

—19 October 1957

Lucky Jim's Political Testament

ON THE COVER of this pamphlet,* the Fabian Society announces that it has been issued 'as worthy of consideration within the Labour Movement'. Lamentable as it may seem, I think the Fabian Society is right. *Socialism and the Intellectuals* is badly written and muddled to the point of exasperation. In default of a suitable penitentiary here, its author should be sentenced to at least six months' hard labour (as I am sure he would consider it) at the Café des Deux Magots, and there learn how to define his terms, how to state his premises, and how to conduct his arguments in a logical and consequential manner. But this being said, the fact remains that what Mr Amis has written is important and, incidentally, far more interesting than the learned and lifeless political tracts published, all too frequently, by Messrs. Wolheim, Utley, Crosland and others in the pages of *Encounter*.

Mr Amis is a Labour supporter. He has, so far, voted Labour in every election and, 'unless something very unexpected happens', he expects to vote Labour to the end of his days. Come election-time, he even sticks a poster in his window and lends his car to party headquarters to save Swansea voters from trudging to the polls. But – he does not join the party; he finds it difficult to work up any enthusiasm for politics; Suez led him to attend his first political meeting in fifteen years, but this simply served to remind him how boring such meetings were; and, at the end of his essay, he contemplates, with a good deal of complacency, continuing a lifetime of political apathy.

This, in itself, may not be tragic for the Labour Party. Unfortunately, Mr Amis – at least on his own account – is not alone. He claims to speak on behalf of a class: the new welfare state intellectuals. They mass, in their thousands, at his elbow: in Cardiff and

***Socialism and the Intellectuals*. By Kingsley Amis. *Fabian Society*.

Hull, in Exeter and Southampton, in Stoke and Sheffield, lecturers in Geology and Civics, veterinary surgeons and welfare officers, with their long-playing records and their ponytail-haired wives, their bottles of Spanish burgundy and volumes of A. J. Ayer. The university colleges of England echo with the tramp of their apathetic feet. The men who should be the rank-and-file of the progressive intelligentsia, the N.C.O.s of the local party organizations, the subalterns of a new generation of Labour voters, are choosing to stay at home and indulge in the pursuit of Civilization (Tourist Class).

Mr Amis has two comments to make on this phenomenon. First, it does not cause him to 'grieve overmuch'. A characteristic of this school of young intellectuals is that they all dislike each other intensely. Mr Amis obviously loathes the class to which he belongs, indeed he even feels it necessary to employ the classic disclaimer: 'some of my best friends,' he writes, 'are intellectuals.' He sees his colleagues as unreliable nuisances, whose presence in a militant party is more likely to prove an embarrassment than an asset. 'I often feel,' he says, 'that even the intellectual who takes up some sort of political career, attains some power or influence in that field, stands a good chance of being wrong on any given issue, a rather better chance than the ordinary Labour Party or trade union man.' And why is this? Because 'the best and most trustworthy political motive is self-interest'. Since the intellectual's interests are not identical with those of the workers, his presence at their side is therefore irrational, unnatural and unpredictable.

This leads Mr Amis to his second comment. (This is not, strictly speaking, correct: his second point is made first; but I am trying to present his arguments in their most favourable light.) What drives the intellectual to take up the cudgels on behalf of the left, he says, is precisely something irrational: political romanticism. And here Mr Amis feels he has laid his finger on the origins of the present apathy: there is today, he feels, a notable lack of causes which can stir this romanticism and which, at the same time, have a distinct political content. The colour-bar, horror comics, the homosexual laws and capital punishment, on all these the new intellectuals feel strongly; but they are not, strictly speaking, political issues calling for street demonstrations and the overthrow of governments. The welfare state, the decline in unemployment, the taming of the Tories, the international stalemate of the cold war have successfully and, it seems, permanently, lowered the political temperature in Britain; even the outrage of Suez failed to bring it back to the boil, because it simply did not go on long enough. The point can be made quite briefly:

> *Though the Tories may be bad again,*
> *There is* no *substitute for Spain.*

Hence Mr Amis is led to the ultimate stage of Marxist logic: the despairing longing for catastrophe. Things will have to get far, far worse, he says, before intelligent people can be persuaded to get together and make them better. 'What is needed,' he writes, 'is a good, long, steadily worsening crisis out in the open where everyone can see it.' (This, I might add, only a few paragraphs after he attacks Auden for writing of 'the necessary murder'.)

I hope I have presented Mr Amis's arguments correctly. Possibly the inner core of his political thought has escaped me. It may be that I have missed some subtle nuance, concealed in his cloudy syntax. If so, he has my profoundest apologies. I say all this because it seems to me, after reading this pamphlet, that the only thing which prevents him from becoming an active Labour supporter is a regrettable unwillingness to think. The problems he raises can all be answered by the simple statement of self-evident propositions. It is demonstrably untrue that an intellectual is more likely to be wrong on a given political issue than the ordinary voter, if only for the simple reason that he is likely to be in more complete possession of the facts about it. Perhaps I am naïve, but I have always assumed that an educated voter is likely to be more responsible than an uneducated voter; that knowledge is a desirable and useful thing to possess; and that intelligence is an important political asset. Mr Amis employs the word 'intellectual' freely, without attempting to define it. He may have forgotten that it was first used in describing the partisans of Dreyfus, that small band of writers, journalists and lawyers who challenged the power of the French state and army, and risked the fury of the Paris street mobs, because they believed that reason was a better arbiter of human affairs than prejudice; and he may also have forgotten that it was the intellectuals who eventually triumphed.

No wise man, I think, would dispute Mr Amis's contention that self-interest is a healthy political guide. But it is precisely in exposing and propagating self-interest that the art of politics lies. If all British workers had correctly appreciated their interests in 1955, there is no doubt that a Labour government would be in power today. It is here that the intellectual has an important role to play.

It is his job to bring things out into the open where everyone can see them. If he does this successfully, then it doesn't matter much whether he votes himself, or lends his car, or sticks up posters, or even writes pamphlets.

Nor is the intellectual, as Mr Amis supposes, himself disinterested. His politics, too, are guided by self-interest. Mr Amis's evident contempt for humanist values leads him to ignore the fact that such interests need not necessarily be materialistic. In the long run the intellectual takes up a political position not because of the petrol shortage, or the price of Spanish burgundy, or the level of income tax – any of the issues likely to affect his material wellbeing – but because one of the parties soliciting his support is prepared to subscribe, if only in part, to the values in which he believes. In doing so, the intellectual automatically protects his status and his future.

One of these values – the most important – is justice. Justice is the application of reason to the problem of controlling human behaviour, and its interests are identical with those of the intellectual; if they are threatened, his are threatened, too. This, I think, is the answer to the comment made by Mr Amis on 'political romanticism'. He defines it as the 'irrational capacity to become inflamed by interests and causes which are not one's own, that are outside oneself'. In fact, what he means by political romanticism is really a sense of justice, which every true intellectual possesses and this is quite rightly, and quite rationally, aroused whenever and wherever an injustice is committed, whether it be in Spain, in Abyssinia, in Cyprus, in Egypt, or in Britain. In this sense, the intellectual is, by definition, politically committed, and his sympathies will always and in all countries be found, in the main, on the side of the rational, progressive, democratic left.

It is true, of course, that I am talking about the ideal intellectual, whereas Mr Amis is discussing British intellectuals as he believes them to exist today. But is the difference so enormous? I suspect that Mr Amis, like most 'contemporary' young novelists, is slightly out of date. In the years following 1945, there was, I agree, some apathy among the younger intellectuals, particularly in academic circles; an inevitable and probably healthy reaction to a decade of intellectual life dominated by the strident voices of the left. There was even some talk of a 'New Right' (where is it now, I wonder?). This tendency, however, was grossly exaggerated by Mr Amis and others, who used it as a gimmick in their presentation of a certain type of modern hero, generally referred to as Lucky Jim, who enjoyed a certain success with the circulating libraries. Naturally, they have a vested interest in keeping him alive, in persuading people that he is dominating the political horizon with giant, uncommitted strides. But I suspect – in fact I am sure – that Lucky Jim, at least in his political context, is dead, killed on the afternoon of 30 October 1956, by Sir Anthony Eden; and that what Mr Amis has written in this pamphlet is merely Jim's last will and testament. It may be that Mr Amis was not inflamed by the Suez issue; but in that case he is the one intellectual I have heard of who was not. The London air, at least, is loud with the lamentations of intellectuals who now regret having failed to do their full share at the last election to keep the Tories out. Nobody who attended the great Suez demonstration in Trafalgar Square feels the need for another Spain. The rumpus has even invaded the Athenaeum. Never in modern history has the intellectual element in a nation been so united, militant and, I submit, successful. After all, Messrs. Auden, Spender and Co. lost their battle; we won. The present mood, of course, may not last; but for Mr Amis to say it does not exist is sheer, blind ignorance. *Swansea, art tha sleepin' down below?*

—12 January 1957

The New Spectre Haunting Europe

A SPECTRE is haunting Europe – the spectre of student power. As in 1848, each outbreak in each European capital contains the seeds of another elsewhere, as students gain courage from the success and audacity of their foreign brethren, and learn from their mistakes. With each outbreak, the students raise their objectives and widen their horizons. There is no need to speak of a Students' International, for this implies a common organization, a discipline and a programme which simply do not exist. Pavlovian mutterings, by Lords Butler and Alport, about international communist plotters pulling the strings, simply betray the gentlemen's age and ignorance: they are fighting a bogey laid to rest a decade or more ago, and which is now just as frightened of the new apparition as they are themselves – perhaps more so, to judge by the frenzied efforts of the C.P. to exorcise it. Of course there are many and multiplying contacts between students in different countries: exchange of information and techniques, gestures of solidarity, sometimes even active assistance. But the student revolt is both less and more than an international conspiracy: it is spontaneous and systematic at the same time. Spontaneous, because these young men and women do not need to be persuaded, organized or regimented by anyone into doing what they are doing; systematic because they are inspired by common attitudes, grievances, disgusts and doctrines, which leap across the frontiers.

Anyone who is fascinated by political processes and public philosophies, be they students, dons, writers or politicians, should make every effort to go to Paris now. For what is happening there is of great importance not only to France but perhaps, in the long run, to the world. To be there is a political education in itself, to watch the birth-pangs (perhaps, soon, the murder or even suicide) of a new approach to the organization of human societies. That is such a rare event in history that we are fortunate to be alive to witness it. For too long, those of us who care about politics have been imprisoned in the sterile triangle formed by communism, fascism and bourgeois democracy. Appalled by the choice between the two authoritarianisms, most of us have struggled wearily to humanize the third, cobbling together every ramshackle variety of 'democratic socialism' in the vain attempt to combine material progress, on a mass basis, with a raised quality of life. Often enough we have got neither. Here in Britain, for instance, we have a stagnant economy, in which university students are told we must develop horror weapons in the cause of the export trade, and workers are stampeded by ignorance and demagogy into howling abuse at an even more exploited section of the population, the blacks. No wonder young people look for a fourth choice: and in Paris, it seems to me, they are beginning to find one.

We might have expected that the French, who have given more to political thought than any other nation, would have a unique contribution to make to the student phenomenon. When the students moved in Prague, Warsaw, Berlin, Rome, Madrid, the United States, even in Britain, how could France – above all Paris – lag behind? Had the French, buried for a decade in paternalism and apathy, lost their taste for debating the way in which society should be organized, and their capacity to suggest fresh solutions? I had myself asked this question some weeks ago, being ignorant of the ferment already boiling in a dozen French universities. I need not have worried. When the moment came in France, it was all the more explosive for having been delayed. The French movement, now that it has broken the surface, is seen to be far more sophisticated than its equivalent elsewhere; more deeply grounded in philosophical principles, more adult in its grasp of the strategy and tactics of political action; more violent – much more violent – coming from a race which respects intransigence and pronounces lovingly the words of Danton: *De l'audace, toujours de l'audace!* Above all, the French movement has *style*, a certain elegant flourish to all that it does, which catches the heart and makes one appreciate that politics is not just a utilitarian science, but also an art, whose satisfactions are aesthetic as well as moral.

In the courtyard of the Faculty of Letters, the heart and brain of the movement, a thousand flowers not only bloom but load the spring air with intellectual incense. Young socialists, Marxist Christians, Maoists, anti-C.P. Marxist-Leninists, Guevarists, Fidelistos, Breton nationalists, Young Workers, Portuguese democrats,

Basques and Spaniards, young people from Germany and France and Britain, shout their wares and debate their principles. On the walls, posters – some of great beauty, hand-painted in the Ecole des Beaux Arts – proclaim a score of different creeds. In the overflowing lecture halls and corridors, every conceivable topic is examined: forms of revolutionary action, birth control, the nature of the state, how to fight the police, workers' control, free love, the role of parents, the uses of exams, Vietnam, marriage and divorce, the nature of the university. There is, appropriately, a pentecostal mood, in which those speaking different tongues evoke a common understanding. Workers come there to argue and listen, and so do old men and housewives, and foreigners and Deputies and writers and journalists. The debating groups spill out into nearby streets and crowd the vast Odéon Theatre. De Gaulle, falling back, in his rage, on the vernacular of a young subaltern, has called it a 'dog's breakfast'. Perhaps it is, in a sense: France has brought up its Gaullist vomit and now feels better.

But the disparate debate is underpinned by a powerful thread of logic, which has transformed the French movement from a student revolt into a political event. Most of us, all along, have missed the real significance of the students' demands, partly through blindness, partly because they were not clearly articulated. Yes, we say, we agree you have a right to reforms in your universities, to greater control in their direction and more say in their curricula; but what has this to do with more general political action? Why don't you stick to your own business? It has taken the French to get the argument across, and I doubt if even they could have done it without the leadership of Cohn-Bendit. This jovial young Robespierre, with his flaming red hair and piercing blue eyes, has the true revolutionary's gift of combining a philosophy which can be reasoned, slogans which can be shouted and a mad-dog taste for taking positions by frontal assault. When he speaks, men listen; where he leads, they follow. He makes the impossible become possible simply by doing it. It wouldn't surprise me if he beats the ban on his return to France.

Well, say the students of the 22 March – now transformed into *Les Enfants de Marx et du 13 Mai* – why don't we stick to reforming the universities? Because to do so would be futile. There are now 600,000 students in France; there will be more every year. Society has laid it down that those of sufficient intelligence, who work hard enough at high school, may automatically enter university. Needless to say, no provision is made for them when they get there. There are not enough teachers, lecture rooms, halls of residence, libraries, laboratories. The courses laid down for them are, for the most part, idiotic, the teaching old-fashioned, the exam. system medieval or at best 19th century. But all these problems are secondary; even if they can be reformed by student agitation – and students have to descend into the streets to get any concessions whatever; so much for 'peaceful progress' – they leave the wider problem untouched. What is the point of improving the structure of higher education by reformism, if the rest of society remains the same? Paris University, for instance, can now churn out 5,000 sociologists a year. They are, of course, taught in a silly way. But supposing you revolutionize their teaching, you are still left with the problem of what they are to do in the world outside. The cleverer ones become teachers, and churn out more sociologists; the others become public-relations advisers in factories, and suchlike, or scrabble around to get a toehold in another profession: at worst flunkeys, at best privileged acolytes serving the altars of capitalism, helping to buttress a rotten society which pursues consumption for its own sake.

Can you reform the medical school without at the same time questioning the assumptions on which the medical profession is organized and the functions of medicine in society? How to 'improve' science courses without at the same time asking what science is supposed to do for mankind? Can you replan the Political Science Faculty without at the same time replanning the political system? After all, the university is the matrix of society, the institution which produces its élites, assumptions and objectives. Will a *real* reform of the matrix be permitted, entailing as it must the eventual transformation of society outside? Not on your life. Therefore student reforms are organically linked to the transformation of the adult world. Student agitation is meaningless unless it can join forces with the workers, the fall-guys in any consumer society, whether on the capitalist or the communist model.

I hasten to add that the students cannot produce all the answers (or rather they produce a bewildering variety of them). But they are asking questions which have never been posed before in the context of a political offensive, and with a stridency which makes it impossible for their elders to brush them aside. For here comes the second contribution of the Paris movement. It is not enough, they say, to debate the questions and formulate the answers, then allow them slowly to percolate: debate and formulation are inseparable from action – and action in the street. The methods of the idealist intellectuals must be *la démocratie de la rue*. The power of the bourgeois-communist or bourgeois-capitalist state will not surrender unless directly challenged. A wild theory? Yes: but it works! The students fought all night on the barricades on 10 May; the next day the government capitulated. And not just a Fourth Republic government, hanging onto a trembling majority in the Assembly, but the arrogant and authoritarian Gaullist state, armed to the teeth with statutory powers and the physical apparatus of repression.

It was at this point that the student movement passed into the mainstream of politics, indeed history. Beneath the thin veneer of Gaullist 'stability and prosperity', practically every large group in France has a grievance, long cherished through years of futile negotiations. Real wages have not risen, have actually fallen in some cases, over the past two years. There is growing official unemployment, much concealed unemployment and underemployment. The peasants fear for their prices when the last E.E.C. barriers fall. Railwaymen, civil servants, busmen, miners, and a score of other categories are underpaid. The Bretons are angry, and so are men in Auvergne, in Provence, in the Pas de Calais. Even the police have their claims.

The police, indeed, are an interesting case. They are badly paid, and recruited, for the most part, from the most exploited classes. During the student agitation, the government treated them like robots. Ordered here, ordered there; one minute told to exercise ultimate restraint, the next to attack ferociously. When the big clash came, the riot police had been on duty for three days, without relief; some had been transported overnight from Brittany, where they had been holding down the nationalists. They were stood to at twelve o'clock on the Friday morning; many got no food or rest for the next fourteen and a quarter hours. They were next told that the students' demands could not be met, and ordered to attack. They fought for four hours and sustained over 400 casualties, many of them serious; they were excoriated by almost the entire population. They then heard, on the evening of that day, that the government had conceded all the students' demands, and they were to be withdrawn in ignominy. If, in the last resort, the consumer state relies on the police to preserve itself, it must learn to treat them, at least, as human beings!

So all those with a grievance have begun to follow the students' precepts, and if the police are bolshy, who is to stop them? Any state must make enemies; the art is to avoid a conflict with all of them simultaneously. Any state must sometimes use force and sometimes appeasement. The art is to avoid doing both together, and thus losing both respect and popularity. One of the reasons why France today must fascinate any student of politics is that the Gaullist government has contrived to make every mistake in the book. (It's fair to add that it has some distinguished precursors, notably the governments of Louis XVI, Charles X, Louis-Philippe and Louis-Napoleon.) Another reason is that, in its distress, the régime is looking for succour to what, in classic political terms, is its natural enemy: the Communist Party bureaucracy. Yes: but only in classical terms. In terms of the new realities expressed by Cohn-Bendit and his friends, which reflect the deeper realities of a mass-movement sickened by the incompetence and complacency of all traditional political forces, the C.P. and the Gaullists are natural allies. Both have forgotten nothing and learnt nothing. Both are rooted in 19th-century concepts. Both have a stake in society – in the status quo – and a good deal to lose by radical change. Both look to Moscow, in their different ways; to maintain the continuity of Gaullist foreign policy is almost as important to Moscow as to De Gaulle himself. Both are entombed mummies, which a breath of ideological fresh air could reduce to powder.

Thus we have the extraordinary antics of the C.P. and the C.G.T. over the last fortnight. Not even De Gaulle himself could hate Cohn-Bendit more than *vieux routiers* like Waldeck-Rochet and Benoît Frachon, men grown grey in the service of Stalinism. First they dismissed Cohn-Bendit and his group as unimportant. Then they were terrified to hear that bodies of young workers were joining the students on the barricades. Then, grinding their teeth, they slammed *l'Humanité* into full-astern, in a desperate effort to capture the movement and asphyxiate it. They jumped on the bandwaggon in order to put on the brakes, but found themselves careering down the slope. They failed to envelop the great demonstration of 13 May, even though the *service d'ordre* (significant phrase) of the C.G.T. prevented most of the workers from joining the students in a rush on the ministerial quarter of the Left Bank. Their men stopped the workers from joining hands with the students in taking over factories. But they could not halt the take-overs themselves, and were obliged to cover such action with their authority. At every stage their orders and appeals have been for calmness, discipline, etc. As such they have been praised for their moderation and sense of responsibility by the *Figaro*, organ of the French bourgeoisie, and given eager publicity by the Gaullist TV-radio network. What a fate for any C.P. which hopes for a long-term future! And, worst of all, they know that, by taking this line, they are confirming, in theory and in practice, everything that Cohn-Bendit and his friends have always said about them. I wrote last week that the Fifth Republic would never be the same again; nor, I think, will Moscow communism either. It now has powerful enemies on the Left, in the heart of Europe. Once again, the French have given birth to a new revolutionary spirit, which will ultimately enrich the lives of all of us. I would like to think, without much hope, that Britain had a contribution to make.

—24 May 1968

How Danny saved the Dollar

WHAT EXACTLY HAPPENED in France this May? Was it an extreme manifestation of a worldwide pattern and a portent for the future? Or a historical throwback, produced by a unique and unrepeatable conjunction of events? Or was it simply a weird aberration, an event *sui generis*? A case can be made – and is made by Tom Nairn (*The Beginning of the End*. By Angelo Quattrocchi and Tom Nairn. Panther. 6*s*.) – that the success of the student rebellion, and the way in which it served to detonate a *levée en masse* of the French working class, proves that there is still a place for revolutionary politics in advanced capitalist societies. Perhaps optimistically, he argues that the Paris Commune of 1871 was the last of the 'old' French revolutions, created by the *menu peuple* or victims of capitalism, and looking back to a pre-capitalist past, doomed to defeat; and 1968 the first 'new' revolution, born of capitalism's triumphant survival of its contradictions.

All the same, it's odd that no one should have noted this possibility before a handful of French students actually demonstrated it. Mr Nairn neatly avoids the problem by observing that, confronted with 'such radical novelties', 'theory has to be very audacious merely to catch up with practice'. But in fact the mainstream of political theorizing, on both sides of the Iron Curtain, had complacently assumed that the violent overthrow of the existing order in developed industrial states was no longer on the cards. Revolutions might, indeed almost certainly would, occur in the Third World; but in the West, trade unions and social democrats, by successful 'reformism', had dulled the edge of proletarian hunger and given the majority of the working class a vested interest in maintaining society. France, above all, seemed to confirm this new perspective: for here, a traditionally turbulent and politically adventurous people had apparently accepted a paternalist regime as a reasonable price to pay for steady economic growth within a framework of political stability. France had 'died' politically; were not other western democracies likely to follow suit?

True, some writers, like Marcuse, had predicted new forms of social explosion. But it was difficult to see these occurring in the actual context of 1968 or even in the foreseeable future. In the U.S. and West Germany, the only countries where Marcuse was at all widely read, student revolts had not merely failed to ignite the working class but had even produced a hostile reaction. It is significant, indeed, that the leaders of the May revolt (*The Student Revolt: the Activists Speak*. Panther. 6*s*.) specifically repudiate Marcuse's influence. Cohn-Bendit is crushingly emphatic: 'Some people have tried to force Marcuse on us as a mentor; that is a joke. None of us has read Marcuse.' He goes on:

> 'Some have read Marx, of course, perhaps Bakunin, and of the moderns Althusser, Mao, Guevara, Lefebvre. Nearly all the militants of the 22 March movement have read Sartre. But no writer could be regarded as the inspiration of the movement.'

My impression at the time confirms this. The intellectual background to the revolt was essentially eclectic. The students were willing to borrow ideas from anyone, but strictly on their own terms, and they had a positive horror of being classified. Like some primitive tribes who equate being named or photographed with an assault on their personality, loss of freedom, even death, they fought any attempt to drag them back (recuperate them, as they put it) into the system, any system. This was one of the reasons, though not the only one, why they declined to publish a positive programme of action, which could then have been stolen by more traditional groups. They wanted to create theory through action, confident that they were part of an organic process which would see the new society arise like a phoenix from the ashes of the old. By this I don't mean they were metaphysicians; on the contrary, they were pragmatists, believing that the process of constant debate, renewed each day in the light of that day's experience, would illuminate the constructive objects of the revolution *pari passu* with its work of demolition.

But despite their reluctance to commit themselves to theory, they did articulate three principles. Firstly, they rejected the traditional economic aims of revolution: the transfer or redistribution of property and power. Classic socialism, to them the inverted mirror of capitalism, is inadequate because it merely changes the governance of society, leaving its false values intact or even strengthened. As one of them puts it: 'We are not interested in transforming the relations of production but in transforming the very notion of economic labour.' This is accompanied by the proposition that the acquisition of power is not the object of political activity; power itself is to be distrusted, especially when expressed through bureaucracies and hierarchies. Nothing is more repulsive and self-defeating than a tightly-knit group of politically-motivated men, in the Leninist tradition, scheming to acquire and hold power, however pure their ostensible motives. The revolution must be used to liberate and to destroy the necessity for the exercise of power, which is itself an act of inhuman brutality. There is something of anarchism in this theory, perhaps also a residual memory of Marx's 'withering away' of the state. The students themselves did their best to operate in a collective manner, repudiating leadership and (despite the efforts of the Press) the cult of personality; and it is encouraging that the absence of hierarchies in their organization in no way diminished their effectiveness.

Secondly, and more practically, the students were simply concerned to show the exploited that revolution could be made to work even, and especially, in 1968. Of course the students never claimed to be able to 'make' a revolution; they would merely, like John the Baptist, show the way. It would then be up to the workers to seize the opportunities opened to them. In May the CP, in a last spasm of bureaucratic conservatism, prevented the workers from overthrowing the regime. But this was a measure of the weakness of the bourgeoisie, that they were forced, in the last resort, to rely on their Fifth Column in the working-class movement and thus oblige it to 'break cover'.

Lastly, the students seem to grasp the true importance of the educational system in the new politics. 'Education,' remarked Jacques Sauvageot, 'is going to be of crucial importance for the growth of every economic system today; whether we like it or not, every aim we put forward will lead us into politics.' It is the policy of all advanced societies to make higher education available to all; soon the universities will be turning out tens, scores, even hundreds of millions of graduates, who will become the dominant element in all societies, as well as a significant fraction of the total population. The type of higher education they receive will thus become the matrix of the type of society they govern. The idea of the university and the idea of society are inseparable; to transform one is to transform the other. If Waterloo was won on the playing fields of Eton, the 20th century revolution will be won on the campus. This seems to me by far the most interesting train of thought to come out of the May adventure, and its chief claim to be the harbinger of things to come.

In the meantime, there is its effect on Gaullist France to be considered. The mere narrative of events (*French Revolution 1968* by Patrick Seale and Maureen McConville Penguin 6*s*.) suggests the following sequence: astonishing moment of revolutionary success; faltering of the regime; recovery of will by De Gaulle, detonating a defensive mobilization of the bourgeosie; Gaullist triumph at the election, leaving the parliamentary Left eclipsed and the regime stronger than before. But in reality, the revolution killed Gaullism. It had been based on consensus and maintained by self-confidence, not bayonets. In May both consensus and self-confidence were shattered beyond recovery. De Gaulle now runs a traditional authoritarian regime of the Right, openly kept in power by the formal apparatus of a police state. It has no future, can have no progeny.

Equally decisive was the manner in which the students ended De Gaulle's vision of a great-power role for France. This, too, had been a confidence trick but a highly successful one, which was beginning to take in more and more people. The essence of De Gaulle's policy had always been to demonstrate France's ability, by acting on the tide of history, to inflict defeat and humiliation on the United States at the point where it was most sensitive – its currency. He had smashed the first line of defence, sterling, in November; next he forced the Americans to suspend sales of gold to all except central banks. How near he would have got to forcing a dollar devaluation we shall never know, but my guess is that the momentum he had built up was becoming irresistible, and that the dam would have broken once it became apparent that the Vietnam peace talks (which started the week the students really got going) could not end the war. The consequences would have been incalculable: perhaps the complete destruction of the international monetary system and a world slump. The student revolt and the general strike ended that game, I think for good. No one now believes that France is an economic Samson capable of pulling down the temple. How ironic that Danny le Rouge should have been instrumental in saving Western capitalism and its chief talisman, the dollar!

—18 October 1968

Young John Bull, 1969

LAST FRIDAY, a retired Colonel, living in Eastbourne, pleaded guilty to causing actual bodily harm to a long-haired art student, called John Bull. Bull, he thought, was a bad influence over his daughter, Anna. After the case the Colonel is quoted as saying:

> '[Bull] says he is against society and goes around giving out papers against the government. He calls the police fascist, but the first thing he did when I hit him was to run to the police and complain about the offence. Good heavens, when I was his age no fifty-four-year-old bald-headed father would have hit me and got away with it. I'd have hit him back again immediately. But all Mr Bull did was to shout for help from my daughter: "Anna, Anna, your father is hitting me!" '

Now what is instructive about this episode is not merely the symbolism of the student's name – which I find particularly satisfying – but the fascinating confusion in the minds of both parties to the dispute. The Colonel, feeling that he was acting as the custodian of law, order and authority, used violence – and indeed appeared contemptuous when his antagonist did not respond in kind. Young John Bull, I take it, is of a revolutionary cast of mind, but recoiled in horror at becoming personally involved in a violent act.

This confusion is one of the salient characteristics of our society. Middle-aged Berliners, outraged at the defiance by students of the due forms of law, actually beat them up, if the odds are favourable. De Gaulle distributed the Legion d'Honneur by the képi-full to the riot police who brutalized, and in one case murdered, unarmed students last May. Equally, the young advocates of the violent overthrow of society would not, in practice, participate in the cruelty and mass-slaughter their theoretical policies demand. Tariq Ali, who edits one of these volumes, (*New Revolutionaries* edited by

Tariq Ali. Owen 38*s*.) is quite open on page 72 about the need for violence, though he calls it 'defensive'; but with exquisite timing, he did not return to Pakistan, where a truly revolutionary situation had developed, until President Ayub had surrendered and the crucial phase of violence was over. I am not accusing him of pusillanimity, but merely suggesting that there is a credibility gap between the words and the actions of the new revolutionaries. Equally, Alexander Cockburn, who co-edits the second volume, is eloquent in analyzing the ills of our rotten capitalist society. (*Student Power* edited by Alexander Cockburn and Robin Blackburn Penguin 7*s*.) He is also happily married to the rich and beautiful daughter of a Scottish peer, and good luck to him. (In this he is following in his father's footsteps, for that veteran communist Claud Cockburn was the only member of the *Daily Worker* staff who managed to enjoy a generous expense account, and is married to a delightful lady who hunts twice a week in the season.)

Joking apart, however, these two books fill me with sadness. They contain, it is true, some excellent things. *New Revolutionaries* begins with Régis Debray's moving speech at the end of his trial, in which he showed both humility and humanity, and courage in facing the truth, however wretched it might be:

> 'Revolutionary war is not a question of individuals facing individuals – everyone has a family, parents, sons, loved ones, a childhood. They are but mere representatives of two irreconcilable orders. These acts of war are the fruits of social, economic and moral antagonisms existing independently of the will of the actors and preceding them. No one has created these antagonisms and no one can take them away, but they should indeed be surmounted and settled. Naturally, the tragedy is that we do not kill objects, numbers, instruments, but, precisely, on both sides, irreplacable individuals, essentially innocent, unique for those who have loved, bred, esteemed them. This is the tragedy of history, of any history of any revolution. It is not individuals who are placed face to face in these battles, but class interests and ideas, but those who fall in them, those who die, are persons, are men. We cannot avoid this contradiction, escape from this pain.'

It seems to me that Debray is here, unconsciously, stating the case for social democracy, where it is a viable alternative to revolution. For, as an incurable social democrat, I state with absolute conviction that anything to the Left of social democracy, as a political theory, must to a greater or lesser extent be totalitarian, and therefore traffic in violence. And the victims of violence must almost invariably be innocent.

Here is a dilemma which none of these new revolutionaries seems prepared to face – perhaps wisely, because they cannot, and know they cannot, resolve it. Throughout these two books, there is reiterated clamour for freedom, 'greater freedom', 'total freedom'; the word is often employed in capital letters, thus: FREEDOM. But what has their favourite *guru,* Herbert Marcuse, to say on the subject?

> 'The whole post-fascist period is one of clear and present danger. Consequently true pacification requires the withdrawal of tolerance before the deed, at the stage of communication in word, print and picture. Such extreme suspension of the right of free speech and free assembly is indeed justified only if the whole of society is in extreme danger. I maintain that our society is in such an emergency situation, and that it has become the normal state of affairs.'

I doubt if the two Polish students, who write so perceptively of their country in Mr Ali's volume (and who are both in prison) would endorse this; nor would Pierre Frank, who provides an excellent, though depressing, analysis of the Czech situation. The truth is that such outrageous invasions of our basic rights are never justified in any situation whatsoever, and no really socialist debate can start from any other premise.

Secondly, there is much abuse, in these volumes, of social democracy as an instrument of change. 'Further progress,' writes Mr Tom Fawthrop, 'along the path of socialism means throwing aside the rotting corpse of social democracy, upon which the vultures of Fabianism, careerism and orthodox communism are still sustaining themselves.' These three have a 'necrophiliac passion for a dead social democracy'. I wasn't aware that official communists were particularly attached to social democracy, but let it pass. Moreover, I must tell Mr Fawthrop that social democracy, far from being a rotting corpse, is alive and well, and living in Great Turnstile. Elsewhere we are told that 'socialism cannot be reached by the path of social democracy' (i.e., by democratic methods – otherwise the phrase is meaningless, which of course it may well be anyway). But supposing we concede Mr Fawthrop's point: social democracy is dead and, where living, wholly ineffective or even a tool of monopoly capitalism. What, then, must we do? Throughout Mr Cockburn's volume, which I must add contains a good deal of closely-meshed, though often raucous and unconvincing, argument, there is an uneasy feeling that student power, now it has come into existence, may waste its energies by failing to operate upon society as a whole. The 'corrupt reformism' of official student organizations is reviled. Mr Cockburn writes: 'student power has only acquired a truly *revolutionary* character where students have rejected the notion that higher education is a world of its own.' True, and welcome. He adds: 'However subjectively subversive students may be they cannot by themselves bring the whole social process to a halt, as can the actions of the working class.' True again, but the great question is: how can students act as the instrument of the working-class awakening which alone can bring about radical change?

Both books face this problem and fail to solve it. I doubt if there can be a revolutionary alliance between students and workers, except in very special circumstances. In West Germany and the United States (even to some extent here) student activism has, if anything, created a working-class backlash. The alliance between workers and students in France last May and June was both temporary and uneasy, and this was by no means entirely due to the deliberate sabotage of the CP; nor, since last June, has it been followed by a more durable union. On the contrary the CP seems to have fully reestablished its grip on the organized industrial workers. The only country in which students and workers have been amalgamated as a political and social force is China; and this was an act of government, carried out through the apparatus of the most authoritarian state the world has ever known, and at immense cost to China's culture and technology. Nor was the result successful, as an observer, quoted in *New Revolutionaries,* points out:

> 'The only lasting product was increased tension and animosity between the workers, former conservatives, and the students, extreme rebels. This situation appears in many respects to be typical of the situation throughout China now.'

There are certain natural antagonisms, and indeed genuine conflicts of interest between students and workers, which we ignore at our peril. They can sometimes be made to disappear. Students and workers in Poland have on many occasions worked together against Gomulka's Stalinist tyranny. Novotny, in his last days of power, strove unsuccessfully to incite the industrial workers against his student enemies. Indeed, throughout the Czech crisis, students and workers have shown almost complete solidarity, despite sustained efforts to separate them. But, of course, in Poland and still more in Czechoslovakia, the enemy is essentially *external*. This, it seems to me, makes all the difference.

There is, however, one way in which radical students can disseminate the religion of change among the workers. But it is a dull, arduous and painfully slow way, which I fear is wholly unattractive to the contributors to these volumes. I mean, needless to say, the unexciting methods of Fabianism, in which those who have had the privilege of higher education (for it is still, alas, a privilege) use their brains and energies not to descend into the streets – for the workers will not follow them there – but to write books, pamphlets, articles, give TV and radio broadcasts, lecture, attend local party meetings, and thus forward the leavening of progressive ideas in society. Students should not be guerrilla fighters; they are no good at it, as the tragic story of Bolivia shows. They should be apostles, preaching the gospel of socialism by using their natural weapons – the written and spoken word. In an appendix to *Student Power*, Marcuse says, in one devastating aside: 'As a whole the existing situation has always been bad.' True enough, but not so bad that the cult of violence cannot make it even worse. It may be square to say so, but if we believe in helping mankind to improve its miserable condition, there is no substitute for social democracy.

—7 March 1969

Part 4

CROWNS AND CORONETS

Coronation Street

QUEEN VICTORIA has never had an official biographer. She is known to the public chiefly through a selection of her letters, published in eleven volumes, and Lytton Strachey's sentimental and unreliable portrait. Most of the scores of books written about aspects of her life and reign are worthless. In recent years the need for a full-length reappraisal has been growing: scholarly biographies of many of her leading contemporaries have appeared; the Royal Family now permits far more generous access to the Windsor archives; and several huge collections are open to public inspection. The process of examining all these documents and relating them to Victoria's own life and career is a vast undertaking, beyond the capacity of any single scholar. Lady Longford's new biography, (*Victoria R.I.* by Elizabeth Longford. Weidenfeld & Nicolson, 63*s*.) despite its great length, should therefore be regarded more as a pioneering than a definitive work, and she has prudently devoted most of her attention to the personal side of the Queen's reign, sketching the political background lightly. Her book is elegant, painstaking, often shrewd and invariably readable, and seems sure to attract many readers. Whether it presents a complete portrait of Victoria is another matter.

Two distinct pitfalls confront the biographer of Victoria, and into both Lady Longford occasionally stumbles. The first arises from the extraordinary number of the Queen's relatives. Through no fault of her own, she inherited an unusually large family connection; and, thanks to the ministrations of her consort, she expanded this brood on what can only be termed a geometrical scale. The births, activities, virtues, failings, illnesses and deaths of these people, both English and Germanic, naturally interested her, though they are clearly not of commensurate concern to us today. The point about Victoria's relatives is not that they were intrinsically boring but that they are inclined to occupy an excessive amount of space, and Lady Longford is insufficiently strict in relegating them to their proper historic importance. Their mild personal dramas tend to obtrude and at times give the narrative something of the episodic quality of an elevated *Coronation Street*.

The second difficulty concerns Victoria's own worth as a witness. Lady Longford is inclined to accept statements in Victoria's letters and diaries at their face value, preferring them to other evidence, if contradictory. Thus, where the Queen's account of events conflicts with, say, Greville's, the latter is dismissed as a malicious gossip, though on other occasions, where Greville is the only authority, he is accepted without demur. The truth is that Victoria was a highly emotional woman, whose subjective attitude to the truth must always be treated with reserve. Her letters are frequently tendentious and her diaries are open to the further objection that the originals were destroyed and that all we possess are edited transcripts prepared by her daughter, Princess Beatrice. We do not even know on what principles the Princess carried out her task, and some entries may therefore be edifying inventions.

By generating an atmosphere of family cosiness and by attaching too much weight to Victoria's own writings, Lady Longford provides an unduly favourable portrait of the Queen, both as a woman and as a monarch. She tends, in fact, to perpetuate the version that Victoria, despite certain foibles, was a monument of robust common sense, who epitomized the moral principles and public attitudes of her worthiest subjects. I can find little evidence to support this view.

Victoria was not favoured by nature. She had sound teeth and, despite a tendency to hypochondria which produced convenient psychosomatic symptoms at tense political moments, she enjoyed excellent general health. But she had weak eyesight, a receding chin, listless hair and a prominent, aggressive nose. Her short, plump legs supported a dumpy body and an unsuitably large bust (her hands and feet were small and neat). Victoria was very conscious of her physical limitations and suffered from shyness throughout her life. Though excitable and acutely susceptible to masculine attractions, she does not seem to have achieved sexual fulfilment. The Prince Consort, like many Germans of his class, appears to have been a dutiful but inconsiderate lover, and her letters to her eldest daughter make it plain that she derived little but discomfort from the sexual side of her marriage. She greatly feared childbirth and detested her frequent pregnancies. Her relations with her children were, in consequence, uneasy and sometimes venomous.

Her life with Albert was bedevilled by frequent and, it would seem, awe-inspiring outbreaks of temper. The Queen would follow her spouse from room to room, berating him. Albert's response was silence followed by lengthy memoranda. Despite his efforts, and her own repeated attempts at self-discipline, the Queen's temper was never finally overcome. Even in old age, she was liable to sweep all the objects off her desk (including presentation pieces in massive silver-gilt) on the receipt of unwelcome news. These outbreaks were so severe that at times both Victoria and her doctors feared she would succumb to the insanity which, they believed, was hereditary in her family. Victoria was constantly haunted by the shadow of George III.

She was also obsessed by death. However much she might despise people during their life, she relished the awesome moment when they left it, and the demise of comparatively minor politicians (or relatives) got the full treatment in her journal. In another incarnation she must surely have proved a gifted obituarist. Her lamentations, however, suggest an insincere and superficial nature. In life, she treated her mother with a mixture of cruelty and condescension; but she set up an impressive caterwauling when, in due course, the poor lady died. And this was merely a curtain-raiser for the obsequies of Albert, which occupied an entire decade. Towards the end of her life, Victoria's palaces were filled with busts of the dear departed, her calendar heavy with lugubrious anniversaries.

It is not to be expected that a woman of such unstable temperament would bring much wisdom to the conduct of public affairs. On all the great political issues of her day, and most of the minor ones, she proved herself either confused or wrong. Apart from an instinctive conservatism, and a certain class loyalty as a paid-up member of the monarchs' trades union, it is impossible to discover any salient principles behind her political attitudes. Indeed, like her grandfather, she had a marked dislike for public men who acted on principle. Her animosity towards Gladstone probably dates from his high-minded resignation in 1845. She simply could not understand the attitude of the Tories who overthrew Peel for betraying a cause he was elected to defend. Salisbury's resignation in 1867 was a black mark against him, and she was outraged by Lord Randolph Churchill's departure in 1886, more particularly since it was signalized by a letter written on Windsor Castle notepaper.

Victoria never understood the constitution or the part she ought to play in it. She does not seem to have grasped the importance of the Second and Third Reform Bills, both of which she accepted without much argument. On the other hand she repeatedly insisted that she had 'no intention' of becoming 'sovereign of a democracy', and in 1892, when the Tories were turned out, she summed up her real feelings neatly:

> 'These are trying moments & seems to me a defect in our much famed Constitution, to have to part with an admirable Govt like Ld Salisbury's for no question of any importance, or any particular reason, merely on account of the number of votes.'

Until 1868, Victoria belonged, strictly speaking, to neither party, giving her allegiance to the man who caught her fancy. But after her first experience of Gladstone as Prime Minister she became a rabid Tory. Disraeli encouraged her to communicate privately with him on state matters even when out of office, and she continued the practice with Salisbury – to the extent of asking him when it would be most convenient to the Tory Party for her to put pressure on Gladstone to dissolve parliament. But it would be pointless to list the occasions on which Victoria, through prejudice, obstinacy or sheer malice, degraded her office. It was left to her despised son, Edward VII, to inaugurate the practice of constitutional monarchy.

Victoria's greatest achievement, it is often maintained, was to place the British monarchy on a sound footing of personal morality. There is some truth in this, though Edward VII's escapades do not seem to have done him much harm with the public. Victoria was probably a chaste woman herself, but her attitude to sexual morals was curiously ambivalent. She always had a ready ear for salacious gossip, particularly about those she already disliked for other reasons. Her two favourite Prime Ministers, Melbourne and Disraeli, were both of loose morals and shifty about money, too. But Gladstone, the pillar of rectitude – indeed the embodiment of the supposedly Victorian virtues – was rejected, almost entirely on personal grounds. The Queen may have hated the sin but she certainly loved the sinner. Indeed, her attachment to the oafish and drunken John Brown is difficult to explain unless we assume there was something improper (not necessarily indecent) in their relationship. Lady Longford quotes verses Victoria sent Brown on New Year's Day, 1877:

I send my serving maiden
With New Year letter laden,
Its words will prove
My faith and love
To you my heart's best treasure.
Then smile on her and smile on me
And let your answer loving be
And give me pleasure.

On the back was written: 'To my best friend J.B., from his best friend V.R.I.' Lady Longford calls this and similar messages 'artless and innocent'. With the best will in the world, it is hard to agree.

—11 September 1964

Square Deal for Bertie

EDWARD VII, the egregious Bertie, has always had a bad press. During his long career as Heir Apparent he was subjected to every variety of journalistic criticism, from street lampoons to solemn admonishments in *Times* leaders. Even while he was on the throne, Fleet Street held a watching brief and never hesitated to rap his pudgy knuckles. After his death, nemesis descended. Certainly, a two-volume official life appeared, in which Sir Sidney Lee conscientiously extolled his virtues; but few read it, then or since. Bertie never patronized literary men, and the confraternity took its revenge. Kipling dismissed him in a telling half-truth – 'a corpulent voluptuary'. Beerbohm made him the painful butt of a gallery of cartoons. Belloc wrote a savage set of verses which, though never published in full, have been gleefully recited at select dinner-parties for the last half-century. Younger writers probed his life merely to unearth squalid love affairs. And then, after Bertie's shade might well have felt a truce overdue, Christopher Sykes published his *Four Studies in Loyalty,* which told the horrid tale of how Edward VII humiliated and finally ruined his most faithful friend.

It is only just, then, that Bertie should at last get a square deal. In the light of the experience of the Kitchener family, the Queen is to be commended for her courage in throwing open the royal archives to the strict scrutiny of Sir Philip Magnus. True, after Bertie's death, the most compromising documents were reluctantly burnt by his secretary, Lord Knollys – another episode in the sad history of Hanoverian holocausts. But a great deal remains on the record nonetheless, and Sir Philip has not hesitated to discuss it. The cautionary story of Nellie Clifden, the actress smuggled into his tent at the Curragh; the affair of Lady Aylesford's letters; the mysterious row with Lord Charles Beresford over Lady Brooke – all these, and much else, are elucidated and told in plain language. But if Sir Philip is thorough he is also fair, and he has an accurate sense of perspective. This lengthy book (*King Edward VII,* Murray. 50*s*.) is not a recital of royal scandals, but a portrait in the round. Sir Philip provides neither a *réquisitoire* nor a plea for the defence, but a judicious and detailed summing-up from the Bench.

The jury's verdict, I think, is likely to be favourable. If, like any other delinquent, Bertie is allowed to plead early upbringing and environment in his defence, then he has a strong case. His birth gave his mother, as they say, 'a bad time', and she resented it. He was severely and secretly beaten by a spiteful nannie. Scarcely out of the nursery, he was made the lonely subject, by his solemn father, of one of the most ill-conceived experiments in the history of education. The love affair – his first – with Nellie Clifden was, his mother came to believe, the direct cause of Albert's death (in reality the drains at Windsor Castle were to blame), and for some years she treated him with hostility verging on hatred. At all times she made it plain that she preferred the company of her other children and trusted their judgement in preference to his. Bertie's can be regarded as a classic case of a childhood starved of affection, understanding and even friendship.

From this sprang his many faults and deficiencies. His father's educational system left him with an abiding distaste for books of any kind. He seemed incapable of actually reading one, even at the dictates of common prudence. In 1884, on the advice of friends scarcely more literate than himself, he wrote to the Queen complaining of her failure to mention him in her *Highland Journal*. Back came the acid response: his name was, in fact, mentioned on pages 1, 5, 8, 331 and 378: never was careless reviewer more thoroughly rebuked by wrathful author.

Bertie's childhood was also, I suspect, responsible for his infrequent but extremely violent outbursts of rage (a characteristic he has passed on to many of his descendants) and his extraordinary passion for food. Bertie ate four enormous meals a day, interspersed by substantial snacks. His usual dinner consisted of eleven courses, with frequent second helpings. Sir Philip tells us that his favourite dishes included pheasant stuffed with snipe, themselves stuffed with truffles and garnished with a rich sauce; ortolans cooked in brandy; snipe stuffed with foie gras and cooked with truffles and madeira, and grilled oysters. All were bolted, as he admitted to his doctors, without mastication, and eating on this scale went on to the very eve of his death. One's sympathy goes out to Queen Alexandra, a professional beauty whose eighteen-inch waist was not achieved without the most stringent dieting, and who was forced to watch these daily orgies.

Bertie, in short, was not a pretty picture. His sallow youthful looks quickly turned into obesity. Though trilingual, he spoke English with a guttural accent. He was restless and easily bored. Most of his life he was in debt, and he was always anxious to make a fast buck, whether by gambling or on the stock-exchange. For his first sixty years he was without a job of any kind, for Victoria, despite the harassed entreaties of her ministers, who knew well that an idle Bertie was certain to get himself into trouble, resolutely refused him employment.

In the light of all this it is, perhaps, remarkable that Bertie did not turn out to be a monster. In fact he was, on the whole, a rather nice man and an extremely successful monarch. Both can be ascribed to his possession of that supreme virtue, tolerance. Where he got it from is hard to say: such a quality is rare among royalty and unprecedented in his own family. But Bertie had it. Where his parents were narrow-minded, priggish, unforgiving and bigoted, he was expansive, warm-hearted, easy-going and indulgent. He liked to be happy and, above all, he liked to see those around him happy as well. He drew his friends from an unusually wide circle: they included painters and diplomats, musicians and actors, bankers and jockeys, soldiers and politicians. He persuaded high society to accept Jews, detested race-prejudice and treated minority religions with respect. Almost anyone was welcome in his circle provided they had good manners and fat purses. Unlike most of his contemporaries, he was particularly kind to children; his treatment of his own was an example which his heir, alas, failed to follow.

Bertie, in fact, though impulsive and often vehement in his opinions, was fundamentally open-minded. He made a friend of Dilke when the latter was an avowed republican, and he helped to re-establish him in society and politics after his disgrace. Many of his friends and household officials were Liberals, and as early as 1894 he was convinced by Rosebery that a moderate reform of the Lords was necessary. Bertie was quick to quarrel, but quick to forgive too, and he could apologize handsomely when persuaded he was wrong. Sir Philip gives some fresh details about the famous breach with Lord Randolph Churchill, including the shocking fact that Churchill showed Bertie's correspondence with Lady Aylesford to the Princess of Wales. Most men would regard such conduct as unforgivable, but Bertie in time restored Churchill to favour and later treated his son with unusual affection.

In one respect Bertie was fortunate in being denied the throne for so long. He improved with age, and at his accession he was already in his 60th year, had learnt the lessons of most of his mistakes, and had acquired a wide knowledge of men and affairs. The courts and chancelleries of Europe he knew intimately, and his judgement on foreign policy, as anyone who studies his minutes on the published documents can testify, was usually shrewd. While not the instigator of the *Entente Cordiale,* he gave it warmth and colour. He was adept at smoothing the ruffled feathers of the royal peacocks who strutted across the Continent, and had he still been alive in 1914 it is just possible that his personal intervention might have averted catastrophe, at any rate for a time.

On home affairs he was an old-fashioned conservative, but not in all things. He supported Fisher's revolution at the Admiralty, though Service and society opinion was overwhelmingly against it; indeed, at a time when Campbell-Bannerman was dying and Lord Tweedmouth, the First Lord, insane, his vigorous backing saved both Fisher and the *Dreadnought* programme. As a rule, Bertie got on better with Liberal than Conservative ministers and, though he huffed and puffed a bit, he raised no real obstacles to the social revolution which began in 1906. His handling of the crisis over the Lords was, on the whole, well-judged, though he was given some absurd advice by Knollys. All this would have been inconceivable in Victoria's day. Indeed, I think it can fairly be said that Bertie, through a combination of laziness and tolerance, inaugurated the modern practices of constitutional monarchy. We should all be grateful to him.

In one respect, however, Bertie was bigoted, even fanatical. This was in matters of dress. Sir Philip does not mention the fact that Bertie's father was the grandson, on his mother's side, of Emil Augustus, Duke of Saxe-Gotha and Altenburg, a notorious transvestite, whose name and habits figure prominently in manuals of sexual psychology. It is, perhaps, from this personage that Bertie inherited an obsessive interest in clothes which earned his parents' outspoken disapproval at an early age, and which later, under the administration of a gifted theatrical tailor, blossomed into a positive passion. Bertie invariably changed his clothes at least four times a day, and on occasions no fewer than eight variations of costume were required before his urges, no less than his sense of fitness, were satisfied. On those who failed to share his enthusiasm a baleful, and often unforgiving, eye was cast. Trouser-creases, curly-brimmed bowlers, the position of buttons, knee-breeches, the vexed question of turn-ups, the exact attire suitable to a private view – on these and kindred matters the King's mind constantly brooded. His natural aptitudes fitted him, perhaps better than anything else, to be an expert adviser to a chain of multiple tailors. My one real complaint about Sir Philip's magnificent biography is that it devotes insufficient attention to this facet of Bertie's character, which, if the truth were told, probably exercised his limited faculties more than any other aspect of human existence.

—20 March 1964

A Lady in Mid-career

NO HUMAN BEING in history has been so completely and so continuously exposed to the public gaze. For more than sixteen years she has fulfilled an annual average of 150 engagements, most of which have been filmed and many televised. Scores of books, hundreds of thousands of magazine articles have sought to provide intimate glimpses of her life and personality. Yet the glimpses are purely of externals; the intimacy has eluded court scribes and gossip columnists alike. The Queen is an unknown woman. Her secrets – if there be any – are as closely kept as were those of the Widow of Windsor in her lifetime. Mid-brown hair, grey eyes, a pretty, high complexion, powerful, arched eyebrows, long neck, a good, carefully preserved figure, a thin, high voice – all these are familiar. So, too, is the taste for those unlovable corgis, the fondness for certain conventional rustic symbols. 'The Queen likes horses, dogs and dukes – in that order,' says a friend. The late Mr Horace Smith, who taught her to ride, states in his autobiography, *A Horseman through Six Reigns,* that she once confided to him that her ambition, had she not been Queen, was 'to be a lady living in the country, with lots of horses and dogs'. Surprise, surprise! But can this lady-of-the-manor image be the whole story? After all, other members of her family present sharply-differentiated characters, as instantly recognizable as the cards in Happy Families. Uncle Windsor, the eternal juvenile lead, with his posh cockney accent and talent for sartorial invention, forever doomed to re-enact the idylls of the Bright Young People. Or Uncle Gloucester, that fine specimen of Hanoverian manhood, puffing and panting through a thousand regimental inspections. Or kid sister Margaret, stamping her imperious little foot and trailing, a little breathlessly, in the wake of contemporary fashion. Or the Queen Mother, dispensing a comfortable lavender-scented charm and being considerate to the servants, a Jolly Good Sort. These are – or seem to be – genuine individuals, creatures of flesh and blood. Can the Queen really be so dull and featureless as she seems?

The truth is that dull is the wrong word: formidable is more apt. The Queen is the 42nd monarch of this kingdom, dating from William the Conqueror, and, beneath the shyness and charm (both marked characteristics of Queen Victoria), is fully conscious of her status and heredity. She exacts her due. She speaks her mind. She tolerates no familiarity. She has been on the throne a decade and a half and knows her business thoroughly, far better, indeed, than most of those who surround her, in politics or the court. No successful businesswoman in mid-career can outdo her in settled habit and fixed opinions. In the sphere of authority which the constitution still allows her, she is very much the boss.

And this sphere is tenaciously protected from democratic intrusion. The British monarchy is representational; there is no nonsense about it being popular. The Queen entertains between 20,000-30,000 people a year, of all classes. But her household and friends are chosen, virtually without exception, from the ranks of the territorial aristocracy. She inherited her courtiers from her father; changes have arisen solely through death or retirement. Their qualifications repeat the same monotonous litany: Eton, Oxford, the Guards; Harrow, Oxford, the Guards; Eton, the Greenjackets; Eton, the Royal Navy; Eton, the Hussars; Eton, the Guards; Eton, the Guards; Eton, the Guards. The Queen's ladies are duchesses or countesses, or the daughters of such. The style in which the Queen lives is totally alien to that of any of her subjects, including the richest. Buckingham Palace is the largest inhabited palace in the world, Windsor the largest inhabited castle. Sandringham, her own personal property, on which a fortune is currently being spent, is the most valuable agricultural estate in the kingdom. Thanks to the freedom from death duties which the monarch enjoys, her possessions are unique in the world, in both value and variety: the finest and largest collection of paintings in private custody; the most valuable collection of jewellery, of silver, of porcelain and of many other treasures, including stamps; and a private fortune of not less than £100 million. The catalogue exhausts the superlatives. There are the unique touches, too, which decisively separate the ruler from the ruled: the absence of number-plates from the royal Rolls Royces and Daimlers, the carefully-prescribed garments in which flunkeys and servants surround her. Her footmen wear powdered hair, scarlet livery decorated with gold braid, scarlet plush knee-breeches, pink stockings and black buckled shoes; the senior servants, black-and-gold braid livery with white wool cloth breeches, white stockings and black buckled shoes. The royal rituals have changed surprisingly little in the past half-century. The decision to end the presentation of debutantes was taken more to suit royal convenience than from any democratic motive. The Queen spends a good deal of her time in expert discussion of ceremonies, uniforms, cap-badges, regimental buttons, medals and insignia. Much attention is paid to harnesses, bridles, bits, snaffles and other stable-wear. The subject of saddles is of paramount importance. The Queen's own cost £450 each and involve as many as eight sittings – though happily a lady of birth who has the same-shaped seat spares the monarch the need to be fitted in person. The uniform in which the Queen attends the trooping of the colour is of her own design and shows a pretty taste in the art of military costume – no doubt inherited from her great-grandfather, who might in private life have made a successful theatrical tailor.

The pattern of royal duties shows no particular rapport with a nation supposedly obsessed with exports, technology and productivity. Of course, the Queen attends a wide variety of functions, but the list of annual fixtures, reflecting her sense of priorities, is as follows: twelve investitures of medals; Maundy Thursday ceremony; Queen's Scout Parade; Cup Final; Queen's Birthday Parade; Epsom Derby; Ascot; visit to Holyroodhouse; annual Garden Service; annual Thistle Service; garden parties; Goodwood races; Braemar; opening of Parliament; British Legion ceremony; Armistice Day Service; Diplomatic Corps party; Christmas Day broadcast (canned). Her private relaxations, enjoyed on her own estates or those of her titled friends, recall, almost without deviation, those of her grandfather George V, a country gentleman of conservative views, who was already in his mid-thirties when Queen Victoria died; shooting, stalking (but no hunting), riding, bird-watching and messing about with dogs. At private house-parties given or attended by the Queen, a certain amount of romping takes place. There is even a game which consists of both sexes alternately threading each others' garments with a long piece of string, until all are joined in happy conviviality. This doubtless is used to break the ice; but no familiarity is permitted. Conversation on public matters is rare, for the Queen is discretion itself; it is well informed but usually flows through unexciting channels. According to her mother, the Queen can sustain the talk throughout dinner on the subject of sparking-plugs. One up to J. Bonnington Jagworth!

The Queen, in short, conforms strongly to one of the two marked behaviour-patterns of British monarchs of the past two centuries. There are the gifted, the frivolous, the gay, the artistic, the irresponsible, who sometimes come a cropper: George IV, Edward VII, the Duke of Windsor. In her own generation, a bat's squeak echo of this strain is, perhaps, to be found in Princess Margaret. On the other hand, there are the proper, solid, unimaginative and conscientious monarchs: George III, Victoria, George V, George VI. The Queen is firmly and irrevocably ranked among the latter. Her admiration for her father, a decent and unambitious man unwillingly yoked to the royal juggernaut, is limitless. She will abide by his example in all things. Narrowly educated, unoriginal and by no means clever, she nevertheless has a perfect sense of duty, as she conceives it. The British monarchy, with all its faults and virtues, is in safe hands so long as she lives.

Yet its powers have already suffered a major erosion during her reign. The right, in certain circumstances, to choose a prime minister has always been a royal prerogative. When, in 1963, Mr Macmillan resigned, the Queen foolishly acceded to his wish to carry out soundings about his successor himself. She accepted the verdict of his masterful memorandum and failed to seek advice beyond it, though a majority of her cabinet did not agree with its findings. The controversy which followed led the Tory Party to adopt an elective system of leadership similar to Labour's. Hence the chief remaining power of the British monarchy has been allowed to lapse, almost certainly for good. No doubt it is better so, though the Queen's heirs may not see it in quite that light; indeed it may well be that, when the archives are opened, the political influence of the monarch will be found to have steadily diminished during the present reign. It is significant that, throughout the Rhodesian crisis, in which the Queen is directly involved, Mr Wilson has, step by step, carried her with him as a robust supporter of his policies, against what we might suppose to be her natural inclinations. Nor is it likely that she will raise much opposition when he abolishes the hereditary basis of the House of Lords; she has already accepted the principle.

All the same, she is a formidable woman, and likely to become more so. A British monarch's theoretical powers do not increase with the duration of the reign – on the contrary – but the personality becomes much more difficult to handle. The Queen already possesses more public experience than most of her ministers. The time will come when her premiers are her juniors in age, too, and vastly her juniors in service. Her health is excellent. She may well still be on the throne at the end of the century, advised by men now at school. The example of Queen Victoria, whom she resembles in more ways than one, suggests that they will be made to earn their emoluments.

—23 August 1968

Uncle Taffy

IN 1911 MR LLOYD GEORGE, Chancellor of the Exchequer, Constable of Caernarvon Castle, Member for the Caernarvon Boroughs, and a brilliant exponent of personal publicity, conceived the stunning idea of formally installing the heir to the throne as Prince of Wales in the castle of which he himself was custodian. The ceremony was normally performed, as a routine matter, by the Monarch in the House of Lords; indeed the last occasion on which the event had taken place as a public occasion, in 1611, had proved of ill augury: for the young prince later became Charles I and contrived to have his head chopped off by his indignant subjects. In 1911, however, on the very spot where Edward I had presented his son (later to die by having a red-hot poker inserted up his anus) to a crowd of beaten and sullen Welshmen, all went well. It is true that Edward VIII was later to lose his throne. But he kept his life. Indeed, he had some claims to his principality. Of all the 21 Princes of Wales, he was the only one to bear a Welsh Christian name, David, by which he was commonly, though not officially, called; and as king he expressed a transient sympathy for the plight of unemployed Welsh miners, much to the annoyance of Mr Baldwin. A photograph of the ceremony shows him looking extremely bothered in a cocoon of hefty regal garments, flanked by his father and mother, and surrounded by hordes of flunkeys in preposterous hats. Lloyd George is nowhere to be seen; but before, during and after the event, he skilfully extracted the maximum personal kudos from this symbolic union of the two nations – for was not young Prince David, however remotely, descended from such exotic characters as Gruffydd ap Cynan, Owain Gwynedd, Llywelyn the Great, Maelgywyn Fychan, Maredudd ab Owain and Llywelyn ab Owain, to say nothing of the Tudors?

On the first of next month the ceremony is to be re-enacted. The idea seemingly came from the Queen, though no doubt that crafty

Scotsman, Harold Macmillan, had something to do with it. It has now, however, been taken over, lock, stock and pennant, by another Welshman whose flair for publicity rivals that of Lloyd George himself: the present Constable of the Castle, Anthony Armstrong-Jones, Earl of Snowdon. It is true that the man officially in charge is the Earl Marshal, the Duke of Norfolk, and the greatest expert on ceremonial nonsense outside the Vatican. But there are various if subtle signs that a battle for power has been taking place behind the scenes, and that Snowdon has Norfolk on the hip. Norfolk fancies a ceremony that would have brought a glint of approval to the traditionalist and all-observant eye of George V; Snowdon would prefer the approbation of a Mary Quant. Norfolk and Snowdon: one could search the universe in vain for two men who have less in common, apart from an obstinate determination to get their own way. The Duke, indeed, has the chief formal authority; but in the struggle the Earl possesses many enviable advantages. The Duke knows the exact degree of precedence between, say, an Irish countess and the eldest son of an English baronet; he can spot an incorrectly-dressed Herald Extraordinary at a hundred yards flat; but he has neither the desire nor the talent for designing canopies and pennants, has no knowledge of modern textiles and the uses to which they can be put; he is not trendy and has no wish to be. Moreover Snowdon is unquestionably Welsh, and can claim descent, if a little fancifully, from Dafydd ap Einion, who led the Men of Harlech, Llewelyn the Great, Prince of North Wales, and Rhys ap Gruffydd, Prince of the South; he is married to the Queen's sister to whom, according to a genealogical table at Clarence House, he is twelfth cousin twice removed; best of all, he is Welsh Uncle, and constant mentor, of the star of the ceremony himself.

Careful comparison between the original arrangements for the investiture, issued by the Duke on 13 February, and the final souvenir programme, published recently, show the extent of the Earl's victory. He has not, to be sure, had it all his own way. The programme has a laugh in every line and, at five bob, is worth more than a year's subscription to *Private Eye* and *Punch* combined. Ecumenism has run riot – prelates from the Church of Wales will move freely with representatives of the Free Churches and even with the Archdruid. All present are invited to recite the Lord's Prayer in either Welsh or English, and innumerable songs and hymns will be sung in both languages simultaneously, though few will know the tunes and fewer still the words. Gorgeous popinjays will make 'three separate obeyances', trumpets will 'sound' and flags will be 'broken'. But reference is no longer made to various mayors 'and their suites', the Queen will no longer 'alight' from her 'motor car', and there is a colour gouache of the 'set' for the ceremony, which might well have been a backcloth for a fashionable Ken Tynan production of Marlowe's *Edward II*. Most significant of all, those responsible for the programme conspicuously thank Lord Snowdon for his 'assistance'.

This trivial, but no doubt hotly contested, triumph should surprise no one. A photograph, or rather 'study', taken by Yevonde, of the six-month-old Tony in the arms of his mother, shows a remarkably plain but determined baby, with the long upper lip already prominent. Eight years later he is seen in a smart 'Prince-of-Wales-check' coat and jodphurs. Tony's origins are slightly ambiguous, in the sense that he comes from an uneasy mixture of the professional, Forsytian upper-middle class, and the minor aristocracy. His paternal grandfather was a doctor specializing in mental diseases, who may have numbered among his patients Jack the Ripper, in search of whom he spent his holidays inspecting mental hospitals in Norway, Italy, Switzerland, Austria and France, even going so far as to visit a model institution in Nijni-Novgorod; he occupied nearly a column in *Who's Who*. Tony's father was a wealthy barrister. But the ambience of Tony's childhood owed more to his mother's background; Nanny Gunner and Governess 'Marty'; a house in Eaton Terrace, decorated in baroque by Syrie Maugham, to which Uncle Oliver Messel added some characteristic fashionable touches, shooting and riding; a smart prep-school (Sandroyd) and Eton. His parents' wedding, at St Margaret's, was a Forsyte affair, a Slade student recalling that 'some of the choicest fish of medicine and the law, of parliament and Welsh local government, City business and Chelsea art, swam about happily for a time in a ferment of goodwill'.

There was a certain note of social uneasiness about it all. Though Grandfather Jones had been knighted, the hyphenation of the family name had only been arranged by deed-poll as recently as 1913; Anne Messel had been presented at court under the auspices of a Mrs Cyril Potter, and at the wedding the guard of honour was formed by the Handcross and Staplefield Girl Guides. But Tony's christening was a different matter. A few months before, a Lady Maud Warrender had reported that 'little Mrs Armstrong-Jones did wonders with just a cook-housekeeper, a houseman and a maid'. But extra servants were speedily engaged, and the godparents at the christening included Sir Michael Duff, Colonel Wingfield Digby, Lady Forres, Lady North and the Countess of Seafield, the richest woman in Britain. Armstrong-Jones senior felt a little lost in this set-up; indeed the marriage was aptly described as an 'apple pudding set in a soufflé'. It broke up in 1935, the wife moving upwards into the aristocracy, the husband opting for the theatre in the shape of the actress Carol Combe.

Tony does not seem to have been unduly shaken by this broken marriage, remaining on excellent terms with both parents and their spouses. But he was always secretive, a little solitary, a man who could keep but not give a confidence. He enjoyed experimenting with Carol's old make-up box, and has occasionally shown a skill for dressing in drag. He has been thrown into a slimy goldfish pond by hearty louts, but in some ways is aggressively masculine, boxing successfully for Eton (he also coxed the winning Cambridge eight). In other respects he did well neither at school nor university. An Eton master wrote in an end-of-term report: 'Maybe he is interested in some subject, but it is not a subject we teach here.' At Eton he never made 'Pop'; at Cambridge he was sent down after twice failing exams.

What, then, to do with Tony? He had wanted to be a photographer ever since seeing the remarkable collection of 13,000 photographs which his great-grandfather, Sambourne, had formed for use in drawing his *Punch* cartoons. There was some opposition, but eventually he was apprenticed to the court photographer, Baron, for a fee of 500 guineas.* There he swiftly turned from a rank amateur into a thorough professional, learning the complex mechanical and electrical techniques of the craft. The artistic mysteries cannot be taught, but Tony was clearly familiar with them already. Indeed, it should be said at once that he is rightly ranked as one of the half-dozen best photographers in the country. He will never be a genius, like Cartier-Bresson, but he has a remarkably wide range, is full of inventiveness, is extremely hard-working and has all the urges of a perfectionist.

---

*For this and much other information the author is greatly indebted to Helen Cathcart's biography (*Lord Snowdon,* W. H. Allen, 30s) which appeared last year. Despite the fulsome tone, and occasional solecisms ('Sir Bertrand Russell'), it contains a mass of factual data and, for a work of its type, is not unduly discreet.

But it is one thing to be talented, professionally trained and industrious; quite another to get a foothold in a highly competitive trade. For some years Tony had a hard time of it. But, though not intelligent in any academic sense, he is clever, cunning, ruthless and pertinacious. He is tough and courageous, having survived a devastating attack of polio at sixteen, which still gives him pain in his left leg. He has nerve and is not easily rebuffed. Rebuked by a bossy headwaiter for photographing a minor royal at a public function, he promptly approached the lady, asked, and got, her permission. (But he is also sensitive: he keeps an album in which are pasted embarrassing or critical letters, headed by one from the headmaster of Eton, Birley, for photographing Eton boys without consent.) Tony's first breakthrough came when he made the lead page of the old *Tatler* with 'Cockle Hunting at Blakeney Point', and for a long time the magazine was his chief vehicle; he shamelessly exploited his family connections to supply it with photographic gossip-fodder. His next break, a crucial one, came with the death of Baron, which left a gap in the ranks of royal photographers. Tony was approached by the Duke of Kent, and got a commission. He was soon photographing the Queen's children, and in the big league; the demand from magazines, newspapers and private clients was more than he could handle, and he was even publishing commissioned albums of photographs and contemplating an exhibition.

Meanwhile, socially, he was slowly but steadily moving upwards from the third eleven of the smart set. He still seemed to know people rather better than they knew him, but it was no longer quite safe to throw him into a fish-pond. Most men did not particularly like him; most women did. They liked to listen to him talk, and, even more, they liked the intelligent and sympathetic way in which he listened to them, and then gave them practical advice about make-up, hair-styles, clothes, jewellery. But he was not entirely satisfactory. He certainly had girl-friends, but randy debs who went to his studio unchaperoned were mildly disappointed to find that, unlike many young photographers today, he kept his dealings with them on a strictly professional basis. He also had a taste for secret hideaways, as at Rotherhithe, which few – very few – were permitted to enter, or even know about.

The stages by which Tony gained the acquaintance, then won the intimacy, of Princess Margaret would require the subtlety of a Proust to relate. Once the Peter Townsend affair had ended in fiasco, it was pretty clear to a clever lad like Tony, with an instinctive understanding of women, that the Princess would want to marry soon, and that, being an obstinate young woman, she might decline to marry from the accepted circles. Tony held very few cards, but he played them faultlessly. He was also assisted from very unexpected quarters, for Margaret's intimates, above all her sister, were worried about her; they wanted her to marry a man who knew how to handle difficult women. The Queen by now had had some dealings with Tony, and admired his tact and discretion. Certainly she took no steps to discourage what was clearly becoming a friendship and might speedily become more. All the same, it was uphill work. Tony would be the first Welshman to marry into English royalty since Owen Glendower; she would be the first princess close to the throne to marry a commoner since 1503. There were practical problems, too. Tony was good at secrecy: that was all right. But the vernacular of courtship? German princes, of impeccable lineage and with a thorough grounding in protocol, have found it hard enough to get to the point with royal English ladies. At what stage could Tony risk calling her 'Ma'am' as a joke rather than a duty; and when – Margaret being a girl who wants the best of both worlds – could he drop the 'Ma'am' altogether and call her 'ducky'? When, in the darkness of the basement cinema at Clarence House, could he cross the final Rubicon and clasp that hot little hand?

But Tony never put a foot, or a hand, wrong. He got the Queen on his side and, equally important, the Queen Mother. Prince Philip had no objection, or in any event expressed none: if Margaret liked that kind of arty world, as she evidently did, then she was welcome to it. The Mountbattens, always influential, had connections with bits of Tony's complicated family. As for the girl herself, the crucial moment may have come when Tony held an exhibition. She must be an expert on such things, he said – after all she had opened enough of them. Should he have a lot of little rooms or one big room? Probably no one had ever asked her advice before on a serious, professional matter; as an act of flattery it was a masterstroke, and it did the trick. The Princess told the Queen; the Queen told Mr Macmillan. Against all odds, Tony had done it. Bagehot wrote that 'a royal marriage is a representation of a great universal truth'; in this case, the truth undoubtedly is, to paraphrase J. M. Barrie: 'There is nothing quite so impressive as a Welshman on the make.'

The marriage itself was somewhat lacking in serenity. It was immediately preceded by a crop of inconvenient deaths, both of minor royalty and among Tony's family. And on the wedding day itself Tony's auntie had her jewels pinched. The best man, Jeremy Fry, was suddenly unavailable, and replaced by an astonished Roger Gilliatt. There was Labour grumbling about the provision of the expensive royal yacht, always a sore point with them, being used for the honeymoon. And Margaret's stipend was put up from £6,000 a year to £15,000; after all, as someone pointed out, was not the Armstrong-Jones family motto '*A noddo Duw a Noddir*' – 'To Support God is to be Supported'. It just so happened that Tony's last cover for *Vogue* coincided with the wedding; as someone from *Vogue* pointed out, the issue 'sang from the bookstalls'. Ironically, there was trouble from photographers, chiefly nasty French ones. Then there was the question of accommodation. Their first home, in Kensington Palace, a sort of doll's house put up by George III, proved too small. Tony spotted a much bigger one, next door and dreadfully dilapidated. It was done up at an admitted expense of £85,000. The Queen contributed £20,000; but the public had to provide the rest, on the grounds that the Ministry of Works had a duty to preserve architectural masterpieces. But as the basement included the most elaborate, and costly photographic studio in Kensington, the public began to suspect that they had been saddled with some very expensive royals. This impression was confirmed by the Jones's junket to America, which of course did our exports a power of good, or so it was claimed, but which cost the Foreign Office £30,000, and which happened to coincide with the launching in the States of Tony's latest book of snaps. An embarrassed Foreign Office minister was obliged to answer an awkward question in the House.

After all, it was not as if Tony was completely without means of his own. After much anxious consultation behind the scenes, and to the vociferous and righteous indignation of the *Observer,* Tony joined the staff of the *Sunday Times*. Tony not only took much-publicised photographs; he also jazzed up the office of the Editor-in-Chief, Denis Hamilton, with black leather trays, low sofas, glass-topped tables, Chinese lamps and other smart knick-knacks. Lord Thomson saw it, jealously asked for the same to be done to his office, then grumbled at the expense. But he probably got value for money: Tony is the archetypal do-it-yourself man. Honest craftsmen would starve if there were more like him around. He can stitch and lay carpets, knock up bookshelves and cupboards in no time, paint walls, hang wallpaper with professional skill, operate an acetylene cutter for kitchen steelwork, repair and re-upholster furniture, and is a dab hand with curtains, cushions and hangings of all descriptions. He can, indeed, transform a bare room into a colour-supplement fantasy before you can say String-along.

Where lies the future? Some old but inconvenient friends of Tony's have been pronounced incapable of keeping up with the Joneses and quietly but firmly dropped. As Mark Boxer, who is sufficiently in Tony's confidence to know, put it, certain people in future would 'not drop in quite so casually for breakfast'. Tony turned down an earldom on marriage, but later accepted it 'for the sake of the children': this is odd, as the Queen could easily have made Margaret a duchess in her own right, thus ensuring courtesy titles for her kids. Perhaps Tony thought an earldom was not quite the rate for the job; but the Queen can be obstinate too. Then there is a certain tendency, among the Snowdons, to be accident-prone. The very title, Snowdon, is unfortunate: a lot of Welshmen, who not unreasonably decline to regard Jones the Earl as one of themselves, resent his appropriation of their principal protuberance, which he has probably never ascended except by the railway; and he is liable to be confused with a tiresome Labour turncoat, the late Viscount Snowden. There was the errant butler, who left the Snowdons' service in dudgeon, because, he alleged, he resented his master's interference and parsimony; and, what is worse, wrote for the papers about it. A wax effigy of Jones was mysteriously stolen from Madame Tussaud's and later found propped up in a telephone kiosk. And a few hours before Tony was due to attend the first conference on the investiture in Cardiff, a home-made time-bomb exploded, damaging the façade of the 'Temple of Peace'. What will happen on 1 July, God alone knows, though the Special Branch are doing their best.

All the same, the future for Tony looks rosy enough, though less so for his wife. Tony, so successful in improving the dress-sense of such women as his stepmother, has abysmally failed with his Margaret, who has strong will-power and an indestructible taste for spangly dresses and suchlike. As a royal beauty, she has been decisively upstaged by the young Duchess of Kent and, still more gallingly, by her niece, Princess Anne who, despite her equine features, has captured the photographers' imagination, and hence the public's, by her extraordinary hats. Margaret dislikes formal engagements, and makes her feelings plain. Her husband, on the other hand, is now a confident royal performer. He retains his youthful panache. He has plenty of charm, when he finds it politic to exercise it. Tony in action was neatly described by Queen Ena of Spain, an experienced judge, whom he was deputed to look after on the occasion of the Duke of Kent's wedding:

> 'He proved a charming escort during the journey. He seemed far removed from the incorrigible eccentric described by the newspapers. He was the picture of correctness and of the English gentleman. His speech is soft, his gestures are pleasing and precise and he wears a pleasant and perpetual smile. My curiosity was satisfied on every point.'

One wonders how easy it will be to maintain the 'perpetual smile' as Margaret moves inexorably into the bitter regions of middle age. Tony has hit the jackpot, but the price he will eventually have to pay may prove a heavy one, even for such a resourceful and resilient man as he undoubtedly is. Meanwhile, on to Caernarvon! Tony has won the first round and is confident of success; he has a firm avuncular hand on young Charles's shoulder, and their mutual passion for the theatre is a distinct asset. But Norfolk, though bruised, is by no means down and out, and he comes of fighting stock. Observers of the royal scene will hope that the best man wins.

—27 June 1969

Part 5

MEN AND HISTORY

The Historian as Radical

WHAT ARE THE QUALITIES of a great historian? I find myself asking this question after re-reading some of the scores of historical classics, many of them hitherto out of print, which are a small but valuable tributary of the paperback flood. (*Domesday Book and Beyond*. By F. W. Maitland. Collins. 8*s*. 6*d*. *F. W. Maitland: Selections from His Writings*. Cambridge: California. 13*s*. 6*d*. *Medieval Village, Manor and Monastery*. By G. G. Coulton. Harper. 18*s*. *Queen Elizabeth I*. By J. E. Neale. Penguin. 5*s*.) The answer, I think, can best be provided by analyzing the scholarship of Frederick William Maitland, the supreme medievalist. Why Maitland? The choice can be justified on the following grounds. From the departure of the Romans until modern times, English history provides a process of continuous evolution which is quite unique in Europe, above all in the legal framework which determines (and reflects) the nature of society. Further, the most important element in the social structure, at any rate until the second half of the nineteenth century, was the ownership of land; and the only occasion on which land-ownership in England underwent something tantamount to a revolution was in the generation following the Battle of Hastings. How did this come about? Was it, indeed, a revolution, or merely forced evolution? This is the central, as well as the most difficult, problem in English history; by making it his life-work – and by very largely solving it – Maitland can claim the authorship, I believe, of the largest single contribution to English historical studies. His professional principles, therefore, are of paramount importance.

Firstly, Maitland never attempted to narrate the progress of society as a whole. Narration, indeed, is the enemy of good scholarship, for it entails a constant series of judgements as to motives, which can rarely be supported by evidence: it places, moreover, an altogether exaggerated emphasis on the actions of the central power, indeed of individuals. Even an outstanding example of modern narrative history, such as Professor Neale's *Queen Elizabeth* I, must necessarily mislead, for by failing to portray Elizabethan society in depth it invites the reader's judgement on actions taken out of their historical context.

Narration has a further drawback. It presupposes a stable density of evidence, and is based on the assumption that history can be built like a pyramid, the superstructure of one period resting securely on the foundations of its predecessor. In fact, the volume and quality of evidence diminish steadily as time recedes, and the narrative historian inevitably (and largely unconsciously) finds himself remedying the deficiency by projecting into the past the known conceptions of a later age. Historians today are slowly recognizing that history must be the examination of a fixed point, from which light radiates into the surrounding years. Sir Lewis Namier is popularly credited with this fundamental discovery; in fact, it had been a decisive technique among medieval historians for two generations, and Maitland was its greatest practitioner.

Indeed, he brought it to a peculiarly useful refinement, which was the principal instrument of his historical method. History, he argued, should be approached backwards, proceeding from the later known to the earlier unknown. As he put it: 'We must accustom our eyes to the twilight before we go out into the night.' It must be said that Maitland did not actually invent this technique, which had earlier been used by Seebohm; but in *Domesday Book and Beyond* he employed and perfected it on an unprecedented scale. In Domesday Book and its related documents he recognized the crowning administrative achievement of the Middle Ages: its sheer detail and comprehensiveness, its functional accuracy, make it the most valuable historical manuscript in the world. Maitland saw it as an immense armoury of weapons, to be selected at need to hack into the thickets of the past; or, to vary the metaphor, as a battery of searchlights to probe the Anglo-Saxon night behind it. And, conversely, once the differentiations between late Anglo-Saxon and Early Norman society had been established, the way was prepared for a reconnaissance into the future, via the beacons of the early pipe-rolls, chancery-rolls and court-rolls, until we reach the lighted thoroughfares of the statutes and parliamentary records of the later Plantagenets.

It follows from this that Maitland never for one instant permitted his mind to wander far from the evidence. His imagination was ceaselessly employed in piecing it together, but rarely creatively, that is, subjectively. Each wafer of conclusion rested on solid evidential masonry. His detailed findings have often been faulted, but as a rule merely by the emergence of fresh evidence. Indeed, he was scrupulously careful to point out the lacunae in his case, and to warn the reader that there is no finality in historical research. The salient flavour of his writing is its humility.

Maitland deplored controversy, and was perhaps unduly mild in rebuking erring contemporaries, many of whom were arrogant and spiteful. But with one fault he had no patience, for it contradicted his entire methodology. He termed this 'anachronism', or 'after-mindedness' – the imposition of later ideas and concepts on a period to which they were alien:

> 'Against many kinds of anachronism we now guard ourselves. We are careful of costume, of armour and architecture, of words and forms of speech. But it is far easier to be careful of these things than to prevent the intrusion of untimely ideas. In particular there is a besetting danger for us in the barbarian's use of a language which is too good for his thought. Mistakes then are easy, and when committed they will be fatal and fundamental mistakes. If, for example, we introduce the *persona ficta* too soon, we shall be doing worse than if we armed Hengist and Horsa with machine-guns, or pictured the Venerable Bede correcting proofs for the press . . .'

The merits of Maitland's scholarship can be better appreciated by contrasting them with the faults of another formidable, though distinctly inferior scholar, Dr Coulton. To an important degree, Coulton shared the same approach as Maitland: the function of history was to discover facts, and facts could only be based on contemporary evidence; all else was error. Coulton indeed was an impoverished schoolmaster, who obtained recognition late in life (he was elected a Fellow of St John's, Cambridge, at the age of sixty-one) largely because of his extraordinarily wide knowledge of medieval records. For most of his career Coulton was engaged in furious controversy with Catholic pseudo-scholars, such as Belloc and Cardinal Gasquet; he was concerned to demolish their pre-conceived view of the Middle Ages as a peasant's paradise by forcing them to look awkward sources in the eye. To this extent he reflected Maitland's virtues.

But there the resemblance dwindles. Unlike Maitland, Coulton was primarily a controversialist: for him, victory came to seem more important than truth. He thus fell into the cardinal sin of collecting evidence to prove a point, rather than allowing the point to emerge from the collection of evidence. This led him into the corollary vice, anachronism. Evidence was wrenched not only out of its historical, but even its geographical context, and strung together into a case which could convince only the layman. To take one example of many: seeking to demonstrate the low value which feudal society placed on the life of a serf, he cites an English document of 1284, a German of 1172, other English documents of 1200 and 1240, a North-Italian chronicler of 1400, a Vatican document of 1440, a German court-case of 1444, an English case of 1514 and, among others, a French parish *cahier* of 1789! At no point does he evaluate, either historically or textually: he was concerned with quantity, not quality. Curiously enough, on this very point, he was unconsciously rebuked by Maitland himself, more than a quarter of a century before, in a characteristically witty aside. Expressing surprise that eleventh-century society should have assessed the value of a ceorl's life as high as 200 shillings (or the price of twenty-four to thirty oxen), Maitland adds: 'The sons of a *villanus* who had but two oxen must have been under some temptation to wish that their father would get himself killed by a solvent thegn.'

Despite their varying professional standards, however, both men were at one in viewing contemporary society with a radical eye, and each for interesting reasons. Coulton had a passionate devotion to the peasant, medieval or modern, English or foreign: he regarded his own relentless exposure of the wrongs the medieval villein had suffered as an integral factor in securing better conditions for his present-day successors. He delved into the past because he hated the land-owning classes; and he hated the land-owning classes with added venom because he had studied the past. History for him was thus a living *continuum*: this made him imperfect as a historian, but, no doubt, a better human being.

Maitland also favoured reform, but in a logical, unemotional fashion. Unlike Coulton, he regarded the past as largely irrelevant to the politics of the present, for he believed, correctly, that while knowledge of the present can illuminate the past, to apply the lessons of the past to the present is to invite disaster. Like many other late-Victorian academics, he moved on the fringe of affairs: he was a member of the Leslie Stephen circle and a brother-in-law of H. A. L. Fisher, the Liberal minister and scholar. His contacts with public men must have helped him to appreciate the administrative achievements of Henry II or Edward I. But he was progressive-minded, I think, not because of his Liberal friends, but because he felt this to be the logical and therefore proper professional posture for a historian. If, his mind reasoned, it was wrong to project anachronisms into the past, it was equally wrong to maintain them in the present. Society must evolve and change its institutions to suit its particular needs. To preserve for the sake of preservation was mere sentimentality, which a scholar should avoid like the plague. This tempts me to point a sly moral. The historian whose work draws him to conservatism is likely to be, for this very reason, a poor scholar. The true historian has a functional inclination to the left.

—6 January 1961

The Dark Youth of Disraeli

'FAILURE, FAILURE, failure, partial success, renewed failure, ultimate and complete victory.' So Lord Randolph Churchill summed up the career of Disraeli. More than fifty biographies have told the story of his long battle, after he had broken Peel, to re-create the Tory Party and restore it to office; but the first thirty-four years of his life, until his election to Maidstone in 1837, have always been curiously shrouded. We know that they were painful and, in some respects, disreputable; we also know that, after his rise to fame and the tightening-up of public morality in the 1840's, Disraeli did his best to cover up his earlier traces. He bowdlerised new editions of his novels and toned down his sartorial excesses (he even went so far as to deny, in a newspaper letter, that he had ever possessed green trousers; a palpable lie or, perhaps, a convenient collapse of memory). Towards the end of his life, he seems to have burned batches of letters and censored his secret diary. He left instructions to his executors to destroy certain papers. These were never carried out, at any rate in full, but his great biographer, Moneypenny, writing shortly after the turn of the century, still judged it necessary to suppress evidence of some of his early financial transactions and of all his illicit love affairs. Subsequent biographers were able to add little.

Recently, however, virtually all the known Disraeli papers have become available for public inspection. These include not only thirty boxes of papers – including the mutilated diary – at Hughenden, but an important series of letters he wrote to Benjamin Austen, one of his principal creditors, and Austen's wife Sara, who launched him as a literary prodigy. First in the field to examine them is an enterprising American scholar, Mr B. R. Jerman, who has shown considerable ingenuity in tracking down a number of related manuscripts. Though he appears to have overlooked one fascinating batch of papers – the letters which Disraeli and his mother wrote to John Murray, the publisher – and though his handling of the material is often, from a literary viewpoint, clumsy and insensitive, his book (*The Young Disraeli.* By B. R. Jerman. Oxford: Princeton. 35*s*.) is of first-rate interest.

The dynamic of Disraeli's early years appears to me to have been his ambivalent attitude towards his father. Isaac D'Israeli was the son of a philistine merchant and stockbroker. He revolted sharply against his father's attempt to chain him to business (his earliest literary work was a poetic denunciation of commerce) and eventually, after anguished family debates, became a professional man of letters. He was, however, essentially a passive figure, retiring and contemplative, whose work was primarily a descant on the researches of others. Characteristically, his breach with the synagogue was brought about by the insistence of the elders that he should hold office. Disraeli respected his father for his gentleness but also, one feels, despised him for his timidity towards the world. For Benjamin's one aim, in his first thirty years, was to become a man of action, a romantic executive. The compulsive hero of his youth was Byron, and it is not until the Byronic echoes begin to fade that the mature Disraeli emerges.

But what sort of action? Disraeli did not know; and his father being unable or unwilling to supply guidance, he spent his youth in a tragic series of follies, the consequences of which were to burden him for decades. His father had little money to give him: his first object, therefore, was to make it, fast. While still an articled solicitor's clerk, at the age of eighteen, he became heavily involved in the South American mining speculations of the mid-1820's, writing a series of shady commercial pamphlets and investing his hypothetical earnings in disastrous stocks. How he met his City friends we do not know; but he appears to have had, from the earliest age, an extraordinarily wide and dubious acquaintance. At the same time, he contracted with John Murray to become editor and co-proprietor of a daily newspaper, *The Representative*. Both ventures crashed within months. Murray lost over £20,000. Disraeli went into debt, with two other young men, for £7,000.

From this initial calamity, Disraeli's finances never recovered. At no time in his life did his earnings exceed his expenditure and when, in 1839, he steered into the safe financial haven of marriage to Mrs Wyndham Lewis, a comfortable widow with some £5,000 a year, his debts were around £20,000. During the intervening period, his overwhelming but undirected ambition necessarily took the forms most likely to bring him ready cash. This was the chief reason why he became a novelist. *Vivian Grey*, his debut, was a scandalous success, but the sums he received from it were immediately absorbed in settling his more pressing debts, and he was never able to hit the jackpot again, though he threshed about in various directions – including translation and even poetry.

Indeed, he was only able to keep afloat by two devices: borrowing expensive City money and touching his acquaintances. The first merely increased the seriousness of his position, the second led to bitterness and lost friendships. His long correspondence with Benjamin Austen traces the familiar pattern of admiration for a youthful genius gradually changing to cold contempt for a cheat and a liar; and Austen was lucky – he eventually got his money back. Others fared far worse. In 1830, it seems, Disraeli had to be rescued from a sponging-house; throughout this period, he often had to change his address to avoid sheriff's officers, and on one occasion narrowly escaped arrest in his father's house.

He later described this period as 'my miserable youth', and certainly his letters at the time often express desperation. But I doubt if Disraeli suffered as much as his anxious family and creditors. His temperament was incorrigibly sanguine: he invariably overrated his expectations – of selling a copyright for thousands, of getting elected to parliament, of bringing off a coup in the City. This must have been a constant source of irritation to his friends, but it kept his spirit unbroken until the luck finally changed. At the height of his mining-stock difficulties, we find him engaged in abortive negotiations for the purchase of a country estate at Stockton, which included a pocket borough. Again, in 1835, while in need of the odd £5, he embarked on the creation of a financial empire in The Hague, which inevitably collapsed in expensive ruin. His personal adornments, in lace and rings, do not seem to have suffered from financial calamity; Disraeli was always broke but never shabby.

Moreover, all his frenzied difficulties were unable to prevent the emergence of two new and insistent themes: love and politics. That Disraeli had early affairs seems likely; and it is certain that, at the age of twenty-eight, he was the lover of Mrs Clara Bolton, the wife of a doctor. But it was not until the next year that he fell in love – in a passionate, sexual sense – for the first and only time in his life. This mistress, Henrietta, Lady Sykes, was the wife of an unpleasant and eccentric baronet, and outwardly at least the affair was extraordinarily sordid. Henrietta undoubtedly also slept with Lord

Lyndhurst, Disraeli's first political patron, and it was widely believed that Disraeli had acted as her pimp to secure Lyndhurst's help. Moreover, Henrietta seems to have come to an agreement with her husband that her intimacy with Disraeli would be condoned provided that she, in return, would not object to his affair with Mrs Bolton, Disraeli's discarded mistress. Certainly, the Baronet was unusually complaisant, travelling abroad while Disraeli lived in his wife's house.

Despite this, there is no doubt that Disraeli really loved her, and she him. Her letters are vigorous specimens of late-romanticism, while his devotion was reflected in his best 'straight' novel, *Henrietta Temple*. During this period, he even contemplated, as his secret diary reveals, giving up the active life and surrendering to sensual calm. But the spell was broken by Henrietta's infidelity: she was discovered in bed with Maclise, the painter, by the Baronet himself, who proceeded to denounce her on the front page of the *Morning Chronicle*. After this, the theme of love dies away: Disraeli's marriage to Mary Anne Lewis was a convenient arrangement, which only slowly burgeoned into affection and never into passion.

But the political theme grew, with ever-increasing resonance. There is something both moving and inspiring about the progressive emergence, in the midst of Disraeli's financial and sexual jungle, of the great political certitudes which were to dominate his public life and re-vitalize the Tory Party. Again, this development has, at a superficial level, a sordid side. After three unsuccessful contests, he abandoned his optimistic belief that he could crash parliament as an independent Tory radical, and as the decade progresses we find him beginning to toe the party line, and to win favour with Peel and the Carlton by emerging as a party pamphleteer and even as a leader-writer on the *Morning Post*. By these means he got himself a safe seat at Maidstone and – two years later – a rich wife. But such concessions to the established powers were marginal: never for one instant did Disraeli deviate from his growing conviction that the first object of Toryism must be the maintenance of the essential character of the English countryside, and it was this passionate belief, far more than his personal dislike of Peel, which dominated the battles of the Forties. For it was linked to an even more central article of faith: Disraeli's realization that the masses were fundamentally conservative too, that a wider suffrage could become an instrument of stability – a barrier to a hideous industrial society enslaved by small-minded capitalists. Hence, it was during his agonizing experiment in youthful careerism that Disraeli, by a series of intuitive flashes, which he gradually rationalized into coherent theory, hit upon the dominant paradox of modern politics: the successful Tory democracy.

But he never really lived to reap its fruits, which were left to lesser men like Salisbury, Baldwin and Macmillan. Lord Randolph's summary is misleading: there was no ultimate triumph. Even by the time Disraeli entered parliament, much of his energy had been irretrievably consumed: the quest for fame had taken its toll. And then, for more than three decades, industrialism was in unrestricted power. Out of forty years in parliament, Disraeli held office for less than ten, and by the time he acquired power with a reliable majority, he was a frail figure in his late sixties. His one great triumph – at the Congress of Berlin – was nothing more than a lucky incident, which had no relevance to his main political beliefs. Apart from his Suffrage Act of 1867 (which brought him abuse and electoral defeat) he was never able to translate his theories into law. During his early struggles, he repeatedly reassured himself that failure did not matter, provided time was still on his side: time was the working capital of fortune. His tragedy is that when success finally arrived, time had run out.

—17 December 1960

The Dumb Colossus

SIR PHILIP MAGNUS has written a biographical masterpiece (*Kitchener: Portrait of an Imperialist.* By Philip Magnus. Murray. 30*s*.), but it can give little pleasure to the Kitchener family, to whom he confesses himself deeply indebted. In the course of 380 superbly documented pages, every particle of the great general's reputation is mercilessly ground to powder, and the cumulative effect is all the more appalling in that Sir Philip virtually refrains from comment and allows the deadly facts to speak for themselves. With the possible exception of Wellington, no British general has enjoyed, in his own lifetime, anything approaching Kitchener's reputation. This had always seemed to me mysterious. In the light of this new biography, it can only be called a gigantic confidence trick.

How did he do it? In the first place, the age was in his favour. In the second half of the nineteenth century, spectacular colonial acquisitions could be made at negligible cost in lives and money, and the generals got the credit for them. The politicians, with their eyes on future diplomatic complications, were normally opposed to forward policies; but to the soldiers they represented the only hope of promotion and wealth. Hence governments, Conservative and Liberal alike, were dragged into the imperial adventures by professional heroes frantic for glory and publicity. The public – far more imperialist than its leaders – appreciated that it was the soldiers, rather than the traders, who were building the empire. Kitchener was a public hero long before Omdurman because he was known to be the leading advocate of reconquering the Sudan. And once a general became a front-page figure he had the politicians at his mercy. Over a period of twenty years, successive Cabinets spent a great deal of their time devising commands sufficiently grandiose to tempt Kitchener to accept them. Both Balfour's and

Asquith's governments were in repeated peril at the threat of his resignation.

Kitchener exploited his natural advantages ruthlessly. Through his father and his friends, all energetic club lobbyists, he obtained constant mention in the press. His good looks and growing reputation got him a foothold, which he assiduously extended, in the great Tory houses, and through the medium of private correspondence – chiefly with Salisbury's daughter-in-law – he was able to put his views directly to the Cabinet (he did not scruple to send copies of secret operational plans and memoranda to Tory hostesses). Politicians who had to work closely with him grew to distrust him intensely; but in general he made a good impression in political circles for one simple, and characteristically Victorian, reason: he was economical. By using forced African labour, by cutting down medical supplies, and by employing mainly bachelor officers he fought his campaigns on a shoestring: the re-conquest of the Sudan cost the exchequer a mere £800,000.

As a field commander of small formations, where he could personally control all units, Kitchener was excellent. At Omdurman, he rode furiously all over the field, giving orders direct to battalion commanders. But anything larger was beyond him, for he could not grasp the principle of a chain of command and he had no knowledge of staff work. He hated anything written on paper, believing that all essential details could be carried in his head. When he arrived in Delhi to take over the India command, he instructed his A.D.C.s to pound all files into *papier-mâché*, which he used as the raw material for a new ornate ceiling in his house. By the time of the Boer war, when he was commanding large formations, and fighting white troops with a roughly equivalent fire-power, his faults had begun to catch up with him. He lost the battle of Paardeberg by trying to repeat his galloping exploits at Omdurman. His defects finally came home to roost in 1914 when he was made Secretary of State and placed in charge of the operational conduct of the war. He refused to use the General Staff – which already existed in rudimentary form – and tried to take over direct command of the B.E.F. when Sir John French got in a muddle. He did not know how to draw up a plan, and his orders to Hamilton for the Dardanelles expedition consisted of six vague paragraphs; hence, as the inquiry later made clear, he was the principal architect of the disaster.

Even more serious was his chronic indecision. As early as 1896, he astonished Cromer by asking his views on how to conduct the Sudan campaign. He was baffled by the far more drastic alternatives of the Great War, and the indecisiveness for which Asquith was later blamed and overthrown can be traced to the habits ingrained in the War Committee by Kitchener. By this time, of course, the politicians were getting wise to him. They recognized he had certain flashes of insight: he alone prophesied, for instance, that the war would last for years and that millions of men would have to be raised. But they grew increasingly alarmed by his inability to take decisions or to supply them with the information on which they could take them for him. Lloyd George described him as 'one of those revolving lighthouses which radiate momentary gleams of revealing light far out into the surrounding gloom, and then suddenly relapse into complete darkness'. In Cabinet, totally unable to put his thoughts into words, he remained dumb, glaring furiously at the baffled politicians. As 1915 progressed, Asquith became convinced that Kitchener was losing the war, but he dared not dismiss him for fear of public opinion; instead, he gradually stripped him of his responsibilities, and sent him off on futile tours of the war zones – anything to get him out of Whitehall. His death on the *Hampshire* brought merciful release.

Kitchener had no personal qualities to offset his professional inadequacy. His father mercilessly beat his children and encouraged them to do the same: Kitchener's mother once found him crucified by croquet hoops in the blazing sun. As a result, Kitchener had a cruel streak throughout his life. He was often kind to A.D.C.s, particularly if they were good looking, but he treated his men with contempt and indifference. The Army, officers and men alike, loathed him. A ruthless snob, he made no bones about preferring the company of Tory aristocrats, with Oriental millionaires as a *pis aller*. He was not even honest. In every campaign he looted unmercifully (in South Africa he stole a number of life-size municipal statues for his private park). He exploited his personal position to browbeat the Governor of Kenya into giving him an excessive slice of free land and paying for its operating costs. When famous cities presented him with their freedoms in ornate caskets, he rudely retorted: 'I need gold plate'.

Unlike most phoney heroes, Kitchener was caught out in his own lifetime. Throughout the Victorian age, the generals had been steadily increasing their power at the expense of Parliament, and it took the blood bath of the Great War to expose them for the hollow idols they were. Kitchener, the greatest of them, was the first to go; his accidental death made it far easier for Lloyd George to smash or neutralize the rest, and to restore the constitutional power of the Cabinet. Since then, we have had little trouble from our generals. Montgomery's memoirs reveal that cold egotism is still their hallmark; but at least they are now required to possess a minimum of professional competence.

—25 October 1958

The Case for Curzon

FOR MORE than a generation, Lord Beaverbrook has been seeking to establish, as definitive history, his version of men and events in the years 1914-1925. With this object he has painstakingly cornered a huge slice of the documents, published, and republished his own notes and jottings, and promoted a succession of biographical studies to give his personal orthodoxy the depth of a multiple vision. Not since the great days of the Whig school has there been such a persistent and successful effort in historical brainwashing. In general, it appears to me that the Beaverbrook version is sound, but there are some deplorable lapses in objectivity, notably the consistent denigration of Lord Curzon. This has now culminated in a hostile biography (*Curzon: the End of an Epoch*. By Leonard Mosley. Longmans. 30*s*.), based on the Curzon papers which Beaverbrook holds, and written by the film critic of the *Daily Express*. The author has not so much sought to attack Curzon's public life as to ignore it completely, except where it supplies ludicrous incidents to highlight his relentless exposures of Curzon's private failings and unhappiness.

True, the critical biography is a feature of our age; and based as it is on personal revelations which official biographers usually choose to ignore, it often serves a purpose in explaining historical mysteries. When carried out with discipline, as in Sir Philip Magnus's *Kitchener,* it can make a permanent contribution to knowledge. Even the exposure of Lloyd George's private life, recently published by his son, (*Lloyd George*. By Earl Lloyd George of Dwyfor. Muller, 21*s*.) might be defended on the grounds that it helps to explain – by revealing the magnitude of Lloyd George's sexual promiscuity – the curious collapse in his public energy after his downfall in 1922 and his tragic failure to make a political come-back. This new biography of Curzon, however, has the opposite effect: it darkens the screen of history. By portraying Curzon as a pathetic buffoon, and by virtually ignoring his achievements, it turns his remarkable career into a complete mystery. Why, the innocent reader may ask on finishing the book, can anyone ever have been taken in by this man? Why did his contemporaries regard him as a great (if limited) minister? Why did they want him in their cabinets; and why did the majority of them expect him to become premier?

It is possible, of course, to present him as a horror. He was a compulsive letter-writer and autobiographer, baring his heart with almost Boswellian abandon. From the mass of documents he left behind him, it is easy to select the ammunition of ridicule. He was absurdly vain, often sly. He was mean about money, treated his servants scandalously, bullied his subordinates and even tried to diddle his daughters out of their inheritance. He was often cowardly, occasionally disloyal and put too high a value on titles. He held displeasing views on women, Indians and the working-class (I notice, though, that Mr Mosley does not quote his famous remark, on seeing soldiers bathing: 'I always thought the lower classes were covered in thick black hair'; nor his sartorial maxim: 'Gentlemen never wear brown').

On the other hand, even at a personal level, one can make out a strong case for him. He loved to amuse, to give pleasure. Margot Asquith records the enormous trouble he took to entertain his guests; even late in life, as a sick man, he exerted himself to make the younger generation laugh. An acquaintance in affliction could always be sure of a consoling letter from him (Sir Henry Wilson, who narrowly escaped death in a yachting accident, noted grimly that Curzon was the only politician who wrote to congratulate him on his escape). He treated his first wife as a piece of property: but he loved her and made her a happy woman. With his second wife, who seems to have treated him coldly, he exercised extraordinary patience. Mean in small things, he spent lavishly on preserving the past.

But of course the debate should not be conducted on this level. Curzon was the most consciously public man of recent times; he seldom thought of his life in any other terms, and it is primarily on his political accomplishments that he must be judged. Two points are worth emphasizing if we are to understand the man. Curzon had an overriding sense of duty. Born into the ruling class, gifted with unusual abilities, he genuinely believed he had an imperative obligation to devote himself to the service of the nation;

this explains why, even in the face of personal humiliation, he clung to office, for resignation was to him an egotistical dereliction of duty. Secondly, he took his responsibilities very seriously indeed and prepared himself rigorously to discharge them. Not since Gladstone had any public man worked so hard at the sheer thankless task of acquiring knowledge. He travelled the world with this end in view, wrote copious notes, pored over books and reports in solitary study. Unlike the vast majority of politicians, he believed facts were paramount. To him, the source of political wisdom was not a knowledge of human nature, but the British Museum, 'that haven of Elysian study and intellectual delight'. 'I can still hear', he wrote, 'the tinkle of the great arc light as it was lit towards evening in the centre of the big glass dome of the Reading Room.' Coming from a man who was welcome in every house in Mayfair, such discipline, enhanced by an emotional respect for discovered truth, is not only admirable but moving.

But, it may be argued, this pedantry merely added a further touch of ridicule, made Curzon into another Plantagenet Palliser, seeking to cut human beings to the pattern of Blue Books. This, certainly, is the impression Mr Mosley seems to convey. But it is not borne out by the facts. Curzon was regarded as a 'difficult colleague in cabinet, but a valuable one nonetheless. 'Why Curzon?' asked Lord Riddell. Lloyd George replied: 'He has travelled a lot. He has read a lot. He is full of knowledge which none of us possesses. He is useful in council'. Leopold Amery, a sharp-eyed participant in the various cabinet committees which won the war, makes the same point again and again in his memoirs. Though by no means an unqualified admirer of Curzon, (he was instrumental in depriving him of the premiership, though not in the malignant manner Mr Mosley suggests) Amery recognized him as the type of man essential to professional government. He refers repeatedly to his 'able steering', to his 'unwearying industry, vast knowledge and power of draughtsmanship'.

Indeed, despite his astonishing ignorance of people, Curzon's judgement was vindicated by events surprisingly often. His Indian reforms – which Mr Mosley treats with cavalier brevity – were generally sensible and just. A highly unsympathetic critic, H. W. Nevinson, wrote: 'He has proved himself efficient in every department – education, irrigation, commerce, land-assessment, the control of plague and famine and the preservation of Indian arts'. As Viceroy, too, he pushed through the Kuwait treaty, now responsible for the biggest single contribution to Sterling Area reserves; and he capped this, twenty years later, by negotiations ensuring that the great Iraqi oil fields would remain in the British orbit.

His notorious 'surrender' over the House of Lords in the 1910 crisis has drawn scornful charges of 'ratting' both at the time and since (Mr Mosley inevitably, and heavily, falls into the trap of comparing him to Halifax the Trimmer); but in fact he acted in the empirical spirit of Peel. As Sir Robert Ensor puts it: 'The situation might well have drifted to catastrophe if a younger man had not stepped in and retrieved it. This was Lord Curzon.' During the war he probably contributed more towards victory than any other politician, except Lloyd George and Milner. As Foreign Secretary, he was handicapped by his dithering incapacity to prevent Lloyd George from meddling; but again – when he was allowed to make them – his decisions were sound, and under Bonar Law he successfully cleared up the mess Lloyd George had left in the Near East. Indeed, his three-month contest with Ismet Pasha at Lausanne was a *tour de force* of professional diplomatic skill.

It is true that Curzon outlived his time, but not in the sense that Mr Mosley understands it. He did not represent the aristocratic conspiracy to rule (his family were traditionally interested in theology rather than affairs): here, Balfour and Derby were far more typical figures. He believed, rather, in a meritocracy selected, indeed, from the wellborn but exercising power by virtue of industry and brains. He was not a Duke of Omnium but a Coningsby. His obsolescence springs from the fact that he was a militant imperialist in an age when the empire was first beginning to contract. He was a Tory who could intone with real conviction, 'Wider still and wider, Shall thy bounds be set', and in India he tried to put this gospel into practice, to the dismay of Salisbury and Balfour. Here we have the key to his ultimate failure. At the dead centre of gravity of the Tory Party lies the unspoken desire for a quiet life. Now Curzon was incapable of quietude; his energy required continual challenge, grist for his midnight mills. He thought big, and carried with him a whiff of grandiose risk. Hence, when the moment came, the king-makers in the party preferred the safe Baldwin.

Curzon was a good loser; his sharp tears were soon dried, and he hastened to congratulate his opponent. He lumbered on in office, among lesser men, because he believed it his duty and because, despite his egotism, he automatically assumed that the nation came before the individual. While Lloyd George sported with his harem, the old Proconsul, strapped in his steel corset, often in great pain, sneered at by the raffish Birkenhead, a regular joke at dinner parties financed by war profits, toiled into the small hours over his cabinet papers. He had not all the equipment of a statesman; but what he had he gave, and the giving killed him. Amery assesses him in a happy sentence: 'Whatever his minor defects and oddities, Curzon was a generous soul and a great public servant'. Much credit he has got for it, poor man, and we can only hope that some day his papers will be examined by a more magnanimous eye and fashioned into the truthful monument his punctilious nature would have respected.

—22 October 1960

The Art of Opposition

'HE HAS SHATTERED his contemporaries, but he will not charm posterity.' Bagehot's verdict on Lord Brougham, written in 1857 when the old volcano was nearly 80, still stands – but not for the reasons he advanced in his essay. He saw Brougham as a windy agitator, full of sound and fury but signifying little by the harsh standards of administrative efficiency with which he judged statesmanship. In fact, Brougham's achievements, even before the publication of Professor New's present study (*The Life of Henry Brougham to 1830*. By Chester New. Oxford 50*s*.), had not gone entirely unrecognized. His character, on the other hand, has until now been savagely misunderstood.

For this his contemporaries are to blame. With few exceptions, they united to give him a bad press. Inveterate opponents like Croker, sly placemen like Creevey and Greville, embittered reactionaries like Wordsworth (and his neurotic sister), envious juniors like Macaulay, cantankerous critics like Hazlitt, each contributed their quota of malice and lies; and they were joined, for a variety of reasons, by reformers such as Ricardo, Place and Bentham, to whom Brougham had given steadfast and disinterested support. The charges against him cover a multitude of sins, many of them mutually exclusive. He was wildly impractical; he was a professional political manipulator. He knew nothing of the law; he was a legal pedant without a soul. He was obstinate; he was vacillating. He was mad and irresponsible; he was cold, cunning and self-seeking. He was a revolutionary; he was an obstacle to radical reform. He was a blind ideologist; he was an unprincipled empiricist. Faced with this mass of conflicting accusations, the bewildered student is tempted to conclude there must have been something seriously wrong with the man. Professor New wearily complains that Brougham's biographer 'has to make his way as best he can through a mass of malice carefully concealed, with its whispers, gibes and sneers, to say nothing of sheer untruths assiduously invented and circulated'.

Fortunately, Professor New possessed the industry, patience and sheer courage to do precisely this. He has stripped off the layers of established misconceptions. He has checked the published sources with the original manuscripts on which they were based, detecting many important errors and omissions. He has explored a wealth of unpublished materials, some of them uncatalogued; and he has performed a miracle of collation and condensation. The book carries the story only to 1830 and it lacks polish (New died before he passed the final proofs) but it is plainly the most valuable English biography to be published for a long time. It not only rehabilitates Brougham as a man; it reveals him as easily the greatest political reformer of the first half of the 19th century.

Reading this book, it is not difficult to see why Brougham aroused such unjustified criticism and why so much of it is contradictory. He bridged two entirely different and mutually hostile worlds. On the one hand were the rabble-rousers and the academic reformers, who had yet to learn Fabian patience and respect for constitutional processes. On the other were the professional politicians, who regarded parliament as the exclusive instrument of change. Brougham saw that reform would degenerate into revolution unless he could persuade the two to work in harness, and he appointed himself the coachman. Naturally, both resented the complementary disciplines he imposed, and for different reasons. The non-parliamentary reformers suspected him as an unscrupulous politician and attributed his willingness for the necessary compromise to self-seeking. The politicians saw him as a demagogue, even an anarchist, conjuring up ungovernable forces which would overwhelm the constitution. The only people who seem to have trusted him were the unrepresented millions, among whom he was wildly popular.

Their instinct was sound. None of the serious charges against Brougham bears examination. He was not an officer-seeker, still less corrupt. Even in 1830, when he had at last brought the Whigs to power, he agreed to become Chancellor only because Grey insisted that a government could not be formed without him. Though far from wealthy, he repeatedly declined lucrative commissions to pursue the cause of reform in the Commons. His parliamentary seat was never secure but he did not hesitate to defy his patrons on issues of principle. In his relentless pursuit of the Liverpool slave-traders and West Indian planters (who together had connections with about 150 MPs), and still more in his offensive against charitable abuses – one of the great scandals of the early 19th century – he aroused implacable enmities, regardless of his own career. In negotiating bills through parliament, he never, so far as I have been able to discover, conceded points for reasons of sheer political (still less personal) expediency.

Equally, the charges of demagoguery will not stick. He would have nothing to do with such utopian schemes as annual parliaments. Popular agitation he regarded as a vital political instrument, when canalized in some practical direction, and he was expert at arousing it. But when, after Peterloo, anarchy threatened, he skilfully assisted the government in restoring order, while steering it away from blind repression. With rare exceptions, his violence of language was carefully calculated.

Nevertheless, his unwillingness to identify himself wholly either with a party, such as the Whigs, or with a reformist pressure-group, such as the Saints or the Benthamites, made him a solitary figure. His contemporaries, no less than posterity, found it impossible to pigeonhole him – a handicap which is liable to be fatal in English public life. The wonder is that he was able to achieve so much. If Wilberforce is fairly given the main credit of carrying the abolition of the slave-trade onto the Statute Book, it was Brougham, with his trained lawyer's brain, who forced through the punitive legislation which in practice eliminated it; it was he who, by constant pressure in the House, persuaded Castlereagh to devise an international system of enforcement; and it was he who carried the campaign to ultimate success by securing the abolition of slavery itself within the Empire.

Brougham not only created Britain's first modern university, he virtually invented state education by persuading the government to devote public funds to a purpose which, until then, had been left to charity or private enterprise. As Dr Arnold told him: 'Upon the general subject of popular education you are the founder and leader of us all.' Brougham broke the power of state censorship and the system of special juries. He revolutionized the criminal law by ensuring the defence equal rights with the prosecution. His reform of the Court of Chancery made possible cheap and speedy justice in civil cases, and thanks to him the conditions described in *Bleak House* had ceased to exist many years before Dickens wrote it.

Most of all, he made the greatest single contribution to the cause of universal suffrage.

What is even more striking, and gives Brougham his real historical significance, is that he accomplished the bulk of this work in opposition – and in the teeth of a huge Tory majority. If Fox established the principle of loyal opposition, Brougham first gave it positive application. His methods are instructive even today. He devised no elaborate party programme, for he recognized he would never get his heterogeneous allies to agree on one; still less did he try to create a theoretical party 'image' (a task as forlorn in 1810 as it is in 1961). What he did was to concentrate on a number of limited, practical objectives on each of which it was possible, by energetic persistence, to force the government to yield. On the basis of these parliamentary victories, a genuine image and a workable programme emerged of themselves.

Equally, Brougham rejected as unreal the debate (which currently divides the Labour Party) between the educationists, who wish to concentrate on the long-term task of converting public opinion to fundamental changes, and the pragmatists, who by placing the first priority on attaining office limit themselves to marginal adjustments. Brougham's career shows that the two strategies can be not merely compatible but complementary. The academic reformers provided him with a steady flow of facts and arguments. He used the *Edinburgh Review* to present them to the politically-conscious, the national and provincial papers to reach the middle classes, and the public platform to arouse the masses. With this symphony of forces behind him, he fought his decisive pitched battles across the floor of the Commons. Thus political education and statutory change went hand-in-hand.

But the art of opposition, as Brougham exercised it, was no magic formula. Its chief ingredients were hard work and ruthless obstinacy. Brougham never neglected his political homework, still less any opportunity to hound and harass the Treasury bench. In a single session he would speak as often as 170 times. Remorselessly, day after day, at Westminster and in the country, he chipped away at the cement which held the Tory edifice together. With each concession he wrung from the government, he eroded its self-confidence and will to survive. With his successful defence of Queen Caroline, he united, for the first time, the popular and parliamentary forces of change. As Professor New argues, it was this, rather than the death of Castlereagh, which inaugurated the Age of

Reform: for it forced the government to veer to the left and so engendered the split in the Tory ranks which in 1830 finally precipitated the Whigs into power. Thus Brougham proved that if you wish to form a government you cannot afford to behave like one; that there is no substitute for root-and-branch opposition, conducted without respite in the House of Commons; that you can stick to your principles – and get office too.

—22 December 1961

The Creed of the Pallisers

IT IS NOT UNCOMMON for rich men to purchase political insurance from their enemies. In Singapore today the communists draw their principle source of income not from Peking but from local Chinese millionaires; in the Lebanon, I know several wealthy men who find it prudent to support socialist politicians and even newspapers. There is, however, no parallel to the role the great Whig landowners played in England's Age of Reform. For almost a century the men who, one might suppose, had most to lose by change arrogated and retained the leadership of the progressive forces, transformed the nation from an agricultural oligarchy to an industrial democracy, and so destroyed the dual basis on which their power resided. Looked at from this distance of time, it can be seen either as a protracted ritual of class suicide – or as an inspired effort to tame revolution into a constitutional animal. But whichever view we take, the phenomenon is unique and has conferred enviable advantages on our modern political system.

Yet oddly enough, until the appearance of this book, (*The Passing of the Whigs*. By Donald Southgate. Macmillan. 50*s*.) it lacked a historian. Dr Southgate's original intention, I imagine, was to analyze the watershed of 1886 and discover why, at that date, the Whigs decided to terminate their historic mission and assume their natural place on the Tory benches. But he has found that 1886, like other years of destiny, seems less portentous on close inspection and was in fact merely the culmination of a process which had been driving the Whigs to the right for half a century. In recording this process, using post-Namier techniques, he has written a book of great distinction, which for the first time makes consistent sense of the central decades of the 19th century.

The initial difficulty in coming to grips with the Whigs is that they lacked an articulate philosophy. Their leaders, when pressed, would quote tags from Locke or Burke; but not even Macaulay, their best PRO, succeeded in defining their creed. The most typical of them, Lord John Russell, went so far as to write an *Essay on the English Government and Constitution,* but the best he could do was to describe Whiggery as 'temperate, gradual and judicious'. Another Whig, Francis Baring, produced a more comprehensive formula:

> 'A body of men connected with high rank and property, bound together by hereditary feelings, party ties, as well as higher motives, who in bad times keep alive the sacred flame of freedom, and when the people are roused stand between the constitution and revolution and go with the people, but not to extremities.'

Yes: but what is an extremity? And when can the people fairly be said to be roused? Inability to give precise answers to either question led to endless confusion in Whig minds, and exasperated Tories and Radicals equally. The truth is that Whiggism could be illustrated but not defined; it was a shadowy ectoplasm generated by the vague ideal of *noblesse oblige*. A true Whig could not tell how he would act or think until something happened; then he knew instinctively. To men like Disraeli, Gladstone or Chamberlain, this was infuriating, even immoral – the 'negation of principle'.

The Whigs did, however, possess one working axiom: that power should go with property. The country should be run by men with a stake in it. If the ownership of property shifted, then the constitution should follow suit. The Whigs promoted reform in 1832 because they believed that only timely concessions could avert revolution but also, and perhaps more fundamentally, because they felt the middle classes had earned a right to political power by their success in amassing wealth. As Brougham pointed out, they were now richer, collectively, than the landed interests. He went on to draw a convenient distinction between 'the people' – that is, responsible, propertied citizens – and 'the populace' or rabble. It was in the interests of the aristocracy and gentry to share power with 'the people' because this would broaden the basis of support for the existing economic system. The first Reform Bill, in fact, was an anti-democratic measure: under it, the number of working-class voters fell, relatively if not absolutely.

No doubt the Whigs hoped this process could be indefinitely prolonged. But they failed to reckon with the demographic revolution – a phenomenon which few 19th-century politicians analysed or even noticed. Canning was right when he foresaw 'a struggle between property and population'. The Whig theory broke down because 'the populace' expanded faster than 'the people': the natural devolution of property which was taking place within the rules of the capitalist system could not possibly keep pace with the fall in the death-rate. Hence when in 1867 Disraeli broke the truce on extending the suffrage he not only 'dished the Whigs' in the narrow, tactical sense, as he intended, but in a strategic one, too. A further extension under Gladstone followed inevitably. By the mid-Eighties, the constitution had shifted from a propertied to a democratic basis: 'the populace' had secured power, with a vested interest in changing the economic structure. It is no accident that at this point the Whigs decided it was no longer possible to protect property from an enfilading position; their only choice was to join the Tories in the citadel. No accident, either, that the actual break came over Ireland. For there Whig theories had never worked.

There is thus no mystery in the Whig decision to abandon the left. What does need explaining is their failure to take over the Tory party – indeed, their disappearance almost overnight. One reason, of course, was that they left the Liberals at the same time as Chamberlain, who brought the Tories an accession of plutocratic strength which was far more valuable than any Whig contribution and, still more important, a modern technique of mass-politics manipulated by professional machines. But the real truth is that the Whigs, by 1886, were only a husk. The men who followed Hartington across the floor were the officers of a vanished army. As Dr Southgate shows, the drift of Whig families to the Tories had been continuous since 1830: Derby, Tankerville, Jersey, Richmond, Caernarvon – nothing could stem the drain of Whig lifeblood. From 1830 onwards, Whig and Liberal governments had a constant problem in raising majorities in the Lords; Granville complained bitterly of the need to dine and wine 'foolish and dull' peers in order to scrape votes together. During this period Whig leaders created over a hundred peers, but not enough to fill the gaps.

There were other sources of weakness. Whigs had always believed in the spoils system, within limits: the 'responsible' classes, in return for governing the country, had a right to stick their hands in the public till and reward their relatives and supporters. As the century progressed it became steadily more difficult to operate such a system: the Gladstonian concept of public accountability, competitive examinations and the new Victorian standards of public probity combined to remove corruption as a source of influence.

It was the same with elections. Labouchère Senior, a characteristic Whig, had cheerfully accepted dishonesty at the polls: 'As the people is rather scoundrel, and business must be carried on, why, they must be bought.' The Secret Ballot and, still more, Gladstone's Corrupt Practices Act put an end to this. The number of Whig seats fell steadily; by 1886 scarcely a score were 'reliable'. The Church, too, deserted them. Archbishop Harcourt was the last great Whig prelate; by 1850 the Establishment was overwhelmingly Tory. Even their chief source of wealth – the land – eventually failed the Whig magnates. By 1886 the price of wheat had fallen to 31*s*. and it later slipped to under £1; in the last decade of the century, half a million acres of the best land went out of cultivation, and landlords' incomes from farm rents dropped from nearly £60 million to just over £40 million. The great Trollopian certitudes were crumbling.

Even so, the primary element in the Whig decline was their arrogance. They never numbered more than 1,000 families, a third of which were titled; yet they showed a persistent hostility to new recruits. Only two members of the middle class, Labouchère Senior and Macaulay, penetrated to the inner circles of Whiggery. Ducal scions were repeatedly allowed to override the claims to office of able men from the professions or commerce; this exclusiveness was still more intense in the social world, where pain goes deeper. Hence among the new men whom they had endowed with a growing measure of constitutional power the Whigs generated a pervasive hostility which can only be compared to anti-semitism.

If the Whigs despised the middle class, they ignored the workers completely. They never even attempted to build up a national political machine; and, when the Liberals did so, the Whigs found it increasingly difficult to get their candidates nominated for safe or winnable seats. So, when the Whigs decamped to the Tories they brought with them nothing but their rent-rolls and their names – a dowry of rapidly diminishing value. The Whigs seem to have assumed, fatalistically, that workers – as opposed to middle-class shopkeepers – could never be converted to moderate courses. Thereby they missed a vital trick, which the Tories scooped up gratefully. For the great merit of Disraeli and Lord Randolph Churchill was to perceive that brutal economic self-interest need not necessarily be the decisive factor in determining how men vote; that even the poorest have conservative instincts; and that, by creating new political emotions, they could persuade men without property to keep its custodians in office.

So the Whigs vanished without a trace. Whether they betrayed their class (as the Tories argued) or in fact made change slower and more acceptable (as they themselves claimed) is still debatable. If the latter, they have found remarkably few imitators elsewhere: the role of the Whigs is one aspect of the British constitution which we have found difficult to export. Only in India, where all things British are divine, is there a faint echo of Whiggery. On the Ganges, stiff-necked Brahmins voluntarily preside over a social and economic revolution which is certain to end in their eclipse. Their self-justification is that thereby violent change may be averted. It may seem bizarre to range Mr Nehru with Lord John Russell, but they share a common predicament. Let us hope that Mr Nehru is not quite so effectively 'dished'.

—17 August 1962

1086 and All That

DID THE NORMAN INVASION transform English society? Or were the Normans merely digested by a civilization whose institutions proved more powerful than their own? For centuries these questions have been recognized as more than academic. The dynamic behind the first great age of Anglo-Saxon studies, in the latter part of the 17th-century, was the quest for ammunition in the contemporary conflict between monarch and parliament – the need to prove that representative institutions in England were of great antiquity, that they not only antedated William the Conqueror's attempt to introduce a 'continental style' monarchy, but triumphantly survived it. Equally, Anglican divines, anxious to demonstrate the comparative modernity of Romish claims, ransacked the documents for evidence that the Anglo-Saxon church was an independent body, and that its unique position was preserved despite the Norman invasion and the Hildebrandine reforms which followed it. In a sense, the controversy is still relevant today, for the emotive assumption of those who would carry us into Europe is that Britain has always possessed a continental destiny, from which it has been unhappily deflected only by historical accident. If therefore, the continuity of our institutions can be proved – and the Norman 'conquest' shown to be a mere transfusion of blood and ideas – the case for maintaining our insular status is powerfully reinforced.

Well, then, did the Normans conquer England? A spate of recent publications (*The Anglo-Saxon Chronicle*. Eyre & Spottiswoode. 50*s*. *The Domesday Geography of South-East England*. Edited by H. C. Darby and E. M. J. Campbell. Cambridge. £6. *The Domesday Inquest*. By R. Welldon Finn. Longmans. 45*s*. *Anglo-Saxon England and the Norman Conquest*. By H. R. Loyn. Longmans. 30*s*. *The Birth of Western Economy*. By Robert Latouche. Translated by E. M. Wilkinson. Methuen. 50*s*.) permits us to approach this question (if not finally to answer it) with far more confidence than in the past. Within the past twelve months alone, we have had

Professor Whitelock's sumptuous definitive edition of the Anglo-Saxon chronicle, a further volume of the geographical reconstruction of Domesday England, a critical summary of the Domesday evidence by Mr Welldon Finn, a new analysis of the economic impact of the Conquest by Mr Loyn, and the English translation of Robert Latouche's brilliant *Origines de l'Economie Occidentale*. Most of the ground which they cover is inevitably the preserve of professional scholars, but we can extract from them some conclusions of wider interest.

Central to the problem of the Conquest are the character and aims of William himself. The monk who wrote version 'E' of the *Chronicle* has given us an unforgettable portrait of this great and unpleasing man. He was a hard, grasping and unforgiving sovereign. He 'loved greediness above all'; he 'obtained a very great amount of money from his men where he had any pretext for it'; he was 'stark', 'very stern and violent', so 'fierce' that 'he cared not for the rancour of them all'; 'he had earls in his fetters, expelled bishops from their sees and abbots from their abbacies.' But he also upheld the rule of law and gave the country 'good security'. While he lived,

> 'any honest man could travel over his kingdom without injury with his bosom full of gold, and no one dared strike another, however much wrong he had done him.'

Behind this portrait we can grasp at the realities of William's position. He was a practical man with an immensely ambitious vision: the creation of a unitary kingdom in which the crown should be self-supporting in war, and in peace be the source of all law and title to land. To do this, the monarch had to become the ultimate beneficiary of the agricultural revolution which was sweeping parts of Western Europe. This was primarily a revolution of technology: the forest clearances, beginning about 1050, were rapidly expanding the area of cultivation. But the corresponding rise in the value of land increased the desire of the great feudal lords to possess it, and they had the physical means to gratify their ambitions. Here, then, was William's dilemma. The feudal society, with its inherent tendency to oligarchy – or, indeed, anarchy – was anathema to his vision of kingship. But it had one indispensable virtue: it was the only form of organization which could produce in sufficient quantities, trained armoured men on horseback, the decisive weapon of 11th-century war.

William must have realized the acuteness of his dilemma when he surveyed his predicament after his initial victory. He had broken the military power of the old Anglo-Saxon state; but he had a mere 4,000 followers to hold down a population of about 1,500,000. In his early years he tried hard to associate the remnants of the Anglo-Saxon ruling class with his government: but the thegns showed themselves unreliable. Gradually, all but a tiny handful were eliminated. The senior native ecclesiastics were dealt with almost as brutally. By the time of Domesday, in 1086, all the ecclesiastical tenancies-in-chief, except for a few minor abbeys, were held by aliens; and out of 180 baronies only two were held by Englishmen – both Quislings, battening on the lands of dispossessed thegns. Domesday reveals how completely the power and wealth of England had been carved up among a handful of aliens. Of the total annual landed value of £73,000, the King had 17¼ per cent, the Norman prelates 26¼ per cent, and the Norman barons 54 per cent. Twenty great Norman families held nearly half England.

Military necessity had thus forced William, in theory, to place his newly-acquired kingdom in pawn to his feudatories. But it was only in theory. He imposed on his prelates and barons, in return for their lands, the enormous burden of providing nearly 5,000 knights for his service – against a mere 750 for all Normandy. They could build castles only as part of a national defence scheme, and under licence. Their lands could be concentrated for military purposes only in the Marches, where defence was paramount.

These devices, of course, were open to any ambitious continental sovereign, anxious to limit the power of his chief subjects. But William had at his disposal an additional instrument – the residual powers of the Anglo-Saxon throne. These were, in theory at least, considerable, and they were by their essence non-feudal, for they brought the crown into direct relationship with the people and undermined the oligarchic concept of the feudal pyramid. The great 'crown-wearings' three times a year, the summoning of national councils, the collection of the *geld* – a direct national tax which had nothing to do with feudal obligations – above all, the right of men, irrespective of their lord, to resort to the king's courts for justice: all these were institutions made to measure for William's ambition, and he eagerly preserved and strengthened them. But because he needed them, he was forced to retain the Anglo-Saxon administrative structure, the shire, the hundred and the hide, without which they were largely unworkable. These cut across the territorial basis of feudalism: Domesday Book, ostensibly a feudal record, was in fact merely a rearrangement under feudal headings of a survey which was Anglo-Saxon in concept and method. In this respect, Domesday was a symbol of the 'conquest' – a feudal, continental veneer on an English structure.

There is no evidence that William attached any value to English institutions as such, or that he had any love for the English people: in all probability he hated and feared them, as they certainly hated and feared him. The process whereby he preserved English society, and so at every turn limited the effects of the 'conquest', was accidental: the by-product of his immediate and pressing needs. Being the thorough man he was, he was no doubt disturbed by the resilience of the society over which he ruled, and anxious that his dominion should bite below the thin feudal crust he had imposed on it. On purely economic grounds, the mass of Englishmen had little reason to regret the conquest: towns were prospering, slavery was disappearing rapidly; as Domesday shows, the real incomes of the peasants were rising, in many cases impressively fast. Recent research indicates that the typical villein held 30 acres, with two horses or oxen: he was thus far better off than the great majority of Asians and Africans, even today. Confronted with the ocular evidence of English prosperity, William, 'who had fallen into avarice', must have become increasingly anxious to enlarge the share of it which seeped into the royal coffers. By the mid-Eighties, he had consolidated his possessions, defeated all his enemies, and completed the 'continentalization' of the upper layer of society. Had not the time come to probe deeper, to introduce a second phase of the conquest?

William was stimulated into action by the failure, in 1084, of his arrangements to billet mercenaries on the shires. To his fury, the incident showed that his administrative machine was woefully ignorant of what was going on in England, and of the complex mixed society which was growing up under his royal nose. To move forward he must know more. Hence at Christmas 1085,

> 'the king had much thought and very deep discussion with his council about this country – how it was occupied and with what sorts of people. Then he sent his men all over England . . .'

The result was Domesday Book – not only the greatest administrative achievement of the Middle Ages, but one well beyond the present-day capacity of governments in, say, Indonesia, Paraguay or

Ethiopia. Its painstaking accuracy aroused the disgust of the Anglo-Saxon chronicler, as well it might. In administration, knowledge is the father of power, and the fact that William, as the chronicler laments, knew how many pigs each of his villeins possessed boded ill for those villeins – they would soon feel his fist on their backs. Historians have argued for generations as to the precise purpose of Domesday. Was it a kind of census, or a *geld*-book, or a survey of feudal obligations, or a legal record of outstanding disputes? It was probably all of these; every page reeks of money and power, the two things the king loved most. But was it not also something else, the administrative preliminary to a design grand enough to justify the magnitude of such a reckoning? Have we here the beginning of the second phase of the conquest, which would stamp Norman power into every hide and virgate – carry it across the threshold of every cottar and ceorl?

If so, the grand design died almost at birth, leaving only its remarkable blueprint. Before the great book was finished, William was dead. The transformation of England might have defeated even him; certainly it was beyond the capacity and vision of his immediate successors. Despite the initial advantage of conquest, and all his avarice, William had failed to secure permanent financial independence for the crown. The Anglo-Saxon institutions he preserved ensured the unity of the kingdom and the means to rule and defend it; but embedded in them was the principle of mutual obligation – the seeds of government by consent. The society William left was fundamentally the same as on 'the day King Edward was alive and dead', and it was travelling in the same direction. Hence the thoroughness with which the conquering Normans were enmeshed in the English integument. Even in the Conqueror's own day, a subtle change overcomes the language with which the English chronicler describes him: from an alien enemy he is slowly transformed into a king – though a harsh and unpopular one – of England. Less than a hundred years later, Henry II's Treasurer wrote that, nowadays, 'it can scarcely be determined, in the case of free men, who is of English and who is of Norman birth'; and, by the mid-13th century, it is the supposedly alien baronage whom we find insisting that castles should not be entrusted to the hands of foreigners, and that English heiresses should not be married 'to men not of the nation of the realm of England'.

—5 October 1962

Hamlet in Downing Street

FEW MEN have been more splendidly endowed by both God and Mammon than the Fifth Earl of Rosebery. Early in life he confessed his ambitions: to marry an heiress, to become prime minister and to win the Derby. He achieved all of them, the last three times over. He inherited an ancient Scottish title, wide estates and £30,000 a year. He captured the richest heiress of his day, Hannah Rothschild, a devoted and docile wife, who brought with her an income of over £100,000 a year and the princely domain of Mentmore. He possessed good looks, good health in the strictly physical sense, a beautiful speaking voice which held vast audiences enraptured, a brain not only quick but profound, an enviable wit and rare powers of expression both with tongue and pen. His interests were wide and judicious, his means to indulge them almost limitless.

Yet his life was a long Calvary of disappointments, the fruits of success turning remorselessly into dead ashes as, with delicate and diffident hand, he sampled them. He was launched in politics as the protégé of Gladstone, as the golden youth who would inherit the mantle. But he enjoyed only two brief spells as Foreign Secretary (the latter disastrous) and a short, humiliating tenure of the premiership, which brought him nothing but anguish. Within ten years he had forfeited the loyalty and even the interest of his party, and entered a protracted, bitter limbo of political impotence. He lingered until 1929, already embalmed in trite textbook phrases as a paradoxical failure, seeking refuge in the most pathetic pursuit of rebuffed politicians – writing lengthy letters to the Press. His many distractions did little to redeem his collapse as a statesman. His artistic collections mounted: but they did not acquire the quality or depth to constitute a life's work. His racing excited, but did not satisfy him. Graceful essays were written; but, somehow, the major book was never attempted. The gloom of Rosebery's existence remained almost unrelieved, and even his tragedy lacked the saving virtue of drama. His life produced nothing but a long text for a sermon on worldly vanity.

How did it happen? What went wrong? Churchill, who knew him well, found no answer in *Great Contemporaries*. Nor did Rosebery's son-in-law, Lord Crewe, who compiled an inadequate official biography in 1930. But Rosebery left ample material for posterity: copies of practically every letter he wrote or received, copious journals and commonplace-books, exhaustive memoranda on virtually every event and conversation in which he took part. These documents (some of which were only unearthed as recently as last year) have now been mastered by an able young historian and woven into a brilliant and convincing narrative. Mr James may not have solved the secret of Rosebery, but he has given us all the clues we need. Those who read this book (*Rosebery*. By Robert Rhodes James. Weidenfeld & Nicolson. 50*s*.) – and they should include anyone who cares for politics – can make up their own minds.

The first clue is that Rosebery was the victim of the least spectacular, but perhaps the most debilitating, of diseases: insomnia. It attacked him early in life and never fully relinquished its grip. It was all very well for Gladstone to write: 'he is *physically* rather too self-conscious, perhaps, for his health'; but Rosebery's private notes abound with comments such as, 'Slept at New Club – or rather, did not sleep'; 'Dined alone – bad night.' Lord Esher noted: 'He lies awake thinking all night . . . terribly painful to witness.' Rosebery's doctor, Sir William Broadbent, described him as the worst case of chronic insomnia he had ever known and even predicted 'a fatal termination'. Rosebery believed that this evil could be diminished by taking lengthy carriage drives, late at night, and his attempts to develop an effective routine make pathetic reading. But the chronological evidence suggests that his insomnia was more the consequence, than the cause, of political frustration. When Rosebery was deeply and wholeheartedly involved in political battle, when he was immersed in work he loved at the F.O., he not only felt well, but slept well.

Rosebery's second natural disadvantage was incurable. He was on the point of negotiating a seat in the Commons when his grandfather's death imprisoned him in the Lords. He thus spent his entire political life as a member of a body he despised and loathed. Immunized from the normal give-and-take of democratic politics, he never had the chance to develop the tough integument essential to sustained success in public life. Worse: from his sterile seat in the Lords, he saw the unpleasant side of the Commons in-fighting without really understanding its compensating excitement, warmth and nobility. So politics remained for him 'an evil-smelling bog'.

But, when all Rosebery's handicaps are listed, the fact remains he was largely responsible for his own failure. His wealth and magnificence made his contemporaries loth to criticize him, especially since, like royalty, he was adept at disarming opponents by an occasional flash of condescension; but he was not a nice man. Hopelessly spoilt from his schooldays, a social, intellectual and money snob, unfeeling and inconsiderate to servants, faithless to his allies, a heavy burden to his colleagues, Rosebery was fairly saddled with the phrase: 'Not a man to go tiger-shooting with.' He had a nasty wit, which he employed on the weak, including his wife ('I leave tonight. Hannah and the rest of the heavy baggage go tomorrow'). He inherited his mother's anti-Semitism, and when entertaining his Rothschild relatives in the very palace their industry had built, cut short the evening with a curt: 'To your tents, O Israel!' He invited guests to his house and then refused to communicate with them except through servants. He would, in fact, have made an apt candidate for the various new Balkan thrones which were going begging at the time; unfortunately (though he admired the race intensely) he was not a German.

Rosebery's pride was such that he would never willingly accept a favour, even if due to him. He wanted the top Liberal brass to beg him on their knees to accept office, for the perverse pleasure of turning them down. He made absurd fusses about the various honours – Garters, Thistles and suchlike – which were showered upon him, and described being appointed Lord Lieutenant of Midlothian as 'an act of mortification'. Yet he had no democratic scruples in such matters. When Asquith threatened to create peers in 1910, Rosebery promptly had himself made Earl of Midlothian and Viscount Mentmore and Epsom to prevent these titles going to middle-class upstarts.

Why the Liberals put up with him for so long is hard to explain. Of course, he had a big following north of the Border: the Scots adored him both as a double-barrelled aristocrat and because he had made off with an heiress. For a time he appeared not only as the natural successor to Gladstone but as the only man who could prevent a split. But Rosebery wanted power without responsibility, to play Achilles in his tent or, rather, Hamlet in Downing Street. As time went on, even his warmest admirers gave him up. Not surprisingly, it was a fellow Scotsman, Campbell-Bannerman, who in the end found him out and dismissed him as a lightweight. Once Bannerman, a sharp Attlee-like figure in sheep's clothing, became Liberal leader, he determined to stand no more nonsense from Rosebery and snuffed out his political career. For all his assumed indifference to success, Rosebery never forgot this. After the landslide of 1906, Bannerman honoured Rosebery's son by asking him to second the Address. Rosebery imposed a savage veto: 'If you accept C.-B.'s invitation, you are no son of mine.'

After Bannerman virtually drove Rosebery out of the Liberal party, he promptly became the reactionary which, by instinct, he had always wanted to be. His tutor at Eton, the remarkable William Cory, had accurately predicted Rosebery's political character:

> 'An ardent reformer is pretty sure to become Conservative when he marries into a worldly family, when he has encumbrances, when he becomes post-prandial. He will be happier at forty or sixty if his mind can fly back to a year of generous impulse and aspiration when he admired a Canning, a Peel, a Manin, a Cavour, a Hampden.'

It was no doubt such a generous impulse which led Rosebery to accept Gladstone's plea to enlist under his standard. At the end of his life he confessed that his chief political mistake was to reject a similar offer from Disraeli. But this judgement rather misses the point. Rosebery was not wrong to join Gladstone; but he should, in all conscience, have left the Liberals with the other Whigs, in 1886. Instead, his invincible powers of indecision led him to hang on for over a decade, growing more and more out of sympathy with everything the Liberals stood for, but still their actual or potential leader.

Rosebery's failure to make a clean break with the Liberals produced his sole contribution to history – characteristically, a negative one. For twelve or more years, his ditherings prevented the Liberals from resolving the problem of the succession and, with it, the fundamental dispute about the nature and aims of the party. Had these issues been firmly settled, the Liberals would not only have been in a position to form a strong government in the Nineties but, far more important, would have been able to crush the efforts of the new Labour party to get a foothold at Westminster. By 1906, when victory came at last, it was too late: Labour was already fifty-strong in the Commons, and was rapidly loosening the Liberal hold on the industrial grassroots. The elimination of the Liberals as the major alternative to the Tories was only a matter of time. Rosebery thus played a considerable, if indirect, role in the rise of the Labour Party. How he would have hated the thought!

—1 March 1963

The Key to Palmerston

IF POLITICAL SUCCESS be judged by sustained mastery of the system, there is no one to beat Lord Palmerston. He sat for fifty-eight years in the House of Commons, all but three of them on the front benches. Three-quarters of his political life was spent in office. He died as Prime Minister, an open dispatch box by his side, a half-finished letter before him. Between 1832 and 1955 a party in office increased its majority on only two occasions: on both Palmerston was its leader.

None of this was achieved by easy words and political pliancy. Palmerston was incapable of dissimulation, reticence or tact; as he said, he disliked 'a low submissive tone'; or, as Bulwer put it, 'he lacked the organ of veneration'. Among the public at large, he was the most loved of all politicians; among his colleagues, the most disliked – though for widely different reasons. Disraeli and Derby hated him because he kept them out of office. Russell was jealous, Cobden and Bright resented his adventurism abroad and his contempt for Manchester economics at home. Gladstone deplored his morals and his belief in large armaments. Aberdeen feared his bellicosity. The Queen and Albert whined because he was not prepared to recognize the monarchs' trade union (or, for that matter, any other). Palmerston got the better of all of them.

In his new study (*The Most English Minister*. By Donald Southgate. Macmillan. 63*s*.), Dr Southgate describes him as 'not a great man' but 'a prominent and important man'. I find this an odd verdict, though not so odd after reading Dr Southgate's book. What we needed, I should have thought, was a full-scale biography of Palmerston based upon the immense collection of papers now available. What we have been given is a long and worthy account of Palmerston's foreign policy, based mainly on printed sources. The man himself is hardly allowed to emerge from the thickets of long-forgotten international disputes with which the author surrounds him. There is nothing about his early years, very little about his domestic policies and only a few tantalising glimpses of his rich and profane private life.

Yet surely Palmerston was one of the most interesting and consistent of our national folk-heroes. It is true, as Bagehot said, that 'he was a statesman for the moment. Whatever was not wanted now, whatever was not practicable now, whatever would not take now, he quite drove out of his mind' (words which apply with equal justice to our present Prime Minister). This, indeed, explains his extraordinary public appeal, in an age when the absence of modern mass-communications made it difficult for a politician to project his personality. But it is not the whole explanation. What ordinary voters require from a statesman are a few big, simple ideas which appeal to their sense of justice and common sagacity. These Palmerston provided. He was in no sense an intellectual. But he had a vision of the world which was clearly thought out, coherent, consistent with the realities of his age, and communicable in plain language. We may dislike it, as did many of his abler contemporaries: but it is there, four-square and solid.

Palmerston, to put it briefly, was a constitutionalist. Nations, he argued, were best-regulated, and property most secure, under a definite set of rules – whether laid down by tradition or statute – which placed everyone under the law and made arbitrary acts of government illegal. If large property-owning classes were excluded from the framing of such rules, they would ultimately exert their power by violence; reform would be pre-empted by revolution. This was why he regarded the Reform Bill of 1832 as necessary, even if undesirable.

> 'Those who seek to check improvements, to cherish abuses, to crush opinions, and to prohibit the human race from thinking, will find their weapon snap short in the hand, when most they need its protection.'

This principle, he felt, should be applied abroad, as well as at home. The promotion of constitutional governments in Europe was in Britain's interests, as well as that of the European peoples: 'I consider the constitutional states to be the natural allies of this country.' In reply to those who argued that constitutional government did not fit all states, he retorted flatly: 'Her Majesty's Government do not happen to recollect any Country in which a Constitutional system of Government has been established that has not on the whole been better off in consequence.' Anyway, he added, adumbrating the sensible principle adopted by Britain since 1945, 'if any nation should be found not fit for constitutional government, the best way to fit such a nation for it would be to give it to them.'

Fine progressive sentiments. But of course their application involved constant interference in the Continental scene, a strong navy, and an aggressive tone adopted towards governments which showed indifference or hostility towards Palmerston's plans for their improvement. In some cases, his liberal instincts degenerated into sheer braggadocio – as with Don Pacifico. In others (the Opium War is the most notorious instance), it is impossible to defend Palmerston's handling of events, least of all on the basis of his own principles. He often indulged in inflated language. 'The sun never sets on the interests of this country.' 'Diplomats and protocols are very good things, but there are no better peacekeepers than well-appointed three-deckers.' (It is interesting to note that Palmerston coined the phraseology both of Edwardian imperialism at its most vulgar and of Harold Wilson's 'peacekeeping' at its most sly.)

But to his critics Palmerston would reply vigorously. 'The real policy of England is to be the champion of justice and right.' If British interference were to be ruled out, how, for instance, was the slave trade to be crushed?

> 'During the many years that I was at the Foreign Office, there was no subject that more constantly or more intensely occupied my thoughts, or constituted the aim of my labours; and though I may boast of having succeeded in accomplishing many good works . . . yet the achievement I look back to with the greatest and the purest pleasure was the forcing the Brazilians to give up their slave trade.'

It can further be argued in Palmerston's defence that he set his face firmly against colonialism. The fact that a territory would be better governed under British rule, he argued, was not a case for its acquisition. To partition Africa would be as disgraceful as the partition of Poland. We want to trade with Egypt, he said, and travel there, but not to govern it. 'Let us try to improve all these countries by the general influence of our commerce, but let us all abstain from a crusade of conquest.' It is arguable, of course, that had Palmerston survived into the heady imperialist climate of the last quarter of the century, he would have surrendered to the popular mood. But this is pure conjecture: there is nothing in his speeches and dispatches to justify any such assumption. He was quite capable of resisting public clamour when he felt that to do so was in the general interest. The only two serious political defeats of his life, in 1851 and 1858, occurred because he felt it right to take an anti-jingo line.

Where Palmerston is more vulnerable to attack is in his domestic conservatism. He regarded the 1832 settlement, in conjunction with the reforms of the 1830s and 1840s, as final – and 1848, when Britain alone stood firm amid the European chaos, as its vindication. In 1859 he presided over the inauguration of the great Liberal Party; but he was opposed to virtually all its aims. The thrusting and energetic Gladstone, itching to get his reforming hands on the anomalies and abuses he saw everywhere, found him an implacable, if increasingly feeble, opponent; the two conducted an epistolary battle rich in comedy and misunderstandings. At the end of Palmerston's life, the young Goschen had a conversation with the P.M.:

> ' "What is to be done about domestic affairs and legislation?" "Oh," he gaily replied, rubbing his hands with an air of comfortable satisfaction, "there is really nothing to be done. We cannot go on adding to the statute book *ad infinitum*. Perhaps we may have a little law reform, or bankruptcy reform; but we cannot go on legislating for ever." '

During the last five years of his life, the political world, and not least his own colleagues, waited impatiently for his departure. There was no question of pushing him; nature must take its course; but this nature seemed reluctant to do. Palmerston had led a full and raffish life, as well as working harder than any politician of his period; what his younger colleagues resented particularly was that he showed no signs of it. They could sneer – 'a retired old croupier from Baden' (Granville), 'a great bundle of sticks' (Clarendon). But the old man defied them. In his 80th year he was cited as a co-respondent in a divorce case. A year later, after lunch on a cold November Sunday, he pulled a ferry-boat across a stream, took a two-hour walk and fell over a tree-stump in the dusk. He dined prodigiously, as Speaker Denison records:

> 'he ate two plates of turtle soup; he was then served very amply to cod and oyster sauce; he then took a paté; afterwards he was helped to two very greasy-looking entrées; he then dispatched a

> plate of roast mutton (two slices) . . . there then appeared before him the largest, and to my mind the hardest, slice of ham that ever figured on the table of a nobleman, yet it disappeared just in time to answer the inquiry of the butler, "Snipe or pheasant, my lord?" He instantly replied "Pheasant".'

Despite gout and deafness, even his wit survived to the last. When Queen Victoria accompanied him on an inspection of the volunteers in Hyde Park, and complained of the men's body odours, he said that that was what was meant by *esprit de corps*. It's not difficult to understand the Churchillian breadth of his appeal. Nothing of what he stood for now survives, happily, no doubt; but the man himself still lives, dyed whiskers and all, and awaits the hand of a great biographer.

—4 February 1962

A Very Bad Man?

WHAT CAN BE DONE for poor John Wilson Croker? Few politicians and men of letters have had such a bad press. He was pilloried by Disraeli as 'Rigby' in *Coningsby,* and by Lady Morgan as 'Conway Crawley' in *Florence Macarthy*. *Fraser's Magazine* called him 'a critic of the most acrimonious and venemous malignity'. 'He was a bigoted Tory,' wrote Edmund Yates, 'a violent partisan and a most malevolent and unscrupulous critic.' 'A bad, a very bad man,' said Macaulay, 'a scandal to politics and to letters.' He was, wrote one obituarist,

> 'a man who would go a hundred miles through sleet and snow, in a December night, to search a parish register, for the sake of showing that a man was illegitimate, or a woman older than she said she was.'

In 1884, nearly thirty years after his death, his old publishers, Murray, tried to rehabilitate him by issuing three volumes of his letters and papers, edited by Louis J. Jennings. These proved of exceptional historical and literary interest, but left Croker where he was: an unattractive and slightly sinister man. In 1940 an American scholar, Myron F. Brightfield, went back to the original documents and produced a full-length defensive biography, which convincingly refutes the worst calumnies against Croker. Now Mr Bernard Pool has condensed the 1,200 pages of the letters and papers to 270 (*The Croker Papers 1808-1857*. Edited by Bernard Pool. Batsford. 50*s*.), and supplied them with a new and kindly introduction. How does this leave old Croker?

He was a politician of some importance. He invented, or at least popularized, the term Conservative. A junior minister at the Admiralty, he was one of the best debaters on the Tory side for over twenty years. He was a friend of Lowther and Hertford, the two biggest borough-owners. For thirty years he was Peel's closest political adviser. In the *Quarterly Review,* he was chief Tory journalistic spokesman for forty years. He privately admitted in 1829:

> 'I have heretofore conveyed to the public articles written by Prime and Cabinet Ministers, and sometimes have composed such articles under their eyes – they supplied the fact and I supplied the tact, and between us we used to produce a considerable effect.'

Such work had to be done 'in the most profound secrecy', the art being 'to throw in, here and there, such a slight mixture of error or apparent ignorance, as should obviate suspicion of its coming from so high a source'. But though the Tories found him useful, he did not get to the top. His ambition never recovered from the death of his only child, a son, in 1820. At his insistence, the party bosses made him a P.C.; but he got neither peerage nor seat in the cabinet. He declined to re-enter the House of Commons when the Reform Bill, which he hated, became law.

Mr Pool's selection is a reasonable one and reveals Croker as a highly entertaining and well-informed gossip. But some of the most remarkable papers are omitted and others truncated. Why is there no reference to the part Croker played in securing the Elgin Marbles? Why is his splendid letter to Robinson, Chancellor of the Exchequer, in which he secured the release of Theodore Hook from prison, left out altogether? His communications with Canning over pocket boroughs – which rightly figure in the *English Historical Documents,* XI, 1783-1832 – are given only in part, and the statistical schedule dropped. Mr Pool's introduction tells us little new about Croker and, in particular, fails to reveal why so many of his contemporaries found him repulsive.

Though not of Irish origin, Croker was born and educated there, spoke with an Irish accent and had some of the less agreeable traits of Dublin littérateurs – critical malice and a taste for attacking friends under a cloak of anonymity. Anonymity was the curse of early 19th-century journalism. In Croker's case, we know exactly what he wrote from the records kept by his publishers; but his contemporaries did not. Anonymity is a two-edged sword. Croker undoubtedly helped to make the *Quarterly* notorious for venomous reviewing. In particular he specialized in what the magazine called 'Fools' – short, dismissive pieces, ridiculing bad books, which were inserted as light relief to the more solemn critical articles. 'Pray help me to a fool,' he wrote to the editor, 'and I will return him to you roasted, broiled, fricassied or devilled, as you may please.' But the result was that the nastier pieces in the review were invariably attributed to Croker, often unjustly. Harriet Martineau, for instance, pursued a vendetta against him even after his death on the strength of two reviews of her books; Croker wrote neither.

His two bitterest enemies were Disraeli and Macaulay. Disraeli savaged him in fiction, rebuffed his attempts at a reconciliation and was responsible for one of the worst of his obituaries. Why? Mr Pool supplies no explanation. But the reasons seem fairly plain. Disraeli's shifty dealings with Murray, the publisher, were known to Croker, who prevented him from getting a toehold on the *Quarterly,* and indeed actually kept his name out of the review until 1848, although Disraeli had then been the most talked-about politician in the country for several years. It must have been irritating, too, for Disraeli to see Croker described, in the *Chronicle*, as the author of *Vivian Grey*. Most important, however, was Disraeli's belief (surely unfounded) that only Croker's opposition prevented Peel from responding to his plea for office in 1841. Hence the venom with which he portrayed 'Rigby' two years later.

As the leading lights of the *Quarterly* and the *Edinburgh*, Croker and Macaulay were clearly cast as antagonists. But they also clashed repeatedly in the Reform Bill debates, with Croker, on the whole, getting the best of it. Macaulay hated 'that impudent, leering Croker'. 'I detest him more than cold boiled veal,' he wrote. 'See whether I do not dust that varlet's jacket for him in the next number of the Blue and Yellow' (the *Edinburgh*). By this he meant his celebrated review of Croker's edition of Boswell. Perhaps the most entertaining, unfair and childish thing Macaulay wrote, it failed to 'smash' (his phrase) the book, which sold 50,000 copies and remained the standard edition for many years; but it kept the fires of hatred blazing until and beyond Croker's death.

Croker's saddest quarrel was with Peel, his intimate friend. Some estrangement over the repeal of the Corn Laws was inevitable; like most Tories, Croker saw it as a betrayal. Afterwards Croker wrote a letter ('My dear Peel') attempting a reconciliation, but received a chilly ('Sir') and dismissive reply. Mr Pool thinks Peel behaved 'rather unreasonably' in objecting to Croker's attack on him in the *Quarterly*, which explicitly acquitted the fallen leader of personal dishonesty. But Greville, for instance, judged it to be written 'with all the malignity and virulence of ungovernable hatred', and 'revolting from its coarse and savage language'. This was Wellington's view, too; he had strongly urged Croker to couch it 'in terms of decency and moderation', and had begged in vain to see it before publication. In view of their past friendship, which had been much warmer on his side, it was absurd for Croker to suppose Peel would forgive him.

Croker was a handsome man with a ready smile (Macaulay called it 'a leer of hatred'), tremendous anecdotes but an overbearing style of conversation: Wellington accused him of 'talking down' Scott and other notables. His bitter jests were relished but a fellow diner had an uneasy, often well-justified, belief that they would be launched in his direction the moment he left the room. But a 'very bad man'? Macaulay based this judgement on Croker's relations with the Marquess of Hertford, the rich voluptuary who figures in *Vanity Fair* and *Coningsby*. For many years Croker acted as his factotum, managing his boroughs and estates. The job was unpaid, but there was a clear understanding that Croker would get a large legacy. Unfortunately, Hertford became mentally unbalanced; he not only began to add a maze of codicils to his will but surrounded himself with a crowd of prostitutes and shady retainers. Croker had to keep up the connection, partly out of past regard but also because otherwise he risked being struck out of the will altogether. In the end he got £21,000, much less than he expected, and was further entangled in a sensational lawsuit with Suisse, the Marquess's rascally valet, who had absconded with much of the money. From the trial an unseemly picture of Croker emerged: willing to dine in private with Hertford's whores, but not to be publicly seen in a carriage with them. Jennings's edition of the papers gave little about Croker's relation with Hertford and one naturally assumed some process of suppression had taken place; but Brightfield, who went over the originals again, found nothing really discreditable – certainly nothing to justify Macaulay's censures. From the historian's viewpoint, much the best thing would be a completely new edition of the papers, re-transcribed from the manuscripts. Meanwhile, Mr Pool's volume, beautifully produced and printed, whets our appetite for more.

—14 April 1967

Aubrey's Brief Life

BEARDSLEY WAS A CHILD of the 1890s who might equally well have been a giant of the 1960s. From his drawings peep out the trendy faces of our age: a Deneuve, a Bardot, a Jackie Kennedy, a Nureyev, an Eartha Kitt. The brilliant exhibition at the Victoria and Albert last year was thus well-timed, and it's a pity that the spate of books it provoked does not include an authoritative edition. (*The Early Work of Aubrey Beardsley: The Later Work of Aubrey Beardsley*. Cass. 5 gns each; *The Best of Beardsley*. Edited by R. A. Walker. Spring Books. 25*s*.; *Aubrey Beardsley*. Tavernor Reproductions. 25*s*.; *Aubrey Beardsley's Erotic Universe*. Edited by Derek Sandford. Four Square. 9*s*. 6*d*.; *Aubrey Beardsley*. By Brien Reade. Victoria and Albert Museum and H.M.S.O. 8*s*. 6*d*.; *Catalogue*. By Brian Reade and Frank Dickinson. Victoria and Albert Museum. 7*s*.) The most comprehensive, with 331 plates, is merely an improved reissue of the *Early and Later Works*, first published at the turn of the century; it lacks critical and explanatory captions and is heavily bowdlerised. One drawing, the *Return of Tannhaüser*, is reversed, the famous self-portrait, *A Footnote*, is printed in the mutilated version, and *Lysistrata Haranguing the Athenian Women* is censored. R. A. Walker's volume, first issued in 1948, is more liberal: it includes the original versions of two *Salome* drawings, one hitherto suppressed, and the other bowdlerised, and the original *A Footnote*. The *Lysistrata Haranguing* is printed uncensored in the Tavernor Reproductions volume, in the V.&A.'s pamphlet by Brian Reade, and in Four Square's *Erotic Universe* (which includes another *Lysistrata* drawing). Unfortunately, the muddle over standards is not confined to erotic drawings. The *Flosshilde* from the *Das Rheingold* series is reversed in either the Walker edition or the *Later Works* – but which? The chief contribution to Beardsley studies the revival has produced is the V.&A. catalogue by Brian Reade and Frank Dickinson which, despite many misprints, contains much new and accurate information. We must hope that Mr Reade's new 500-plate edition – including all the *Lysistrata* set – which Studio Vista will publish in October, clears up all the mysteries and finally does Beardsley justice.

Of course, much of the confusion which surrounds him was inseparable from his methods of work. Many of his drawings were too 'free' for the Nineties and were issued privately. Others were censored by the publisher, or re-drawn by the artist himself, to meet objections. Some publishers found obscenities where none existed. But for this Beardsley himself was partly to blame: he had a sly habit, as Derek Sandford shows, of inserting erotic references which remained undetected until after publication. To complicate matters still further, forgeries, some obscene, were issued after his death.

By contrast, the facts about his life are simple. He was born in 1872, the child of a *mésalliance*. His father's family were goldsmiths, his mother's army-surgeons, related to the Pitts. His father was a failure, his mother dominant and artistic; his sister Mabel was also a strong character. His education, at Brighton Grammar School, was conventionally middle-class, and he then worked for a surveyor and an insurance company; he was already suffering from tuberculosis. In 1891 he showed his drawings to Burne-Jones, who encouraged him to turn professional. He got his first big contract the next year, from John Dent, to illustrate Malory's *Morte d'Arthur*; worked for the *Studio* (1893), illustrated Wilde's *Salome* (1894) and, the same year, was made art editor of the new *Yellow Book*, published by John Lane. After Wilde's conviction in 1895, Lane fired him, and he fell into the hands of a disreputable solicitor and publisher of erotica, Leonard Smithers. Smithers created *The Savoy*, as a rival to the *Yellow Book*, and gave Beardsley continuous employment, though paying him unevenly. But by 1896 the artist's health was already deteriorating fast: in search of sunshine, he moved to Brussels, Bournemouth, Dieppe, Paris and finally Menton, where he died in 1898, aged twenty-five. His professional career lasted only five years.

Beardsley's life was sad enough, in all conscience; and he was dogged by bad luck. His disastrous connection with Wilde was never close; he liked him at their first meeting but soon came to regard him as an unpleasant and absurd figure: indeed he ridiculed Wilde in his *Salome* illustrations. Wilde was never asked to contribute to the *Yellow Book*, which he viewed with hostility. (He described the first issue to Alfred Douglas as 'dull and loathsome: a great failure – I am so glad'.) But when Wilde was arrested he had a French novel, with a yellow cover, under his arm. The Press turned this into the *Yellow Book*, and a mob smashed the windows of John Lane's premises in Vigo Street. Worse still, some of Lane's authors panicked. At the suggestion of Mrs Humphry Ward, they ganged up and deputed William Watson to send a cable to Lane, then in America, which read: WITHDRAW ALL BEARDSLEY DESIGNS OR I WITHDRAW ALL MY BOOKS WATSON. Nothing is more preposterous than a group of second-rate literary people combining together to issue ultimata, (usually, as in this case, on the basis of misinformation). Yet Lane surrendered and Beardsley was out. The latter, not surprisingly, felt that Wilde had brought him nothing but ruin; and this, rather than his conversion to Catholicism, accounts for his own letter to Smithers, two years later, agreeing to edit a proposed new journal provided it were 'quite agreed that Oscar Wilde contributes nothing to the magazine, anonymously, pseudonymously or otherwise'.

Beardsley's other troubles sprang from the nature of his medium and the exigencies of his health. He was a conscientious craftsman, forced to battle continuously against the line-engraving of the Nineties and the carelessness of block-makers. As his TB drove him further from London, his professional agony increased, as his letters to Smithers show.

> 'The distance between London and Bournemouth is driving me crazy . . . Size of page & sort of paper & such questions are beginning to worry me dreadfully.' (1896.)
>
> '*Implore* them to make a careful block. There is by the way some *Chinese white* on the drawing so let it not be touched with india Rubber.' (1897.)
>
> 'Please implore & conjure the blockist to treat them with the utmost care as the least touch will make a smudge, & the least smudge will spoil the picture.' (1898.)

Yet in some respects Beardsley was fortunate. His first big commission, from Dent, obliged him to produce 360 drawings in less than a year. The pressure of work forced him to abandon the prevailing fussiness of detail, to break away from contemporary influences and to develop a bold black-and-white style that was entirely original. This accelerated a process which would have taken place in any case. Beardsley had a fine mind and was well-read. Like Picasso (whom he influenced) he extracted ideas from a mass of influences – Kate Greenaway, Burne-Jones, Lautrec, Mantegna, Wagner, architecture, French and classical literature, Dürer, to mention only a few – without at any point permitting his art to become derivative. What astonishes, again like Picasso, is the speed and relentlessness with which successive phases in his development took place. This may be partly due, paradoxically, to his physical condition: with the onset of each summer, his lungs improved and he had an access of energy and confidence, expressed in an eagerness to embark on experiment: the five major episodes in his work can be correlated in this way. At all times, however, when his health allowed it, he subjected himself to the most rigorous professional discipline. This accounts not only for his prodigious output but for his concentration on the field where he knew he was absolute master. Like Jane Austen, he had a precise estimate of what he could, and could not, do. Beneath the frail exterior of the aesthete ridiculed in *Punch* was a will of iron and a ferocious intellectual self-discipline.

Even so, his art might not have succeeded without a powerful sexual dynamic. He was not, as Roger Fry put it, 'The Fra Angelico of Satanism'; he was too clear-headed to be taken in by the mumbo-jumbo of the Nineties. But he was plainly interested in sex to a quite unusual degree, fascinated by women's breasts of all shapes and dimensions, by buttocks large and small and, above all, by sexual symbols. He was capable of seeing a phallic presence even in a recently-extracted tooth; hermaphrodites, flagellation and, above all, bestiality intrigued him. His health deprived him of a normal sexual life, but according to Rothenstein did not eliminate it altogether. He was surely not a homosexual, as many contemporaries supposed. Both his work and his own circumstances suggest that his primary sexual concern was with masterful women – not surprising in a semi-invalid whose life revolved around his mother and sister. According to Reade and Dickinson, there is 'some probability of intimacy between Mabel and Aubrey Beardsley in earlier years' but no evidence that an alleged son of Aubrey's, known as 'Mr Watkins', was by his sister. In any event it is clear that most of his sexual energy went into his work and enormously enriched it.

Beardsley was such a considerable artist, his work so clearly capable of development, that his early death was a universal, as well as a personal, tragedy. He died on the eve of an artistic revolution in which he would surely have been a major participant and influence. All the same, it is interesting to speculate whether even his will-power and self-discipline would have been proof against the pressures to which the 20th century subjects an artist of such exploitable talents. Imagine him alive today! His gift for inventing wholly new trends in women's fashions, theatrical costumes and sets, furniture, interior decoration, book and magazine covers – every conceivable variety of applied art – together with his modish obsession with sex, a face and personality ideally suited to television, and a line in conversation tailored to a society exploring the frontiers of the permissible, would have made him a commercial property as valuable as Picasso and the Beatles put together. The prospect fills one with a certain distaste. Better to be labelled the Fra Angelico of Satanism than to become the Michelangelo of the Miniskirt, the Botticelli of B.B.C.-2.

—4 August 1967

The Sound and the Fury

THOUGH MANY HAVE TRIED, no one has succeeded in writing a satisfactory biography of Lloyd George. Perhaps this is inevitable. It is impossible to analyze his political philosophy because any theory built up on his words and actions is invalidated by episodes in his life which cannot be reconciled to the theme. A Welsh democrat; a Liberal; a non-party radical; an anti-party man of the Centre; a natural progressive corrupted by power and money; a pure opportunist from start to finish; a simple patriot – you can begin to assemble the evidence to prove any one of these propositions, but bits of it obstinately refuse to fit, and the result is invariably a ragged and confusing mosaic, defying any system of logic or consistency. It would be monstrously unjust to dismiss him as a bad man; impossible by any accepted standards of morality to call him a good man. He was a great man; but not an admirable man. He changed history, yet his career ended in futility and failure. He was very human, yet at times superhuman, at others inhuman. It was as though an obscure by-election in a Welsh borough in 1890 took the stopper from a magic bottle and unleashed a genie whose marvellous powers acted on the political scene for good and evil; thirty-two years later, in 1922, the genie was somehow got back into his bottle and the whole stoppered up; he hissed and fretted inside but never got out again. A tragic waste of potency, or a merciful deliverance, or both?

Keynes, who observed him closely at his apogee – it was, characteristically, a frustrated apogee – during the Versailles peace conference, described him in his *Essays in Biography*:

> 'Lloyd George is rooted in nothing; he is void and without content; he lives and feeds on his immediate surroundings; he is an instrument and player at the same time which plays on the company and is played on by them too; he is a prism, as I have

heard him described, which collects light and distorts it and is most brilliant if the light comes from many quarters at once; a vampire and a medium in one.'

This is true enough as far as it goes, but it is really a clever way of evading the issue: Keynes is merely putting, in more sophisticated language, the vulgar proposition that Lloyd George was 'a Welsh wizard'. So he was, no doubt; but he was also a practical politician and man of action who changed the society of his time, and a more prosaic judgement is called for.

Lloyd George came into politics as a solicitor, the easiest channel by which a member of the dispossessed Welsh nation could enter national life. He was an underdog who spoke for the underdogs on the two issues which dominated Welsh public consciousness – the secular revolt against the squirearchy and the religious revolt against the Anglican establishment. The second issue, in particular, was the dominant theme of the first phase of his political life, and expressed itself not only in the cause of Welsh Disestablishment but in the opposition to Balfour's Education Act of 1902, which first secured Lloyd George's claim to cabinet office. But he was a Welsh nonconformist rather than a Christian. His favourite book was not the Bible but Hugo's *Les Misérables*, which he read and re-read and carried around with him throughout his life. Though he knew the Bible well, he regarded it not as divine revelation but as a social and political tract: '. . . the most democratic book in the world. Its heroes are David the Shepherd and Jesus the Carpenter. Indeed it is extraordinary that respectable people can tolerate it: its terrible condemnation of oppression and riches, its magnification of poverty.' Lloyd George enjoyed hearing sermons, of which he was a connoisseur, and singing hymns. He was interested in para-religious causes, such as the limitation of the drink-trade. But there is no evidence that religion played any role in his private life, or public actions, and he could equally well be described as a pantheist or a pagan or an agnostic or a hedonist. He could and did lecture ardently on the virtues of the Bible as an instrument of moral, social and literary training, and insist on its central position in any school curriculum. But he had few scruples and no settled moral convictions. His sexual life may not have been so lurid as his eldest son has described it; but it was consistently promiscuous, and on several occasions brought him near to public disaster. He was not a crook; but on money matters he skated on some pretty thin ice. It is hard to prove he lied; but he seldom told the whole, unvarnished truth: the truth to him was a matter of imaginative creation. As Haldane put it, 'Lloyd George uses statistics like adjectives' – a saying which delighted L.G.

Much closer to Lloyd George's heart was the first of the two political impulses: the hatred of the landowning aristocracy which was the corollary of the Welsh peasant's passionate attachment to the land. If there is one theme which runs through his life it is the belief that the widest possible spread of land-ownership was essential to true democracy and the key to the full utilization of the nation's greatest natural resource. He was the born leader of a peasant's revolt, and the land-owning duke held the place of honour in his demonology. His 1909 budget was the collective work of the Liberal cabinet, and L.G. the mere instrument of its presentation; but it is no accident that he contrived to make the comparatively minor issue of the new land taxes the chief battleground, and so precipitated the conflict with the House of Lords; no accident, either, that he tempted the dukes to join the debate in person. Lloyd George was at his best and most effective when he could invest political controversy with the simple shape and strong moral contrasts of a fairy-tale: the dukes on the one side, the landless on the other was the kind of equation he needed. There is a photograph, rich in irony, taken in 1921, when L.G. was Prime Minister: he sits, bolt upright, and triumphant, on a Highland pony, which a duke is humbly leading by a halter. Lloyd George never forgave the aristocracy and was uniquely impervious to its blandishments. He exploited the honours system, perhaps with relish, more probably with scornful indifference. It was a pleasure to him to ennoble a brilliant pirate like F. E. Smith or to humiliate a pretentious grandee like Curzon. He never became a member of the establishment, never joined the ranks of the right-thinking. He acquired, to be sure, an immensely valuable property at Churt, but it was a matter of accumulation rather than outright purchase, a vast smallholding rather than an estate. L.G. worked it himself, for he usually quarrelled with his hirelings; he sniffed and handled and boasted about its produce with the intimacy of a peasant.

It is impossible to read his speeches during the heyday of the Asquith government without believing his passion for social reform to be genuine. Admittedly, in laying the foundations of the welfare state, he was merely executing plans conceived collectively by a whole generation of experts from Sir Robert Morant to the Webbs, but the way in which he breathed life and fire into their dusty schemes reflected an instinctive hatred for injustice as well as a rational conviction that the wit of man could devise remedies. He was not a socialist for he did not believe that a universal panacea could be applied on a practical basis from theoretical principles. But he never doubted the ability and duty of government to alter the harsh economic rules of life. In this sense he could not properly be called a Liberal; and no one, except his most partisan Liberal critics, ever dared to call him a Conservative. All the same, he would not admit the right of an organized section of society, be it the landed interest or labour, to dictate to government for its own exclusive purposes. As Prime Minister he fought the trades unions with tenacity, occasionally with cynicism, sometimes even with cruelty. He did not equate the trades unionist with the poor or the underdog. Yet his final split with the Asquithians came over his refusal to condemn the General Strike; and he never accepted widespread unemployment as a necessary evil of economic life. If he was a Liberal in any sense, it was as a Liberal-Radical of the Chamberlain variety of the early 1880s. His economic philosophy, in so far as he had one, was optimistic, expansionist, pragmatic: he would have strongly approved of Harold Wilson's aims and have been equally contemptuous of his methods.

Lloyd George was never a nationalist in the narrow sense; not even a Welsh nationalist at the outset of his career. But it is almost impossible to categorize his view of the world. You might argue that he had a strong and permanent regard for the rights of small nations: he showed immense courage in upholding the cause of the Boers, the violation of Belgian neutrality was the decisive factor in persuading him that British intervention in the world war was inevitable, he sacrificed his government and his career on the altar of Greek irredentism. But it is an inconvenient fact that the British Empire reached its widest extent when he was Prime Minister, and that he upheld its ostensible interests with vigour and enthusiasm. Certainly he was the chief architect of the Irish settlement of 1921, achieving something which had defied the best efforts of Gladstone and Asquith. But this was only after he had applied coercion for two years in the most pitiless manner; only after the scandal of the Black and Tans, whom he had shamelessly defended, had become unendurable even to his most hardened Tory supporters; and only after the policy of suppression had manifestly failed. The Lloyd George who defied the blood-crazed jingos at Birmingham Town

Hall in 1900 could, in the context of 1920, sneer at his humanitarian critics as 'Bolshevists and Sinn Féiners and faddists and cranks of all sorts'. He was sneering at his younger self.

Nor is it possible to impose a coherent pattern on Lloyd George's handling of international affairs, though this is by no means entirely his fault. True, he was not above making unscrupulous use of such catch-phrases as 'Hang the Kaiser', and for a time at least in 1918 he gave the public the impression that he wished to impose a 'Carthaginian Peace' on Germany. But the evidence now available suggests that he realized an immoderate settlement could not provide a lasting foundation for European tranquility. Both during the Peace Conference and after he did his best to restrain France. But he was caught between the two millstones of Wilson and Clemenceau – the one a self-righteous and impractical idealist, who lacked knowledge and experience of European affairs and a reliable political base at home, the other a cynical realist obsessed by the need to obtain security at whatever cost for his battered and vengeful nation. Lloyd George had to settle for a patchwork compromise, an uneasy blend of jungle law and modern internationalism, which raised more problems than it solved, which was only signed by Germany under duress, and which rapidly proved inoperable. Lloyd George's subsequent attempts to prevent France from enforcing the penal provisions brought French hostility without winning German friendship. All one can say is that his successors did no better, and in some respects very much worse.

Indeed it can be argued that Lloyd George had more than his share of bad luck, and that his failures were due not so much to the instability of his judgement – though that was a factor – as to the times in which he lived and the inadequacy of the men with whom he had to work. It is a pity, in a way, that the six volumes of his *War Memoirs* are widely regarded as unreadable, and in any case unread. Though uninspired in style, and beyond doubt the presentation of a personal case, they tell us much more about the nature of the Great War than Churchill's more celebrated and polished *World Crisis*. Even Lloyd George's bitterest critics were prepared to admit that he possessed unrivalled powers of energy and organisation and the ability to drive straight to the heart of a problem. The war saw these qualities used to the utmost. The tragedy is that supreme power came to him too late, when two years of unstinted effort had been largely wasted and many irreparable errors made. Lloyd George is categorized as an 'Eastern' strategist, and it is difficult to argue convincingly that his attempts to divert Allied resources to a Balkan front were well-judged. But what is now forgotten is that Lloyd George had long urged that to devote resources – particularly in heavy guns and munitions – to the Russian front would bring quite disproportionate results. His advice went unheeded and by the time he became Prime Minister a Russian collapse was inevitable. Indeed he was unable to influence the strategy of 1917, which had already been largely determined under Asquith, and the first results of his stupendous reorganization of the British war machine were not felt until the following year. These, indeed, ensured that Britain was able to continue to carry the strains of war throughout 1918; and the failure to make similar efforts on the German side led to the collapse of domestic morale which precipitated the German surrender. In that sense Lloyd George was the architect of victory. But it was a victory from which Britain emerged in so exhausted a state as to be unable to reap the fruits of peace either at home or abroad. The failures of the Versailles settlement and the failure of his personal bid to make Britain 'a land fit for heroes' stemmed in great part from the delay in giving Lloyd George the mandate to fight the war on his terms. Had he been able to replace Asquith when the inadequacy of the war-direction first became obvious, early in 1915, the story might have been very different. And the peace would have been dictated from a position of strength rather than fear and weakness, and safeguarded by two powers with the resources and morale to sustain the burden of European peacekeeping. As it was, the Europe of the inter-war years had to be policed by the walking wounded, under the aegis of the League of Nations, which Lloyd George brutally but not altogether unfairly described as 'a wheezing harmonium'.

Lloyd George's tragedy was that he never possessed the permanent party base from which to deploy his extraordinary abilities. His upbringing and background made him a Liberal but he was never at home in the party. He could not have been at home in any party. A party must rest on either dogma or tradition and Lloyd George had no time for either. There is a role to be played by a non-party man in British politics but it is a marginal one. Only the accident of war gave Lloyd George a chance to hold the centre of the stage, and when the war was over it was inevitable that the party spirit should reassert itself. Lloyd George was powerful enough to wreck the Liberal Party but incapable of leading it in unity. Perhaps he sensed this instinctively many years before, for in

August 1910 he produced, out of the blue, a scheme for a coalition government which would unite all the talents behind a vast scheme of social and industrial regeneration. It appealed strongly to other non-party figures like F. E. Smith and Churchill but was smilingly brushed aside by Asquith and Balfour. Lloyd George put it into operation in wartime and tried hard to prolong the coalition spirit into the peace; indeed he and his abler colleagues entertained lingering hopes of a great Centre Party until well into the Twenties; but the habits of British parliamentary democracy could not be broken. Lloyd George kept up his courage for many years in opposition. He prepared and published vast schemes for economic reforms which glittered with original ideas and radiated his own energy and optimism. He never got the chance to apply any of them. Power remained firmly in the hands of the party system and of the supine or vacuous leaders it threw up. The last two decades of Lloyd George's life are a sickening tale of hopes deferred, of matchless abilities gone to waste, and of the progressive degeneration of character and judgement which frustrated exile brings. The sound and the fury gradually died and were seen to signify nothing. Like an ex-heavyweight champ, Lloyd George never made a comeback, and in time the mental muscles went slack. No political talent in British history has been so prodigally squandered by a blind and unimaginative nation.

—19 September 1969

Part 6

BAD NEWS FROM ABROAD

Murder in Caracas

IF I WISHED to have Mr Harold Macmillan assassinated, I should have very little difficulty recruiting a team of experts in the Caribbean – for a consideration. A sum of from £50,000 to £100,000 (preferably payable in gold) would secure me, in any one of half-a-dozen cities, such as Ciudad Trujillo, Port au Prince, Havana, Caracas, or even Miami, a posse of practical assassins, competent to work with pistol, telescopic rifle, machine-gun or high explosive. There is at this moment in Venezuela, for instance, a senior dynamite expert who worked under Peron, and at least three professional small-arms killers. There are dozens of ex-SS officers, two or three members of Mussolini's bodyguard, ex-suicide pilots from Japan, survivors from the Vichy *milice*, and even, it is said, some officers from the Rumanian Iron Guard, at various Caribbean cities.

I gained my small insight into the mechanics of Caribbean assassination during a recent visit to Caracas, when I saw them in action. The incident is worth recounting in some detail, for it also tells us something about Caribbean politics, too. Broadly speaking, politics in this area is the pursuit of money. The object of a political team is to win power, by whatever means are available, in order not only to get its cut out of the state funds, but to avail itself of the *douceurs* which the labyrinthine bureaucracy of Latin-America makes inevitable. As the second largest producer, and largest exporter, of oil in the world, with a budget running near the £1,000 million mark, Venezuela is indeed a prize worth having.

Moreover Venezuela has a history of political violence unique even in South America. Bolivar, who liberated it only to die in poverty, remarked bitterly: 'For these people a constitution is simply a book.' There have been twelve successful *coups d'état* since 1810 and scores of attempted ones. President Betancourt, elected in 1958, is the first constitutionally-elected president in its history to survive for more than a year. Moreover, he himself came to power following a *coup* by the armed forces; with the temporary recession in oil, Venezuela's national income is tending to decline, after doubling during the Fifties; credit is very tight in Caracas, and there is rising unemployment as workers are laid off the Babylonian public works projects launched by ex-Dictator Jimenez. All the elements of violence and discontent are present.

At half-past eight on the morning of Friday 24 June, President Betancourt was driving through Caracas to take the salute at an Army Day parade (an important engagement for a Latin-American president who wishes to complete his term). With him in the Cadillac were his wife, the Defence Minister, General Lopez, and his wife, Betancourt's A.D.C., Colonel Perez, and the chauffeur. As the car passed along the grandiose boulevard which leads to the armed forces memorial a stationary Oldsmobile blew up. The Cadillac was wrecked. Betancourt sustained facial injuries, Lopez, his wife and the chauffeur were seriously burnt. Perez and a passer-by were killed. It was an expert job: the massive quantities of explosive in the Oldsmobile had been detonated by remote-control, by the use of microwaves.

I arrived in Caracas immediately after the *coup* to find an atmosphere of grim panic. I had immense difficulty in entering the country (my passport was immediately impounded on landing by a scarcely literate official, who waved off my protests with an airy '*Manana*'; it took me three days and a so-called 'fee' of £3 to get it back). And, once in Caracas, it proved impossible to get out. All exits by air, sea and land were closed; even Venezuela's 150 fishing-vessels were confined to harbour. At the docks, over 3,000 screaming and frightened passengers were waiting to board liners; by Monday, Pan-American Air Lines alone had 600 stranded. In Caracas the muggy air was tense. Armoured cars cut off the streets to the presidential palace. Scores of troops, toting sub-machine guns, patrolled the streets. It became apparent that neither I nor anyone else was going to get out of the country until most, if not all, the conspirators were behind bars.

Loud, therefore, were the orisons raised to Our Lady of Caracas that week-end; and they were promptly answered. The gang had made one crucial error. They had not stolen the Oldsmobile, nor had they removed or defaced its number plates. Perhaps they imagined nothing identifiable would survive the explosion. The plates were quickly traced to the owner, who promptly gave the name of one Manuel Vicente Yanes Bustamente, to whom he had lent it.

Bustamente was easily picked up and confessed. Immediately this became known, a Captain Chavez, proprietor of a private airline called Ransa, gave himself up. He said that one of his planes, borrowed on a pretext by his sister, had been used in the plot. He was locked up too. That evening, a naval captain called Morales Luengo, who had held official position under Jimanez and had recently been exiled for anti-state activities, was arrested while attempting to seek asylum in the Haitian embassy. Luengo, oddly enough, turned out to be the brother-in-law of Chavez's sister. The rest followed thick and fast: Manuel Sanoja, a professional agent of General Trujillo, the Dominican dictator; the pilot of the plane; and Lorenzo Mercado, one of the two men who actually carried out the dynamite attempt itself. His companion, a radio-technician and explosives expert called Luis Cabrera Sifontes, was finally run to earth a fortnight ago.

All these men, according to the Venezuelan authorities, have now confessed, so that we now possess a detailed account of how the assassination was planned and what would have followed had it succeeded. They were, it goes without saying, as pretty a bunch of pirates as ever infested the Caribbean. Sanoja, the Trujillo agent, has been active in half a dozen Caribbean republics; two of his sons have the distinction of being officers in Trujillo's personal bodyguard. Bustamente was wanted for a bank fraud of £1,500. Luengo had been involved, this spring, in another *coup* against Betancourt, led by General Castro Leon.

Luengo, acting on orders from Trujillo, appears to have planned the operation from his Dominican exile. The main difficulty was how to get himself and the explosives equipment into Venezuelan territory. This he solved through his brother, Angel Luengo, who put up his wife to persuade her brother, Chavez, to lend her a plane. Chavez was told that Captain Luengo was seriously ill in Ciudad Trujillo, and that the family were anxious to visit him without going through all the fuss of getting permission from the government (the two countries have broken off diplomatic relations). Chavez agreed and the plane was lent. It stayed only a few hours in Ciudad Trujillo, long enough to be loaded up with Luengo, Sanoja (plus his $100,000) and the explosive and complex killing equipment. Then it flew back to a remote airstrip in Venezuela. The gang met for the first time in full strength at a country estate some 100 miles from Caracas, chosen because a great deal of blasting was being carried out in the neighbourhood. Here they tested the equipment, blowing up several cars (the remains of which were later found by the police). Then the gang moved to Caracas.

But the conspirators bungled. Sifontes was to work the detonator from some distance away, on receipt of a signal from Lorenzo Mercado, who was to raise his hat when the president's Cadillac reached the target area. In his nervousness, Mercado must have given the signal a second or so too soon: the main impact of the explosion struck the front part of the car, instead of the rear. Secondly, the Cadillac was a heavier car than any used in the test explosion; it was also loaded with six people. The force of the explosion should have turned it over, in which case all six would have been burnt to death. Instead, it remained upright – and the injured were able to escape.

Paradoxically, the assassination attempt has done Betancourt a power of good. Perez, the murdered A.D.C., was a popular figure in the army; his death, and the grave injuries inflicted on General Lopez, caused a wave of anger to sweep through the officer's corps, from which the president has benefited. He was also able to use the attempt to arrange a political truce with the other parties, and he will certainly use it, both at the U.N. and in the Organization of American States, to bring political and economic pressure on the Dominican Republic, and so hasten Trujillo's downfall. All in all, then, it looks as if Betancourt now has a distinct chance of completing his term of office. He may even manage to stay alive.

—*23 July 1960*

The Trouble with Persia

IN THE SUMMER MONTHS, the Shah of Persia takes his family to live in a ramshackle houseboat moored to a stone jetty in the Caspian. Not a very convenient arrangement, you might think, but the King of Kings (otherwise known as the Shadow of the Almighty, Vice-Regent of God, Centre of the Universe and Tenant of the Peacock Throne) has already been shot at several times by his dutiful subjects, and this bizarre holiday-home has distinct advantages from the security point of view. At any rate it took me five hours to argue my way from the entrance to the jetty actually onto the houseboat – during which time I had an opportunity to admire the Crown Prince's pram, which has solid gold handles and trimmings.

The Shah is a not unattractive personality and a distinct cut above most Middle Eastern despots. His father, an upstart general, betrayed megalomaniac tendencies in his later years, including a taste for Nazi Germany and Potemkin villages (he now lies in a tomb modelled on Napoleon's in the Invalides), but he at least gave his heir a decent, if peculiar, education. The Shah speaks excellent English, can rattle off statistics as well as any economics don, holds progressive, *Observer*-like views on the status of women, public housing and irrigation, and is properly solemn about the business of ruling 22,000,000 people. All this is better than one might expect; indeed his chief personal drawback is, quite simply, his family, who conform far more closely than he does to the image of oriental royalty.

At the same time, it would be foolish to imagine he is a radical in any meaningful sense of the word. He speaks with real venom of the Persian ruling class, but this is chiefly because he regards it as a liability. His rule is entirely personal. The constitution invests him with powers somewhat greater than those enjoyed by George III. He can hire and fire his ministers at will, which puts a premium on failure, for he is intensely jealous of other men's popularity with the public. Earlier this year he dismissed his Premier, Amini, and his adventurous Minister for Agriculture, Arsenjani, simply because they were becoming too well known – and liked. The present head of the government, a friendly little body called Alam, who looks rather like a retired juvenile lead, is a palpable cypher. There is no one near the Shah of any great ability or character and, despite his protestations, he shows increasing signs of emulating his father's authoritarian ways. When I asked him if he were ever tempted to throw up his precarious job and go into comfortable exile, he replied – a shade ominously, I thought – 'Less and less.'

The history of Persia, no less than the nature of its people, tends to emphasize the isolation and doom-destiny of the monarch. Wandering among the noble columns and staircases of Persepolis, one becomes physically conscious of the sheer weight of the personal impress the great Archaemenian kings left on their country. The monumental bas-reliefs of Darius and Xerxes, supported by the cowering figures of their satraps, and their transcendental inscriptions still inspire awe after more than two millennia:

> 'If thou thinkest how many were the lands King Darius ruled, then behold this picture. They bear my throne, thereby thou mayest know them . . . I am Xerxes, the Great King, King of Kings, king of the nations with their many peoples, king of the whole earth, even to afar.'

The glittering city of Isfahan, the finest monument to Islamic art on earth, is equally the personal expression of the power of the Safavids; indeed it was largely built by one man. The Persians say, still: 'When we have great kings, we are a great country.' The Shah, despite the recent origins of his dynasty, inherits this tradition of veneration and there is a good deal of elaborate kow-towing, from high and low, wherever he goes.

Needless to say, he does not take this personal popularity, which is undoubted, for granted. He has a huge army, which he himself commands, like Hussein in Jordan, and an elaborate secret police network, called SAVAK. Among other things, this supervises the 'trade unions' and screens the candidates for elections whenever (as this week) the Shah chooses to hold them. The press is impotent; any political party likely to cause trouble is banned; and all genuine opposition leaders are in exile, dead, imprisoned or under house-arrest. The June riots, where 100 people are said to have been shot down by the police and army, showed that the chances of the Tehran mob taking over, as in Mossadeq's time, are now virtually nil – barring a revolt in the army, which seems unlikely at present.

It is far more probable that the Shah himself may prove the architect of his own ruin. His programme of reform, though largely paperwork, does contain potential elements of genuine change. It thus poses a basic contradiction – a conservative régime employing revolutionary instruments – and in the long run this must be resolved, either by abandoning the instruments or by changing the régime. In the meantime, the Shah is alienating certain powerful elements in Persian society, notably the mullahs, who are bitterly opposed to his emancipation of women, and the tribes, who form 10 per cent of the population. When I was in Persia recently, the Shah was harassing the tribes with Sabre-jets supplied by the U.S. for Cento defence, and building military roads across their territory. The Prime Minister claimed that most of the tribesmen thought the Shah was wonderful, and offered to introduce me to their 'loyal' leaders. Could I meet the disloyal ones, I asked. 'Unfortunately, no, as they have been rather hanged.'

None of this would matter very much (at least to the Shah) if there were any prospect that his reforms will work. But so far they have merely aroused exaggerated expectations: in practice they are promoting administrative chaos and economic disaster. Although Persia has an enormous bureaucracy (over 200,000, of whom 30 per cent are said to be illiterate), it is manifestly incapable of enforcing structural change. In a commendable moment of frankness, the Finance Minister told an economic conference this spring that the entire income-tax system was unworkable. The tax-collectors, he said, were dishonest, ignorant or acted *ultra vires*. They were inadequately supervised. The files were quite useless. Anyone who has visited the headquarters of the Persian Inland Revenue, and seen its mountainous stacks of decayed dossiers, creeping like some leprous fungus over walls and corridors, will know exactly what the Minister meant. And what applies to this department is even more valid for some of the others.

Indeed, the land reform – the very core of the Shah's programme – suffers from the elementary handicap that the Ministry of Agriculture has given up as impractical the attempt to produce a trustworthy map. A proper cadastral survey, they say, would take thirty years. Hence, for the first time in history a land reform is being pushed through on a basis of almost complete ignorance. The solution the government has adopted is simply to hand the land to the peasants who work it at present.

In theory, there might be something to be said for this from an economic (if not from an equitable) viewpoint, since it would minimize discontinuity of tenure and consequently reduce the loss of production which land reform almost invariably brings. But until now the prevalent system in Persia has divided the produce into fifths, according to who owns the land and who supplies water, seed, labour and draught animals. In many cases, the landlord took four-fifths, which he had the facilities to market for cash. What will happen now he is being eliminated? Can the peasant, lacking working capital – the promised co-operatives have not yet materialised – keep up production? And if he does can he market the surplus? The answer, I fear, is that in many cases, if not the majority, the peasant will simply eat more and work less, and production will fall accordingly.

Of course it is impossible for anyone to generalise about what is now going on, for the reform is still in its infancy. But here are my notes on four of the villages I visited:

Araj: 100 inhabitants. Wheat and flocks. Land reform imminent. Proprietor at present takes 40 per cent of produce, for marketing in Tehran.

Tork Mazrae: 135 inhabitants, of whom two literate. Wheat, vegetables. No land reform; land already held by villagers. Little surplus.

Shoorkab: 140 inhabitants, 20 literate. Poor. Wheat, vegetables, cattle, sheep, bees. Land reform has taken place, owner of village dispossessed. His cattle-pen, granary, etc. now in ruins, his cattle sold. Probable loss of production: 50 per cent.

Talaw: 120 people (Christians, many with blond hair) of whom only handful literate. V. poor. Moslem landlord, who collects 25 per cent of crops. Reform imminent.

These notes tell their own story. Where reform takes place, there is a distinct tendency for production, especially of marketable surplus, to drop alarmingly. And this, moreover, must be seen against a background of persistent agricultural decline, long before the reforms began to take effect, as the accompanying table shows.

Fall in Agricultural Production
(in '000s of metric tons)

	1958	1959	1960
Wheat	3,050	2,659	2,590
Barley	1,280	1,087	684
Rice	670	550	651
Sugarbeet	805	720	588

With population rising as fast as anywhere in Asia, the growing deficit in food supplies means increased reliance on U.S. surpluses, inflation, pressure on the reserves, spasmodic shortages and the economic disquiet and frustration which agricultural decay invariably brings. Not surprisingly, the whole of the Persian economy is beginning to flag, and only oil and American aid keeps it going at all.

The best thing to be said for the Shah's programme is his attempt – a variant on the Cuban system – to use the army to bring education to the villages. Some 2,800 Persian middle-class youths, instead of doing their military service with regular units, are given a four-month course and sent out, in ones and twos, to open rudimentary schools in the rural areas. I saw a number of these boys in action. They were likeable and (it is, of course, early days) keen on their job. The Shah's motives in promoting this scheme were no doubt mixed: partly a genuine desire to break the back of Persian illiteracy, but partly also a wish to have, at village level, trusted informants responsible to the central machine of security. But it is here that his plans may come unstuck, for the 'Knowledge Corps', as he calls it, is a two-edged weapon.

As I saw for myself, these young conscripts are becoming involved – physically and emotionally – with village life, its problems, its griefs, its complaints. For the first time in their lives they are becoming aware of the poverty and hopelessness in which most of their compatriots live. It is always dangerous to confront idealists with a situation which, to put it mildly, is far from ideal. It would not surprise me if these young conscripts produced another Nasser, and if the Shah went the way of poor old Farouk.

—20 September 1963

In the Heel of Europe

THE *AUTOSTRADA*, which takes the traveller the length of Italy as far as Naples, actually stops (like Christ) at Eboli, a dull and undistinguished town where nothing appears to happen from one end of the year to another. From there I took the road inland to Auletta and entered a different world. Immediately the scenery becomes wild and mountainous; a vast, grim, flat-topped *massif* fills the horizon, purple, distant and threatening. The villages are few or disappear altogether. Even farmhouses or cottages are rarely to be seen: just a few shepherds' huts. Apart from stunted olives or oaks there are hardly any trees. The bones of the rock stick through the thin and patchy skin of earth. It is a parched and desperate country, where the guard dogs wear spiked collars for protection against the wolves.

Sitting by the roadside, I saw something I shall not easily forget. An aged peasant woman, entirely shrouded in black, carried a huge bundle (I imagine of olive-droppings); behind her trailed a little girl, with four emaciated sheep on leads; a fawn-coloured goat followed: and, bringing up the rear, was a young man, carrying on his shoulders a wooden plough, of a type which has been in use, with little modification, for three millennia. It was not yet three o'clock, but it would be dark in less than two hours, and they were trailing back, with the bulk of their worldly goods, to the safety of the small town in which they lived.

Quite apart from the drought, the erosion of the soil, the destructive torrents which suddenly descend in winter, the monstrous and wasteful system of land-tenure, the peasants of the *mezzogiorno* must contend with the daily problem of distance. This land has been swept by pillaging invaders through most of its recorded history. The rule of law has never operated effectively. Survival has been possible at all only by the creation of defensible townships, usually on high hills or rocks, where the peasants could huddle together for mutual protection. You see them dotted about the landscape, absurdly perched on the mountains: bright and glittering at a distance but, on closer inspection, a maze of reeking alleyways, usually with a European main street driven through the centre. The narrow roads weave their way from one town to another, quadrupling distances. This pattern, from habit or continuing fear, persists even into these comparatively settled times. A great part of the peasant's time and energy is thus spent trudging to and from his fields.

Potenza, the capital of this province, with 40,000 people or more, clusters on an absurd hill. The earlier town lay in the valley, and was accordingly destroyed in turn by the Saracens, the Emperor Frederick II and by Charles of Anjou. Retreating up the hill in fact brought no lasting security, for an earthquake smashed it to bits in 1857. But there the town still is, new buildings are going up; the population has doubled since the turn of the century. The pattern seems set and irreversible. At the entrance to the town a vast peasant market was in progress. Every conceivable kind of cheap item was on sale, from rough boots to a multitude of charms to avert the evil eye. Here were peasants of all shapes and sizes, who had come in on mule or horseback or donkey, on battered spindly carts or great antique waggons, even occasionally on a tractor or those three-wheeled tin vans which hold up traffic all over Italy. There were solemn, sad men, women almost invariably in black, swarms of ragged children; knobbly cows, the colour of Siamese cats, a tremendous number of dubious fowls and sometimes, though not often, pigs.

Yet Potenza is a rich town by the standards of this part of Italy, a glittering metropolis with cinemas, bars, even hotels. Life is harder in the smaller towns which perch around it on the mountain spine, towns with a dismal past and seemingly no future, but which continue to exist and, despite emigration, grow. What can government – any government – do for these places? The forest cover has long since been destroyed. The high winds and the rains bring the soil down into the valleys in the form of sludge. One passes the occasional pathetic attempt at forest plantations: too small to be viable in their own right, let alone to create micro-climates. Occasionally, too, state funds have set up small factories, on the valley floor, near the main road; but private capital is chary of venturing here.

Across the mountains lies Matera, an even sadder case. Here the landscape of the Murge Mountains is less spectacular, the colour of elephants. Centuries of erosion have cut the earth into deep gorges, and Matera is perched on one. I should, I suppose, have approached it from the east and caught my first glimpse of it in all its ridiculous beauty. But I drove in from the west, uncovering, as the town unfolded, archeological layers of activity, descending in time. On the outskirts, the 20th century: new buildings are going up – those ambitious blocks of flats and offices which, in Italy, are enthusiastically begun and never quite finished: then through the 19th-century section, the 18th-century, the 17th-, the Renaissance, and finally to the old town perched on the rocks. The beauty and poverty grow *pari passu*. Beneath the 'old' town one descends into classical times, almost pre-history. Here a quarter of the inhabitants live in caves, or *sassi,* cut into the rock, with a great multitude of beasts of all kinds. There are several thousands of these habitations, which are surprisingly clean in their way, though all refuse is simply hurled into the ravine. But is this the way Common Market Man should expect to live – in caves, with his flocks?

Matera has been a poor town since classical times, though it has some fine Baroque churches. On the Sunday evening a band played, but it was a simple affair compared with the splendid forty-piece band which performs in the Naples Galiera, all arrayed in the most extravagant Napoleonic uniforms you can imagine. There were many farmers in town, dark, silent men in brown and black, women scarcely to be seen, except in the churches or caves. Matera is grim, and the mood seems to suit it. As if it did not suffer enough in this life, it boasts a remarkable church called the Purgatorio – death carved in stone. Skulls and skeletons creep up its porch and swarm over the façade, they grin at you from the altars, glitter from the pulpit and peer from the darkest recesses of the interior. Death is almost a way of life in these parts.

Yet one cannot generalize. The patterns of existence, like the landscape, change with startling suddenness. No town is wholly the same, the more substantial ones are utterly different. Here is not so much a country as a collection of cities, each with its area of influence and its satellite towns: the spirit of Magna Graecia survives to this extent. There is a kind of urban pride, a consciousness of history which defies poverty and sometimes overcomes it.

Puglia, for instance, is a new world: flat, with good communications, fine seaports, adequate rainfall: it is the wealthiest of the provinces of the *mezzogiorno,* wealthier even than Campagna, the country round Naples. But it is a strange world all the same. The soil is red-brown and fertile, though broken by an infinity of rocky outcrops. In this land is one of the oddest sights in Europe: literally thousands of farm houses built in the Saracenic style. These *trulli,* as they are called, are cones built of dry-stone, and whitewashed, with flatter stones or slates to form the apex; each is a room in itself, and four or five or more are grouped together to form a house. There is a sizeable town, Alberobello, almost half of which consists of these curious structures – indeed, there is even a church built in the *trulli* style. Is their origin prehistoric? No one seems to know. The locals appear to like them: for the most part they are well maintained, kept sparkling with fresh whitewash: new ones are being built. One can stand on an eminence and see hundreds, perhaps thousands of these farms, each in the centre of its own fields. Perhaps Ireland looked a little like this, before the famine. But again, is this the way in which Common Market Man should live?

In the middle of this is Lecce, a fortunate and elegant town. Lecce has a long history and was an independent state as late as the 15th century. It has escaped the worst of the disasters which befell almost all the cities of the *mezzogiorno.* It has always, I think, been rich, perhaps because it is conveniently near three ports, Brindisi, Bari and Taranto; and today it exudes a certain modest prosperity. There are good shops in the place, selling fine clothes, antiques and jewels. Local elections were going on. In the Piazza San Oronzo, around which life revolves, an accomplished Liberal orator harangued a prosperous crowd of solid citizens. High above, a gigantic bronze effigy of the Saint, who first brought Christianity here, looked down from his tall column of sea-green marble, stolen from Brindisi, and raised his arm in a gesture, though whether of encouragement, exhortation or imprecation it was impossible to say.

Not only are the citizens of Lecce prosperous: they also occupy one of the architectural marvels of Italy. The local limestone, which varies in colour from white to golden yellow, has a rare quality; it is very soft to carve, but afterwards sets hard. In the 17th century, two architects of genius, Zimbalo and his pupil Cino, took full advantage of this and created a masterly ensemble of cathedral, bishop's palace and seminary, which stand together in a fine square – a triumphant flourish of Baroque in a country where the style is unknown or insipid. A century before another genius had built the church of Sta Croce, whose enormous façade swarms with row upon row of cherubs, saints and, above all, beasts both fabulous and real, which has led one writer, Osbert Sitwell, to compare it to the Mappin Terraces in Regent's Park Zoo. Inside, instead of the expected clutter, all is space and purity, with natural stone columns of great size, and carved stone altarpieces in the manner of Bernini. The town has scores of churches and palaces, many almost as remarkable as the buildings I have described.

Lecce illustrates the curious unevenness of life in the *mezzogiorno,* the effect of historical accident and geographical location. Taranto, only twenty miles away, is a great and flourishing seaport, and always has been. Today it reeks from the fumes of its refinery and giant tankers hover on the horizon; but ships have crowded its magnificent natural harbour ever since ancient times. It is one of the very few cities in Southern Italy which has a history of continuous occupation. Yet nothing of beauty survives in it; it has lost all its architectural treasures in one catastrophe or another. Indeed, it was lucky to survive at all, and here we have a key to this part of the world.

West from Taranto stretches the instep of Italy, a great scimitar of coast which sweeps flatly down to the mountains of Calabria. This was one of the richest areas of the ancient world. Its Greek colonists produced huge cities, with expensive fleets and armies, and many satellite colonies. One such had ears of corn on its gold coinage, to symbolize its fertility. The people of another, Sybaris, were so wealthy, and so particular, that their name persists in all European languages. Yet virtually nothing of Sybaris now remains; little of Croton; at Metapontum, just a few columns. What happened seems relatively simple. Appropriated by Rome, they became wholly dependent on the functioning of the empire for their economic survival. When Rome fell and the administration broke down, the countless rivers which flow down from the mountains silted up; marshes formed; they bred malarial mosquitoes; the citizens died of malaria or fled into the mountains to found crazy and uneconomic cities on the tops of hills, out of range of the scourge. Taranto's natural situation – it is virtually an island – saved it from the disease, though not from occasional human attack (notably by the Allies in the last war).

Along this wide and now dreary gulf I must have crossed fifty or sixty of these rivers and streams – or rather their stony beds, for except for a few weeks in the year they are mostly dry. But those few weeks are what matter. For many centuries, unrestricted, these torrents carried away the soil and dumped it into the Ionian

Sea, thus transforming an earthly paradise into near desolation. Now at last attempts are being made to corral these destructive forces into concrete channels. But the damage has been done; for the most part it is irreparable. The mosquitoes have been killed, but, short of afforestation on an immense scale, nothing can restore the soil.

Some forests do, indeed, survive, no doubt because of their inaccessibility. From Rossano, a meagre hilltop town on the Ionian Coast, I went inland into Calabria, straight across the Sila Mountains, which rise to 6,000 feet. Until quite recently few travellers came here at all. The distances – by road, not as the crow flies – are immense; the road snakes and writhes; it is often dangerous and an army of men are kept in constant employment to keep it from crumbling over the cliffs. The upper slopes are covered in an ancient forest of oaks, beech, larch and spruce, and I was fortunate to see it in the one week of the year when it blazed with gold, crimson and emerald. Here are high Alpine valleys which provide good pasture, and big, silent lakes, remarkable for their trout. But there is not much work up here; the people cling to their crumbling hill-top towns lower down. These are dismal places, with names like Cropalati or Lungobucco, built on rocks which are baked in summer and ravaged by wind and rain in winter. A great many men are out of work, which may only be obtainable twenty or even thirty miles from their homes. Existence is thin and vertiginous. Scores of women and children scrabble for fallen olives from trees they do not own. I have seen these tiny and bitter things crushed in the presses: an enormous quantity is required to make a single litre of oil. I hate to think of how many hours of labour are needed to bring these women a single shilling.

Calabria, indeed, is the poorest of all Italy's provinces. Figures recently released for 1966 show that its production per inhabitant is barely half that of Italy as a whole; some of the northern provinces are nearly three times as rich. There are mountains everywhere, with river valleys few and narrow. Yet Calabria, too, was once rich. Dropping down from the Sila, I went to Cosenza, its capital. This was an important place, the junction of two strategic rivers, in Roman times. Alaric came there, with his booty and prisoners, after sacking Rome, and died there of some unknown disease. His barbarians gave him a splendid funeral, as Gibbon describes:

> 'By the labour of a captive multitude, they forcibly diverted the course of the Busentius, a small river that washes the walls of Consentia. The royal sepulchre, adorned with the splendid spoils and trophies of Rome, was constructed in the vacant bed; the waters were then restored to their natural channel; and the secret spot where the remains of Alaric had been deposited, was forever concealed by the inhuman massacre of the prisoners, who had been employed to execute the work.'

A likely tale! It seems to me that, if indeed any gold had been hidden in this wretched river-bed, which certainly has become the depository of rubbish of all kinds, the miserable inhabitants of the town would long since have turned over every pebble until they found it.

Cosenza has led a brutalized existence. Sacked by the Saracens, pillaged by Norman kings, German emperors, popes and Bourbons, it has had earthquakes in 1783, 1854, 1870 and 1905; it was frequently bombed (by us) in 1943. An immense, now ruined, castle still dominates the town. Every variety of misrule has been practised here, with fiendish success. In consequence, the agriculture of the region has struggled to survive at all, and little has been done in recent years to restore the depredation of centuries. While I was there, Rome announced that Calabria was to have a modern university of its own, presumably in Cosenza, with a large engineering faculty which would include special courses on soil preservation and land use. Good news, no doubt, but a little late in the day.

What may of course transform, and will certainly change this area is the *autostrada,* planned to go as far as Reggio, on the Straits of Messina. It is already in an advanced stage and, when complete, will be one of the most astonishing engineering works in Europe. The last few hundred miles travel almost continuously through wild mountains, leaping across valleys and gorges on immense steel-and-concrete stilts, many hundreds of feet high. Some towns, like Cosenza, it must surely hurry into the 20th century; others it will push back into the Middle Ages, which they have scarcely left. But few have considered, still less computed, the detailed effects of this great artifact. Maybe it will just help the tourists and the rich to hurry through Calabria, as the railways did.

Sicily is not, according to the statistics, quite as poor as Calabria, but there are vast tracts of the island where the peasants are, in everything that matters, considerably more miserable. How Sicily, the granary of the ancient world, the prize for which kings, emperors and adventurers fought incessantly, became what it is today is a complex story. In the history of human vicissitudes, it has an unenviable place. Take Messina, its third largest town. This was an important Greek city. It was destroyed by the Carthaginians and again, more than once, by the Saracens. Richard the Lionheart sacked it. It was pillaged by Henry VI. It was devastated by plague (1743), earthquake (1783), naval bombardment (1848), cholera (1854) and earthquake again (1894). In 1908 it was hit by the biggest earthquake in European history, which killed 84,000 of its inhabitants, ruined the entire city, the whole of which sank two feet, and caused a 20-foot tidal wave which travelled as far as Malta. But cities can, at least, be rebuilt – even improved. Noto, in the south-east corner of the island, took advantage of an earthquake to conduct the most remarkable experiment in 18th-century town-planning in all Europe. Thanks to an unknown monk of genius, its palaces, churches, streets and houses form a unity of design and decoration worthy of a great capital.

What cannot so easily be repaired is the plundering of nature. For this the Saracen invader, blamed in all history books, is not responsible. It was the Normans who brought feudalism to Sicily and began the process of destruction; and, once introduced, feudalism proved more persistent here than anywhere else. Its terminology – 'fiefs', 'feudatories', 'barons', 'villani' – survived, along with feudal privileges and courts, well into the 19th century and, in some respects, into the 20th. Elsewhere, feudalism was mitigated or transformed by the growth of central government. But Sicily has never, in the strict sense, been governed since ancient times. The writ of central authority, under Normans, Angevins or Bourbons, and even under the modern Italian state, ran only in the coastal towns. The interior was private property, policed, if at all, by the mounted retainers of the feudal lords. The great bulk of the land, perhaps as much as four-fifths, was divided into *latifundi,* huge estates, often of many thousands of hectares, owned by the 142 princes, 788 marquesses and 1,500 dukes and barons of Sicily. From the 17th to the 19th centuries absentee ownership was the rule; most lords never saw their estates, but lived in Palermo, or even in Naples, Rome or Paris. The *latifundi* were let out to stewards, or *gabelloti,* on three-to-six year leases, and by them to the peasants on a yearly basis.

This incredibly wasteful system of land-management persisted for centuries. No one who worked the land had any interest except to reap a quick profit. The trees were cut down, none planted. Wheat was sown in place of vines, citrus or olives. No irrigation works were built, and those that existed allowed to decay. High land was cleared for wheat, though the yield was often as little as two bushels for each bushel sown. After four or five years it would be abandoned, and erosion would complete the damage.

Attempts at reform were frustrated first by legal devices; later, after the coming of democracy, by the Mafia. On a limited suffrage, the 2 per cent who had the vote returned safe nominees of the church and the landlords. Radical governments in Rome, however concerned by land reform, needed the votes of these deputies: so Sicily became like the Deep South in the United States – the nominal supporter of the progressive party, which in return left it to run its own affairs. The growing power of the Mafia underpinned the feudal system, taking over the role of policing the interior and terrorizing the peasants.

Mussolini declared war on the Mafia but succeeded only in scotching it. Its moment of resurrection came in 1943, when it was instrumental in allowing the Americans to make a rapid conquest of the western half of the island, and was correspondingly rewarded. To a great extent, indeed, the Mafia replaced the aristocrats as the owner, as well as the effective ruler, of large areas of Sicily, especially in the North West.

But it is a mistake, I think, in writing of Sicily, to dwell too much on the Mafia. The tales told of the Mafia are endless, and how many of them are true, God only knows. (There is a startling and highly readable account of their activities in Norman Lewis's *The Honoured Society,* now in Penguins.) The Italian papers, especially in Sicily, are full of sensational Mafia trials and killings. For the past three-and-a-half years a parliamentary commission, the 'Anti-Mafia', has been sitting, and has accumulated mountains of evidence and dossiers, to no great effect. To men of the Right, the Mafia is a myth; to men like Dolci it is all-pervasive, the source of evil. Of course the Mafia exists, and of course it is powerful, but today its American operations are probably more important, with Sicily merely a link in the narcotics chain. In any case the Mafia is a symptom of Sicily's ills, rather than a cause. After so many centuries of mis-government or private oppression or both, there is in the island, or at least some parts of it, a sense of despair and defeatism, a disbelief in the possibility of law or justice, making a

Mafia – or any other moral outrage – possible, even in a sense acceptable.

Last month I travelled inland from the East Coast, along the side-roads which branch off from Piazza Armerina, where the Emperor Maximian built a villa in one of the loveliest valleys in the island (it is, happily, still very much as he must have known it). Apart from such isolated valleys, however, the land is dry as a bone: not a cottage, not a farmhouse, not a tree to be seen for miles: just weary soil, what there is of it, and rock. The towns are unutterably sad, and often half-deserted. At dusk I came across a small, windswept and dingy town, and I shall remember it because I have never seen so many mules in my life, not even in the Spanish Pyrenees. There were thousands of them, bowed down with burdens, trooping along the roads which led to the towns; in the streets of the town itself; in great mule-hostelries where, by flickering firelight, I could see them being fed and watered. The place stank of mule. What were they all doing there? Why were the muleteers so strange and sad and silent? Why was there no light, or the faintest trace of gaiety? I had to remind myself that this was not Africa but Europe, indeed Common Market Europe. There is a feeling of demoralization in these parts. Only a few miles away, in Mazzarino, and less than a decade ago, a band of Franciscan monks, led by their Prior, terrorized the town with a protection racket and murdered its richest citizen, who refused to pay up.

But again, one must not generalize. There are all kinds of towns in Sicily, good, bad and indifferent. There is Palermo itself, an evil, stinking, noisy town, perched between headlands which Goethe called the most beautiful in the world. Here Serpotta created his masterpiece in the tiny Oratory of St Lawrence. Here much of the wartime bomb-damage has never been made good, or even cleared away. Children scamper in the ruins and play, shoeless, over mountains of refuse it seems nobody's job to remove. Some of the palaces have been invaded by slum-dwellers, and there are hideous back-streets where I feared to pry. There are many short, fat, heavily-dressed men in this city, hiding their eyes behind sunglasses even at night. *Mafiosi?* In the cathedral are the remains of Frederick II, *Stupor Mundi,* and Henry VI, encased in giant tombs carved from blocks of porphyry: grim things to remind you of oppressive centuries.

Or there is Agrigento, once a great and rich Greek city, now a dirty and bad-tempered town, where the Mafia is said to be powerful, and whose bishop, in 1945, was shot and nearly killed by a Mafia assassin. Or Cefalu, where a Club Mediterranée has produced a crop of local youths who wear long hair and jeans and listen to pop. Or Caltanisetta, the sulphur town, which looks wealthy and businesslike and ugly. Or Catania, which is far richer – the richest town in Sicily – though its perch at the bottom of Etna makes its very existence precarious. Or there is Salemi, a curious hill-town in the North West. Its people, I believe, are descended from the Sikels, the aboriginals of the island, who were driven inland or enslaved by the first Greek colonists. These are very short folk – not much over four foot, many of them – and when I saw them on a Sunday morning, all the men wore dark sober suits and cloth caps pulled well over their eyes. They stood in the Piazza listening to a ballad-singer and story-teller who, with the help of a huge canvas comic-strip, told them, while they listened rapt, the sad tale of Josephina. It was somewhat modernized – a train came into it – but basically it had the same root as the tale of the woman-doge of Amalfi, which Webster used in the *Duchess of Malfi*. Well, things have happened in Sicily, even recently, which would have given Webster material for a dozen horror-plays.

Of Greek civilization little remains, though what does is often of astonishing beauty. Most remarkable of all is Segesta, whose vast, incomplete but well-preserved temple stands quite alone on a hill in a bowl of mountains. I met here, near the ruins, the thinnest dog I have ever seen. He was friendly, even affectionate, but I thought he must be starving until I visited the archaeological museum in Palermo and saw the splendid metopes removed from the temples of Silenus. Here, tearing Actaeon to pieces, were three creatures exactly like the dog I had met, even perhaps a shade thinner. So the dog could, if he only knew it, reasonably claim that his distant ancestors had hunted for the Greeks in the 5th century before Christ.

And what of Syracuse? Some 2,500 years ago it had half a million inhabitants and owned half Sicily; it overthrew the Athenian expedition and changed the course of ancient history. Plato visited it three times and Archimedes died there, killed by a Roman infantryman. Syracuse cuts little ice now, though people talk of an industrial complex growing up there and at nearby Augusta. Other Italians, and Sicilians too, say that the citizens of Syracuse are stupid. I don't know; it's true, however, that my hotel, a new one, had been built directly over the sea, with its bedrooms all facing the (noisy) street. But Syracuse is an agreeable town; if I'd been born there, only pressing reasons would induce me to leave. The old city is a maze of fine buildings, some, like the Cathedral, incorporating ancient Greek structures. There is a certain leisured gaiety about it all. In the Piazza Archimedes, in the evening, one looks at the fountain, representing Arethusa, with a benign eye. Buildings from the 14th, 18th, 19th and 20th centuries face onto the square. There is the Caffe Spadano and the Caffe Samboneti for the old men; the young gather in a noisy, arguing crowd on the opposite side (but what about the women? That's another story, I fear). Traffic halts for conversation. A small boy dashes across the square, carrying a huge tray of steaming cups of coffee. The great dome of the sky is purple-black, the stars luminous. In reduced circumstances as it now is, one can still see why Pindar and Cicero liked it so much. But then Syracuse, it is said, has always kept out the Mafiia.

Elsewhere, there is less contentment, even on a superficial level, and less reason for it. Between 1901-1913, a million Sicilians emigrated. Again, in the decade 1951-61, for instance, 10 per cent of the population, almost entirely males between 20 and 50, packed up and left. The process continues, unabating and seemingly irreversible. Its consequences can be seen throughout the interior. Miles of agricultural terraces have been simply abandoned: some twenty or thirty years ago, some much more recently. The high slopes on the plateau reminded me of Peru, where you can still see, in the Andes, the faint traces of terrace-farming, abandoned since the Spaniards destroyed the Peruvian economy, 400 years ago. Even the Mafia, seeing that the game is no longer worth it, are leaving the interior for the richer pickings of the coastal cities and plains. Since 1947 the 'transformation of the *latifundio*' has been a fundamental law of the republic, and some land reform has actually taken place. The new regional government and the Cassa del Mezzogiorno have spent a great deal of money. Dolci and his disciples have striven and agitated. But the Sicilian peasant of the interior, if he is able, is leaving, and this, at long last, is destroying the feudal system, which depends above all on supplies of cheap, expendable manpower.

I left Palermo on the good ship *Calabria,* which took me overnight to Naples. A newly-wed couple were on the boat, and the bride's family – I almost said tribe – had gathered on the quay to bid her goodbye. What a noise and shouting there was, what a caterwauling as strong men wept and flowers were thrown! It was all very jolly, but while it was going on, more significant figures were walking up the gangplank, dark little men in threadbare suits with heavy bundles, men who had perhaps never seen a ship before and were preparing to sleep on deck. These men and their forebears had been plundered, like their beautiful island, for a thousand years or more, but now they had had enough. They were going north, into Europe.

—8 December 1967

Trulli near Alberobello (illustration by the author)

Part 7

OFF DUTY

No Path to Rome

IN THE EARLY SUMMER of 1901, Hilaire Belloc made a pilgrimage from Toul, the garrison town where he had passed his military service in the French artillery, to Rome. The rules of his pilgrimage were that he should walk on foot, and in as straight a line as possible between the two towns. In the event, he broke both. He failed to force the great mountain rampart of the Gries, still blocked by late spring snow, crossing the Alps by the Grimsel instead; and in Como, depressed by the cold rain falling endlessly on the soggy Lombardy Plain, he took a train to Milan. But the walk was a stupendous effort, nonetheless, and it gave Belloc his best and most successful book, *The Path to Rome.*

In one respect, this book is more poignant today than when it was written: it catches for us the last flavours of pre-industrial Europe which were still perceptible to Belloc as he tramped along. The narrow, rutted roads, along which trundled only the farm carts and an occasional coach; peasants, dazzled by the sight of a rare stranger, and willing to give him a bed in the hayloft; the gleam in the eye of an innkeeper's wife when Belloc produced a gold coin from his purse; the strongly individual character of each village and region, expressed in dress, manners and speech; the solitude which descended abruptly as soon as the open road was gained – all features of a world that has gone for ever.

Belloc was a poor man and he lived rough. He had only a few sovereigns in his pocket; five more were sent to him when he reached Milan. In Paris, he bought a coat for the journey which cost him seven francs. He lodged for a franc a night, or slept out in the open. A photograph taken in Rome after his arrival shows him dressed in baggy linen trousers and coat, and carrying a tiny haversack, his only luggage (it was usually stuffed with bread, meat and a huge bottle of wine). Yet the peasants thought him a rich man, and at Brienz, on the Swiss frontier, he was able to enjoy what he called 'a magnificent great meal' – six courses, with cognac, vermouth and a cigar – which cost him two shillings and elevenpence.

In 1959 it is quite impossible to repeat Belloc's journey – even if anyone were pious or mad or energetic enough to attempt it. I know this from personal experience. For some years, I have wanted to do a walk on Bellocian scale. Not, of course, from Toul, which has no significance for me (and the eastern French are unlovable now, if not in 1901); or indeed as far as Rome, where I recently spent a disagreeable week while the cardinals bickered over a new pope. But I wanted to cross the Alps on foot, from Geneva to Lugano, and last month I tried to do it.

The difficulties began even before I left London. Belloc's tiny haversack allowed him to stride freely and enjoy the sheer pleasure of walking. But had I landed at Orly dressed and equipped like Belloc, I fear the French authorities would immediately have sent me back to London as a dangerous vagrant. Encumbrances are now essential to legality. Instead, therefore, I had a large and respectable rucksack, which soon became full. Pyjamas, dressing-gowns, endless changes of shirts and underclothes now seem indispensable and evoke suspicion if they are absent. I had, like Belloc, a huge pair of boots; but I also felt I should take a pair of shoes, to wear in the evenings – otherwise I should seem a freak. Shaving and toilet things, too, now seem to take up a lot of room; and there was also a sleeping-bag, for to sleep under a hedge without one, as Belloc did, is nowadays to court arrest by wandering police patrols. The result was that my rucksack weighed twenty-five pounds on the B.E.A. scales. It is not as if I am unduly comfort-loving or sensitive to the suspicious glances of foreigners; the tiniest boy-scout tramping on the continent (mostly by train) is weighed down beneath no less. So walking becomes, if not an agony, a labour.

But this would not have mattered, if there had been anywhere to walk. At Geneva, the road along the lake is jammed by traffic at all hours of the day, the view obscured by hideous villas, hoardings and dull trees, mass-produced to protect the privacy of rich Swiss. Despairing of this, I took the paddle-steamer to Montreux, deciding to start from there. And so I did, walking out of the suburbs along the hot metallic road, with the temperature in the nineties (Belloc complained of the unseasonable cold, but he was probably lucky). I thought I would strike open country soon, but the suburbs merely changed into an endless perspective of villas, hotels, motels, cafés, camping-sites, garages, all hugging the road. Moreover, it was impossible to leave the road. The old paths by the Rhône are now blocked by cement-factories and curious industrial structures, electric fences, barbed wire, walls, hedges without gates and minatory notices.

Confined thus to the main road, I had to endure the torture of the motor-car. One passed me, I calculated, every four seconds, and after half an hour, claustrophobia set in, and soon my mind began to dwell on savage hate-fantasies against cars. This, I found, was reciprocated. I was the only walker on the road. Those in the cars clearly regarded me as insane. As they passed, they goggled at me through the windows. But bewilderment was not their only or main emotion: there was also dislike. To them, I suppose, I was an exception to what they regard as the universal and natural desire of mankind to ride in cars at great speed, and therefore challenged the principle on which their view of happiness is based. Some made obscene gestures at me through the windows; others uttered taunts in half a dozen languages; a few hurled empty cigarette packets and other refuse. It was the *sans-culottes* pelting the carriages of the nobles – in reverse.

Soon, mere discomfort changed to a growing sense of danger. The road is probably no wider than in Belloc's day – though it is as straight as an arrow, with perfect vision. I hugged the side desperately, but there was no path on which to walk, merely the rim of a ditch, littered with road-mending materials and the broken pieces of cars. The flow of traffic hurtled past, sometimes missing me by a margin of less than a foot. The English were the most courteous, so far as their skill would allow them, veering away from me in wide arcs which brought them on to the wrong side of the road and led to angry exchanges with other drivers. The French were relentless, never deviating from course no matter how near they passed. The Italians were positively hostile, hunting me along the road, to see how close they could get without actually killing me.

After I had walked for five hours, one of these Italian cars, which had passed me by a mere six inches, stopped abruptly twenty yards ahead, reversed, and drew level. I assumed it was about to offer me a lift, and was thinking up some polite form of refusal, when the driver, his huge face red with outrage, leaned out of the window and shouted: 'It's people like you who make the roads dangerous!'

My resolution never really survived that first awful day. True, I walked for long stretches; but for most of the distance, ordinary prudence forced me to take trains or buses – to walk over the Simplon, for instance, is to invite an accident. As I descended into Italy, the stupefaction of the inhabitants at my desire to travel on foot deepened. One afternoon, I walked down the splendid Cannobina Valley which leads to Lake Maggiore. There were few cars; for once walking became a delight. At six, I paused for a drink at a tiny wayside inn only a few miles from my destination, and talked to two of the locals. One of them said to me sympathetically: 'You know, you think you'll save a lot of money by walking, but you won't. First, there's the shoe-leather – and those boots of yours look expensive. Then, you get hot and have to stop for drinks like this. It all mounts up.'

'But I'm not trying to save money by walking,' I said. His sympathy changed to bewilderment.

'Then why not take the bus?'

'Come, come,' I tried to joke, 'you're talking like a bus-driver.'

'I *am* a bus-driver,' he said proudly. 'My bus is parked round the back of the inn, and what's more, I'll give you a free lift down to the lake.' My refusal left him puzzled and, I fear, hurt.

So I failed, as I think even Belloc must have failed. There is no longer a path to Rome. And with it have vanished all the incidental delights which made his pilgrimage so rich. There is no variety. The hotels are as alike as the petrol stations. You drink the same mineral water from one end of the Alps to the other: its name screams out from every vacant space, even from the sky, where aeroplanes trace it out in white smoke. Many of the local wines have gone to earth: often, one must make do with synthetic Chianti. The speech is uniform – innkeeper's English, mainly about money. And almost all forms of human activity centre around the car. It – and not mankind – has inherited the earth.

Walking, even under adversity, stimulates thought. My own reflections, as I finished my journey, were gloomy. Europe is growing steadily richer. Socialism has not come to pass, but some of its promises are being fulfilled. Even in Italy – which could, only a few years ago, be classified as an under-developed country – the subsistence level is disappearing. Machines which once seemed hopeless luxuries are now within the reach of the majority. And the chief of them is the car, which has become the symbol not only of prosperity but of happiness itself. Many of the little cars which hunted me in the Rhône Valley were owned by workers; next year, there will be hundreds of thousands more. And as they increase, they are relentlessly destroying everything worth doing or seeing. The workers, scrambling onto the middle-class plateau of enjoyment, find that it has lost all its distinctive features. The disturbing – or perhaps comforting – thing is that they do not care a damn. I have never seen so many happy people.

—15 August 1959

The Pleasures of Fear

ALL RIGHT: I know I wasn't going to tackle the North Face of the Eiger. But by my standards it was a serious expedition nonetheless. At King's Cross I stuck out like a sore thumb: the grey, enveloping *parka*, the Bedford Cord climbing breeches, the pale-blue Chamonix rucksack, the great vulcanized rubber boots, and the 100 feet of gleaming nylon rope, hanging in neat coils – all proclaimed, under the arched, businesslike canopy of the station, a mad devotee of an exotic sport. My porter could not deny himself the classic joke: 'Wot's the rope for, guv'nor? Going to 'ang yerself?'

We went north through the night, awakening to real Scottish porridge and pastel glens and lochs slipping softly by. At Fort William I no longer felt alone: several dirty, be-roped figures joined the train, the high mountains were pressing in. I put on my boots and stamped my feet arrogantly in the corridor. At Mallaig, the ferry-head for Skye, I ceased to be an oddity, becoming a mere unit in a gathering regiment of lunatics. The summits of the Black Cuillin, the most fearsome rocks in Britain (some say in Europe), were already visible across the water.

It took us six more hours, by boat and mountain bus, to get to base, a gaunt stone cottage at the foot of Glen Brittle, the great chasm which separates the Cuillin from civilized, pastoral Skye. This was the headquarters of the mountaineering training centre, a building hallowed in the history of scientific rock-climbing. The pioneers of Skye climbing were two formidable and aptly named Victorians, the Reverend Steeple and Mr Doughty. Accommodation at the cottage was more rudimentary in their day: a fading photograph shows them reclining on truckle beds in the kitchen. In their steps came, at one time or another, the entire galaxy of climbers, from Mallory, the tragic hero of the early Everest expeditions, to Frank Smythe, perhaps the greatest mountaineer of all time. Their fading signatures ring from the guest book, as do comments from visitors from all over the world – including, recently, some Soviet experts from the Caucasus.

I had scrambled, amateurishly, in numerous centres: the Alps and Dolomites, the high Sierras of Spain, the Pyrenees, the Atlas (where a burnoused Arab guide lent me his primitive, hand-made skis). But this was my first attempt to acquire professional status. A city life without regular exercise and fumbling memories of rope-technique left me poorly equipped. My companions on the course seemed an ordinary group: a London lawyer, a Scots schoolteacher ('call me a dominie'), a steelworker from Lancashire, a young collegeboy, a garage-hand. But early on the first day, when we practised belaying (securing the rope while a member of the party is climbing) and absailing (controlled descent of a precipice using a double rope) I realized I was hopelessly outclassed by them all.

The second day, we got down to serious business on the high rocks, a climb called Window Buttress officially classified as 'difficult'. It takes you up a great rib of the central massif of the Cuillin, culminating in a spectacular finish: you squeeze your body through a tiny window in a rock face overlooking a thousand-foot drop. My fears began at the very first pitch, mounting steadily as we spidered our way slowly up the rock-wall. The nervous and physical tension, combined with the sheer muscular effort (bad climbers like myself expend at least twice as much energy as necessary and overwork their arm muscles) lathered me in bitter sweat. Half-way through the last pitch, as I scrambled despairingly over the void, trying to lodge my agonized body upside down in the window, I felt I would have to give in: the instructor, a few feet above me out of sight, commented dryly: 'You must come up. There's no way to get you down.' No doubt it was a similar incentive which drove the Eiger climbers up that last 1,000 feet.

The Black Cuillin are killer mountains. Small by Alpine standards, they are compact, vicious and treacherous. Among the high rocks, altitude ceases to matter. The dark, misty wilderness of the Cuillin is as visibly horrific as the great Chamonix cliffs, mistakes equally easy, the penalties as costly. The main gabro rock is rough and satisfying (though it lacerates the hands), but it is spattered with layers of crumbling basalt, unreliable at all times, murderous in wet weather. None of the summits surrenders without a steadily increasing effort: they are attained by the spinal architecture of the range, razor ridges up which we inched unprotected by ropes (to employ them would have taken too long). As I crawled up them, I confess I was continuously aware of an intense unwillingness to plunge into eternity. Long before we reached the summit of our first climb, I swore bitterly that, once back in Glen Brittle, I would withdraw from the course forthwith.

But then, as we began the descent, and saw, through the mist, the first vestiges of loose stones and eventually mountain grass, a great calmness descended. In mountaineering, as with all great sports, the reward begins when accomplishment ends: the agony is followed by a warm, spreading aftermath, in which physical pleasure becomes a transcending happiness. I found myself indulging in a forgotten habit, which I always, unconsciously, adopt on mountain descents: singing noisily the pirates' shanty from *Treasure Island*. My abrupt transformation from a cringing defeatist to a brash, contented extrovert proved, once again, the truth of the pleasure-pain principle. Peace is meaningless without war; a Churchill nothing without a Hitler; a Coleridge requires a Gray, a Picasso an Ingres. As Clemenceau once remarked: 'There's not much fun in shooting a tiger from an armoured car.'

So I stayed on the course. My physical difficulties declined, at first slowly, then with gratifying speed. Fear remained, as it must, for all climbers. Occasionally it was acute. Bad weather invested the Cuillin with a new dimension of danger. The mist was perpetual above 2,000 feet, cold, torrential rain almost continuous; and there was the most dangerous enemy of all – sharp unexpected gusts of high wind, which can pluck you off the spinal columns and dislodge rock falls down the gullies. There were moments of sheer nightmare, when the saturated rocks seemed to rise up to meet the black sky, and the armour of the mountains – rib and cliff, tower, arch and pinnacle – spun and reverberated with the great elemental forces unleashed upon it and us. We spent hours huddled together, movement paralysed, in caves formed by trapped boulders, or roped to sheer walls. But always, on the descent, came the same release, the post-climactic *catharthis* when the black rock-cliffs receded and the first tokens of tamed nature appeared.

In the evenings, there was nothing much to do except sit around the fire. We were left to ourselves, and conversation, and hot, strong cups of tea, supplemented by the bottles of strange-labelled whisky which appear mysteriously in all Highland cottages. Climbers are classless people, much given to serious discussion of books and ideas. Their jokes are harsh but not cruel, centring round horrific stories of calamity on the rock-faces, falling stones, frayed ropes and frostbite. Like most people who regard danger as acceptable, they have no complexes.

For two weeks we toiled and swung around the black pinnacles. Not once did the mist lift from the summits; I never saw the range from our glen. Then, as we hoisted our rucksacks aboard the bus that would take us out of the wilds, great streamers of ice-wind heeled round from the north, and tore away the cloud-canopy. For a few minutes, the entire jaw of fangs glittered in the pale Hebridean sunlight. Then the rain-clouds pressed down again, and as we drove up the glen, we saw the white cascade streaming down Waterpipe Gully – a twelve-hour climb classified as 'Very Severe' in dry weather, impossible in wet. We felt good and snug in the bus.

Dr Johnson was almost drowned returning from Skye. Our little ferry, too, bobbed and gyrated in the choppy straits; I cast only one backward glance at the Cuillin, imperceptible in the black smudge where rain-swept land met the boiling sea. Then back to London and the ordinary metropolitan hazards. A month later I received a certificate informing me I had passed the course.

I mentioned this, with appropriate diffidence, to an economist acquaintance, a man of Central European extraction and pronounced left-wing views. 'You bloddy Fascist,' he said.

—17 March 1961

The Man who Built a Cathedral

WHEN I WAS FIVE or six the dominant figure in my life was not my mother, or my father, but Father Fitzgerald, the parish priest. He was indissolubly linked, in my mind, with the colossal church he caused to be built. Our house lay under its long shadow, only 100 yards away. It was the centre of my universe and Father Fitzgerald was its inhabiting spirit. He was a squat man, just over five feet, with powerful shoulders and a barrel chest. His face, scorched and withered by the sun, was screwed up round a fierce glass eye, which to me always seemed more terrifyingly real than his good one. He was, everyone said, a rich man, but he lived in an atmosphere of grinding personal austerity; and when he lost his eye, he bought the cheapest glass one available. It fitted his eye socket very badly and caused him, I believe, a good deal of pain. One of the maids – a credulous Irish girl to be sure – told me that, when hearing confessions in his dark cubicle, he frequently took the glass eye out to ease the pain. The thought of a gaping, empty socket staring at me unseeingly in the darkness of the confessional frightened me so much that, in future, instead of going to Father Fitzgerald, I used to confess to his curate.

People were afraid of Father Fitzgerald for other reasons, too. He blazed with the wrath and majesty of God, and treated his humble, working-class parishioners like a Prince-Archbishop from the Rhine. His religion was Old Testimental, compounded of brimstone, thunderbolts, maledictions and threats. His mission, as he saw it, was twofold: first, to bully and goad his flock along the road to salvation, second, to raise huge monuments to the glory of God.

It was the second to which most of his energies were devoted. He came to us from a tiny country village in Yorkshire, where he had built the largest parish hall for miles around. But his great ambition was to build a church, and when he arrived in our parish he saw his opportunity. Our church, we all knew, was not very distinguished, but it drew from Father Fitzgerald, when he saw it, an explosion of earth-shaking contempt. 'A mean, down-at-heel, pagan, Methodist prayerbox,' he said. 'An insult to Almighty God. And this a rich parish too, with 4,000 souls earning good wages in the factories and nothing to do with their pence but go to the pictures.'

His Building Fund was duly launched, with startling publicity in the local paper and a barrage of threats from the pulpit. It soon attained quite astonishing proportions – a fact which Father Fitzgerald took for granted, but which excited the outspoken envy of his Anglican colleague, a disgruntled gentleman from the south who had dry rot in his choir-stalls and could do nothing about it. The next stage was to draw up the plans, and Father Fitzgerald, in his grandiose way, brought down an architect from London, a distinguished R.A. with a beard and spats. But the two soon quarrelled; the architect's ideas were not big enough for Father Fitzgerald ('He's a mean-minded man like all Protestants') and he determined to draw up his own plans. This necessitated a prolonged journey through Germany and Italy in search of a suitable prototype. He failed to find one, but he eventually settled on a design which combined the main features of two cathedrals which had caught his fancy: a gigantic nave, four hundred feet long and topped by three domes in line, and a massive Romanesque tower. It was, in short, an architectural oddity. But it had a certain monumental grandeur, not unlike the Eiffel Tower, in that it represented the triumph of visionary ambition over the laws of nature.

Its construction, however, posed grave practical problems. One of the reasons why the distinguished R.A. had been unable to draw up plans on a scale to which Father Fitzgerald thought God was entitled, was that the site chosen was clay soil, liable to subsidence if too great a weight was put upon it. It was pointed out to him that if he persisted with his present plans, the sheer weight of masonry would cause the church to sink a foot-and-a-half in the first year after completion. This was just before his annual retreat, and during it he met a German Monsignor, who had been a constructional engineer in his youth. This gentleman told him that the problem could be solved by laying a bed of concrete over the site, and he returned triumphantly to confound his critics. But the concrete bed itself was unsuitable to the site, and when the local borough surveyor got wind of it he laid a formal complaint before the town council. If Father Fitzgerald persisted in his mad scheme, he said, the surrounding houses would be pulled out of the vertical and he would not answer for the consequences within ten years. The council promptly forbade Father Fitzgerald to go ahead. He had always hated politicians, and he now joined battle with a violence which, even for him, was unusual. The ensuing commotion, which involved an under-secretary of state, three M.P.s, a geologist and a score of engineers, is difficult to follow, but its one indisputable result was that Father Fitzgerald emerged a clear victor. The concrete bed was laid and the borough surveyor resigned in disgust. (Twenty years later his warnings were amply confirmed, but by this time the church was built and it was too late. Over 400 houses had to be pulled down, most of which were owned by a leading local Freemason, who went bankrupt in consequence. Father Fitzgerald, had he still been alive, would undoubtedly have called this a judgement of God.)

Having swept the board clean, Father Fitzgerald now got down to the more exciting business of construction. As usual, his obstacles were not material ones but the lack of faith of his fellow-men. The parish, by now thoroughly alarmed, had appointed a five-man committee to keep Father Fitzgerald on the side of sanity, and its first decision was to engage an engineer and a reputable firm of builders. The result was a head-on conflict on the first day work began on the site. Wisely, Father Fitzgerald did not attempt to fire the engineer, but concentrated on the committee; for the next five Sundays he delivered violent sermons against them from the pulpit, until three of them resigned, to be promptly replaced by his supporters. He now commanded a majority on the committee, and the dismissal of the engineer and the builders followed as a matter of course.

Slowly the massive church climbed up from its foundations. I spent many hours on the site, watching Father Fitzgerald goading on his minions. He was smart enough to consult experts on all vital technical points, but he refused to employ anyone permanently. He would have no truck with building firms, preferring to engage his labourers himself. He even, after a few weeks, fired the foreman he had appointed, because he considered he did not get enough work out of the men. The labourers, mainly husky Irish lads, went in mortal terror of him, and worked as they had never done before (or, I have no doubt, since). His burly, apocalyptic figure would leap at them from behind sand-pits and heaps of stones just as they were settling down to brew tea; and even when not actually on the site, he would observe it, through field-glasses, from the windows of the presbytery.

When, after three years, the main body of the church was complete, the parish did make a feeble effort to play some part in superintending its decoration. Father Fitzgerald, whose mood by this time was more mellow, allowed them to appoint a Consultant Decorator, a prominent Catholic layman who was an acknowledged expert on ecclesiastical art. But he was, poor man, accustomed to dealing with subtle and enlightened cardinals, and could never bring Father Fitzgerald to accept his advice. After a few ineffectual weeks he left in despair. From then on, Father Fitzgerald presided regally over a court of carpenters, plasterers and painters, occasionally conducting plundering expeditions to Europe, from which he returned with packing-cases loaded with German silver, Spanish crucifixes, vestments from Venice and Bruges, alabaster angels, and Madonnas of Pyrennean basalt.

The completed church, it should be said, entirely vindicated its creator. A famous architect, who visited it, pronounced it a sound piece of construction, and it received an admiring notice in the *Catholic Trumpet*. The Bishop, at the ceremony of consecration, said it was the finest church in his diocese, and fit to be a cathedral. This innocent remark immediately aroused all Father FitzGerald's most atavistic suspicions, since he concluded that the Bishop had designs on his church. In his litany of dislikes, bishops occupied a prominent place – indeed, his contempt for all his ecclesiastical superiors, with the solitary exception of the Pope, was almost limitless. The diocese he regarded as his natural enemy, an impersonal and malevolent force always anxious to come between a parish priest and his flock. He fought its intrusions and buttressed his own privileges with the venom and tenacity of a Hildebrand. The thought that his church – the greatest parish church in the world, as he liked to imagine it – might be seized by some insolent bishop and transformed into a cold cathedral remote from the people, filled him with pain and anger.

In fact, as he ought to have known, his Bishop went in considerable fear of him. He always confined his ceremonial visits to a strict minimum. After the completion of the church, he offered Father Fitzgerald a monsignor's hat (an offer which Father Fitzgerald, who regarded it as the thin end of the wedge and who in any case despised monsignors, rejected in a remarkably unspiritual letter), but it would never have occurred to him to seize the church in the face of Father Fitzgerald's wrath.

The old man, in short, was left to enjoy his creation in peace. From its high pulpit, topped by a canopy containing a sounding-board of his own design, which magnified his already powerful voice into something akin to the Last Trump, he continued to thunder for the rest of his natural days. He had only two sermons, which he knew by heart, and which corresponded with his two alternate moods. By the time he had mounted the pulpit, we always knew which one we were going to have. If his step was jaunty, and his face elated with the mysteries of the universe, we knew he would begin with the words, 'Consider the beauteous, bountiful, everlasting, inexhaustible, infinite goodness of God', and that we would have five short minutes of grateful thanksgiving. But if he went up the stairs slowly, and surveyed the congregation darkly under beetling brows, then we knew he would draw himself up to his full height, lean over the edge of the pulpit, and hiss at us the two terrible words: 'Martin Luther.' Then would follow a philippic against Protestants in general, in which all his current complaints against the administration of the parish and the sinfulness of its members would somehow be inextricably mingled, and which would invariably conclude with a denunciation of converts ('Let them not expect to be received in this parish. I'll not have ex-Protestants in my church, cluttering up the road to salvation'). It never lasted less than half an hour.

When, in due course, Father Fitzgerald died, his funeral procession was nearly a mile long, and was headed by seven bishops (a compliment which would have brought him only rueful satisfaction). He was a wealthy man, and he left £20,000 to the parish; not a penny (or, as he would have termed it, 'not a red halfpenny') went to the diocesan fund. But within a year the Bishop had his revenge, if that is the word. By order of the Cardinal, his sprawling, overcrowded diocese was reorganized, and he was given a suffragan bishop to assist him. But a suffragan bishop has to have a pro-cathedral, and Father Fitzgerald's church was inevitably chosen. The money he left to the parish was used to enlarge the presbytery to accommodate the bishop and his staff. So the old man's worst fears were abundantly confirmed.

But his parishioners don't look at it that way. They have forgotten Father Fitzgerald's prejudices, and can think only of the reflected glory they enjoy in having a cathedral in their midst. As they see it, Father Fitzgerald would have been delighted to see his lifework so fittingly rewarded. Indeed, if you ask them about him, they reply: 'He was a remarkable man. He built our cathedral, you know. All by himself.'

—31 October 1959

The Naked and the Red

THE TALL, ANGULAR ENGLISHMAN standing on the *quai* looked ordinary enough, granted the usual oddities of English people in the south of France. Long, sun-reddened legs, dirty khaki shorts, huge feet encased in thick socks and sandals, a battered rucksack from which a copy of the *Observer* obtruded. But there was something furtive about him, as if he was a provincial visiting Soho for the first time and uncertain where to find a strip-tease joint. I watched him approach a vaguely nautical figure and ask: *'Ou est le bateau pour les nudistes?'*

The sailor (if indeed he was one: the municipalities of these little Riviera 'ports' often hire peasants at 500 francs a day to pose as fishermen) jerked his thumb over in our direction, where we formed a patient queue, waiting for the boat to take us out to the Ile du Levant.

We were a mixed bunch. My wife and I were going out, shall we say, as journalists. There was a thin-lipped youth, whose jaws and arms twitched convulsively, and who might have been a psychopath. A solidly-built Swedish couple, heavily equipped with binoculars and cameras. A good number of Germans, impatient to get their *lederhosen* off, and a sprinkling of French tourists, out, quite frankly, on a day trip *pour voire les naturistes*. At the last moment, a large English party climbed aboard, marshalled by a stern middle-aged schoolmaster with lean bronzed shanks and steel-rimmed spectacles. He held a roll-call, ticking off names in a little green book. 'Where's Angela?' he asked sharply, and the others took up the call, wailing 'Angela, Angela', across the little harbour.

But Angela never turned up; perhaps she had got stage-fright at the last moment. Her companions sat huddled together in the gunwales, chewing ravenously at pieces of bread. One of them turned to me and said: 'I say, where did you manage to buy that copy of the *New Statesman*?' I studied the other travellers with interest: it is a curious sensation, being squashed together in a boat with fifty people, knowing that, in an hour's time, everyone will strip to the skin. Rather like waiting for the Last Judgement, in fact, or being rowed across the Styx by Charon.

In reality, of course, the rules which govern the Ile du Levant are not so severe. It must, indeed, be unique in the world, in that it is a colony where nudists and the merely curious can mix freely. The island has some perfectly ordinary non-nudist residents – a Mayor, a *Syndicat d'Initiative,* hotel-owners and their families as well as a contingent of French sailors, who occupy some sort of naval base on the rocks. Hence, in the area around the little harbour and the village, the nudists are obliged to wear what the notices call *un slip minimum*, which in most cases turned out to be a triangle of cloth tied on with string.

At first glance, therefore, the harbour presents a bizarre appearance: a ballet of bronze girls, naked to the waist, who have come down to meet the boat, and groups of off-duty sailors, leering villainously. Outside this restricted area, however, complete freedom prevails. You can take off all your clothes, or none at all. There is only one condition: you may not take photographs, except with the permission of the nudists who are likely to figure on them.

I came to the Ile du Levant with two preconceptions about nudists. First that they would be mainly fat, middle-aged and ugly, with a predominance of men. Secondly, that the atmosphere in the colony would be rigidly puritanical, with sex kept firmly under control. For I had been misled by nudist propaganda, which centres round the proposition that the naked body is morally neutral, and that uncleanliness lies solely in the mind. It may be that some nudist colonies reflect this curiously naïve view, and are the grim and humourless places I imagine them to be. Not so the Ile du Levant. In fact I found that both my preconceptions were entirely mistaken.

In the first place, the great majority of the nudists were under thirty. The men were vigorous and handsome, the girls for the most part pretty and shapely. The chief aesthetic offence, indeed, is caused by the inevitable mechanics of getting a sun-tan. For most of the girls make the mistake of arriving after they have already sunbathed elsewhere in bikinis. They thus find themselves with white patches on their bottoms and busts, and though these do, in due course, get pink and finally brown, the rest of the body meanwhile gets even browner, so that the odd – and slightly obscene –

discrepancy remains. Lying on the sunbaked rocks, I pondered for some time on this problem, and decided that the only solution would be for them to sunbathe in a garment which exposed only those parts of the body which elsewhere the law decrees must be covered. But this, I imagine, would look even odder.

My second preconception – that nudists are anti-sex – proved equally untrue. Watching their behaviour, on the rocks, in the sea, in the village street, in the cafés and shops, I came to the firm conclusion that most of them are obsessed by sex. The men come there to look at naked girls, and spend most of their time doing so, quite unequivocally; while the girls come there to be looked at, and quite manifestly enjoy it. There is a third group, the least pleasing but fortunately the smallest: men, usually well into middle age, who spend their time exhibiting themselves to women tourists. They tend to creep stealthily all over the island, suddenly popping out at you from behind bushes. They are also disagreeably talkative, haranguing the casual visitor with long lectures about the ancient Greeks, Sparta, etc., usually delivered in a strong German accent. For nudists, like homosexuals and Catholic converts, are the most inveterate of proselytisers.

We did not escape the treatment. No sooner had we found an agreeable rock on which to doze (I retained some of my clothes, not on moral grounds, but for fear of sunburn) than a shadow fell across us, and I looked up into the large, hairy and naked paunch of a Ruhr industrialist. 'Ho,' he said, 'I see that you and your little friend' – nudists, I note, like to pay married couples the compliment of assuming they are living in sin – 'I see that you and your little friend do not see face to face on the Naturalist Question. She does disrobe and you not.' I explained my point about getting burnt, but he brushed it aside. 'It is often so. Sometimes the man has shame, sometimes the woman.' Five minutes later, he was well launched on Sparta, and I was able to terminate the conversation only by jumping into the sea, from whence I watched him plod eagerly over to another group. A nudist colony, I imagine, is a bore's paradise: it's awfully difficult to give anyone the brush-off if both you and he are stark naked.

Indeed, the real drawback to nudism is the sheer monotony. Sunbathing on the rocks, swimming in the sea, it makes sense. But once away from the coast, nudism becomes a ludicrous posture. In the village, I watched naked men and women going shopping, staggering beneath heavy baskets, sometimes wearing hats or with a towel across their shoulders. In the restaurants, they spread their napkin across their knees, not having anything to tuck it into. The waitress who served us, a plump, jolly girl, and obviously a native rather than a *naturiste,* took off her blouse to please the tourists, and very peculiar she looked with her large Provencal breasts bobbing over her pink-and-white apron. The fact is that nudism is not natural, unless you are doing something such as swimming, where clothes are a nuisance. In any other situation, the nudist is a joke, and often an unfunny joke.

On the harbour, as we prepared to embark for the mainland, a solitary policeman was on duty, no doubt to see that the *slip minimum* rule was observed. I should like to report that he, too, was wearing a *slip,* but in fact he wore blue jeans and a beach shirt, crowned by a *képi* as a sign of authority. He had a gun, too. As we passed out of the harbour, an angry argument broke out between a serious French nudist and a huge German tourist, who wanted to take a colour-movie of some naked figures on the rocks. A clipped English voice said: 'Seems odd, doesn't it, to be back in uniform?' Then the sea became very rough indeed, and people began to be sick. In my distress I was consoled to note that a really fanatical German nudist, tanned as dark as his *lederhosen*, went as green as everyone else.

—13 August 1960

Dining with Liz

IT IS NOT one of my favourite Left Bank restaurants, though there is no doubt that the food – mainly fishy things – is good. It was first made famous by that jovial stage-designer, Christian Bérard, known as Baby, who found it was prepared to indulge his passion for eating *sauce hollandaise* with literally everything, and even today its décor reflects the slightly faded chic of the Thirties – Bérard self-portraits, sad pierrots by Jean Cocteau, and Vertès murals. Anyway, there we were last month, having given our order and taking the first sip of wine.

The wine-waiter, a frail little man who keeps a shrewd eye on the world, leaned over our table confidentially. 'You will perceive,' he said, 'that *une invitée de marque* has just arrived.' Indeed she had: there, settling themselves at a nearby table, was the whole Cleopatra circus. The heavy white face, from which the huge eyes stared out like weapons, was unmistakable; so, too, the solid, rugger-playing back of the Welsh escort. And to complete the trio was a small, pudgy girl, offspring of who knows what forgotten union.

The room became suddenly conscious of the importance of flesh. The more personable waiters drifted hurriedly in the direction of the little table, flicking desperately with their napkins at imaginary crumbs. There was a great flourishing of menus, a swift concentration of trolleys bearing fierce spirit-flames. When the notorious appear in person, it is often more interesting to study the anonymous faces of those who stare. The four American ladies on my left, dressed like brightly-coloured insects, rattled their charm bracelets as a preliminary warning of disapproval. Then their hatted heads moved together in conclave, as Miss Taylor's finer points were dissected. A family party of Parisian working-class gourmands – a type often seen, to the indignation of wealthy foreigners, dining magnificently in the most expensive French restaurants – lifted their heads from steaming platters of bouillabaisse and a great roasted fish which reposed in the middle of their table. For the men in the party, at least, lust fought a brief battle with gluttony, and the latter won. Bouillabaisse, after all, requires one's undivided attention.

At a third table, an American businessman tried hard to conceal the light in his eyes behind his bi-focals. This was life, this was what he had come to Paris *for*. You could take your Lido and your Folies Bergères and throw them in the Seine. Unfortunately, still more watchful eyes were on him. The solitary, if prolonged, glance his wife cast at Miss Taylor made it plain that she was regarded as a personal threat to domestic content back in Cleveland, Ohio. There was a sharp exchange of words, and the businessman kept his nose dutifully in his plate, except for brief moments when his wife was too preoccupied with her *sole bonne femme* to detect his surreptitious peeps.

Miss Taylor has a hearty appetite and did full justice to the food which flowed smoothly to her table. Then came the bustle of departure as she, child and escort were bowed out to the waiting Cadillac, its huge tailfins winking with lights like a yacht moored in harbour. At once the restaurant sprang to life, all restraints of courtesy abandoned. The four American ladies craned forward their scraggy necks – hens peering out of a coop. The French workers, the climax of their meal safely past, hurried to the windows joyfully. The businessman, liberated by the fortunate absence of his wife in the powder-room, leapt to his feet: for an instant I thought he was going to cheer. The vast black car swung round in a wide circle and vanished into the Paris night.

Suddenly, I became aware that the Cleopatra circus had arrived fifteen minutes after us, had consumed an ample meal, and had left while we were still waiting for our soufflé. There may be disadvantages in being Miss Taylor, but it certainly gets you service.

—18 October 1963